"Bravo! *LEADERSHIP AND THE CUSTOMER REVOLUTION* says what needs to be said! A fast read, provocative, perfect for any leader looking to change their organizations. It makes me think about what I have done right and what I could have done better."

> —*Dr. Edson Bueno*
> Founder and Chairman of the Board
> Amil

"Leadership, customer loyalty, front-line ownership, Gary Heil rises above the rhetoric on these issues. As a Baldrige Examiner and internationally recognized quality and service expert, he has had a significant impact on American business."

> —*Thomas J. Garvey*
> President
> Chase Manhattan PFS

"Superior customer service, delivered by highly motivated employees, continues to be one of the most powerful competitive weapons in the marketplace. Rick Tate and Gary Heil are two experts who have helped Johnson & Johnson discover how we can differentiate ourselves by serving our customers better than our competition. We look forward to their new book and new insights into this fascinating subject of Customer Service."

> —*Jerry Gilbert*
> Vice President,
> Consumer Sector Customer Relations
> Johnson & Johnson

"This is a terrific book if you're really serious about improving your company. It's straightforward and no-nonsense, visionary and practical. It forces you to look at the way things are, not how you wish they were, and points out areas where significant change can take root."

> —*Sandra Kurtzig*
> Founder and Former Chairman
> The ASK Group

"No business policy or practice escapes scrutiny in *LEADERSHIP AND THE CUSTOMER REVOLUTION*. Drawing from years of experience with all types of businesses, the authors make us question our capacity for success by poking fun at conventional approaches to organizational change. The language is as clear as the message: stop talking about and start acting upon the mandate of change."

—*Karen M. Lage*
Vice President
Management Resources and Development
Merrill Lynch

"I have worked with Gary extensively during my sixteen-year tenure with the Walt Disney Company. Gary is an enormously talented and gifted speaker, facilitator, and catalyst. The strengths he has brought to these and other organizations include a vast database of knowledge and experience acquired through his association with hundreds of organizations, an invaluable role as change agent, challenging people and organizations to think 'out of the box.' *LEADERSHIP AND THE CUSTOMER REVOLUTION* will be an outstanding resource to organizations intent on improving any facet of their operation."

—*Pamela Treski Landwirth*
Formerly General Manager
Walt Disney Company
Currently President, Treski and Associates

"Moving an organization from a less than productive business to a creative, driving operation is a difficult task. Taking an already successful business and bringing it to new levels of excitement and profitability is even more daunting. In both situations, Gary Heil has been very powerful as a consultant, leader, and advisor. Gary has had the uncanny ability to push the leaders of an organization towards developing a vision and living it. Conventional wisdom is not something that is a barrier for Gary, rather an opportunity to excel as a unique, one-of-a-kind organization. *LEADERSHIP AND THE CUSTOMER REVOLUTION* will be a must read for business executives."

—*Art Levitt*
President
Chief Executive Officer
Hard Rock Cafe

"Packed with mind-bending ideas, *LEADERSHIP AND THE CUSTOMER REVOLUTION* may be the best business book this year."

> —*William "Bill" Oncken III*
> President
> The William Oncken Corporation

"I've had the pleasure of working with Rick Tate and Gary Heil for more than ten years. Rick has had significant influence on shaping our service vision and strategies. Rick has a way of translating complicated service issues into concrete specific actions that have—in no small way—contributed to our success and reputation in our industry. It's great to have their team in our corner."

> —*William E. Miller*
> Director of Training and Development
> Cintas Corporation

"*LEADERSHIP AND THE CUSTOMER REVOLUTION* should be required reading for anyone involved in managing people and more particularly, reengineering their operations. The authors' insightful and forthright description of common corporate foibles is very constructive. It clearly points out many of the things which stand in the way of making truly constructive changes in organizations, and should be helpful to many managers in providing the leadership in order to remove those roadblocks."

> —*H. Lee Noble*
> President
> Polymers Division
> Miles, Inc.

"When it comes to customer service, many organizations still talk the walk. For those interested in really doing something about service, this book provides an excellent road map."

> —*Gordon Peters*
> President
> The Institute for Management Studies

"As managers today, we're working harder and faster, yet finding that we're even further behind. In our frenzy to survive, we forget that yesterday's solutions can only deliver yesterday's results.

This book provides ideas that can get today's managers something different. It recommends practical techniques for gaining the loyalty and commitment of our employees—providing the only real competitive advantage.

These are not the times for the faint-hearted," say Heil, Parker, and Tate. I heartily agree. At last, we have some help for the bumpy, scary, exciting rollercoaster ride ahead."

> —*Irene Reskin*
> Educational Development Manger
> Pacific Bell

"*LEADERSHIP AND THE CUSTOMER REVOLUTION* is a book not just of concepts, but of real-life examples of what, why and how. The direction, new ideas and challenges have continually influenced my effectiveness as a leader. I have read, reviewed, absorbed, and practiced various chapters of this work, and can attest to their practical and positive application. We are using materials from the book today, and it works. Learning is a constant need for any organization and it is imperative to learn from teachers like Heil, Tate, and Parker."

> —*Evy M. Smith*
> Vice President of Sales and Marketing
> Cellular One, Indiana, a BellSouth Company

"This book is a call to action. It tells us we have to stop talking about change and start making it happen. It's tough and candid, and filled with provocative ideas and smart suggestions."

> —*Richard B. Thomas*
> EVP and Director
> American Honda

LEADERSHIP AND THE CUSTOMER REVOLUTION

LEADERSHIP AND THE CUSTOMER REVOLUTION

The Messy, Unpredictable, and Inescapably Human Challenge of Making the Rhetoric of Change a Reality

GARY HEIL
TOM PARKER
RICK TATE

 VAN NOSTRAND REINHOLD
I(T)P™ A Division of International Thomson Publishing Inc.

New York • Albany • Bonn • Boston • Detroit • London • Madrid • Melbourne
Mexico City • Paris • San Francisco • Singapore • Tokyo • Toronto

Copyright © 1995 by Gary M. Heil

I(T)P™ A division of International Thomson Publishing Inc.
The ITP logo is a trademark under license

Printed in the United States of America
For more information, contact:

Van Nostrand Reinhold
115 Fifth Avenue
New York, NY 10003

International Thomson Publishing GmbH
Königswinterer Strasse 418
53227 Bonn
Germany

International Thomson Publishing Europe
Berkshire House 168–173
High Holborn
London WCIV 7AA
England

International Thomson Publishing Asia
221 Henderson Road #05–10
Henderson Building
Singapore 0315

Thomas Nelson Australia
102 Dodds Street
South Melbourne, 3205
Victoria, Australia

International Thomson Publishing Japan
Hirakawacho Kyowa Building, 3F
2-2-1 Hirakawacho
Chiyoda-ku, 102 Tokyo
Japan

Nelson Canada
1120 Birchmount Road
Scarborough, Ontario
Canada M1K 5G4

International Thomson Editores
Campos Eliseos 385, Piso 7
Col. Polanco
11560 Mexico D.F. Mexico

1 2 3 4 5 6 7 8 9 10   QEBFF   01 00 99 98 97 96 95 94

Library of Congress Cataloging-in-Publication Data

Heil, Gary, 1950–
    Leadership and the customer revolution : the messy, unpredictable, and inescapably
human challenge of making the rhetoric of change a reality / Gary Heil, Tom Parker,
Rick Tate.
        p. cm.
    Includes index.
    ISBN 0-442-01852-5
    1. Leadership. 2. Organizational change. 3. Customer satisfaction. I. Parker, Tom.
II. Tate, Rick. III. Title.
HD57.7.H4   1994
658.8'12—dc20   94-22980
                                                                                                                CIP

Contents

PART 3   LEADER AS CUSTOMER ADVOCATE

PART 4   LEADER OF PEOPLE

EPILOGUE   LEADER AS HERO

• • • • • • • • •

Foreword: New Year's Eve
Every Night of the Year

I'm lucky. My mentor was different. He believed that a hotel should be built in the shape of a mouse, the best architects would love to design buildings for theme parks, and each individual's capacity for creativity is unlimited. He embraced the notion that achieving world-class levels of innovation requires total commitment and radically different thinking and he was uncompromising in his pledge to quality. The goals he set for himself and others in the organization were—in the words of the authors of this book—"strategically unreasonable." To work with him was to be inspired, to make a maximum contribution—to reach your full potential. I remember every day as both challenging and exhilarating.

Early in my tenure at Disney, I was charged with leading a team to develop a new theme for a part of the property that wasn't performing up to typical Disney standards. My first appearance in this role was at a brainstorming session with a dozen or so team members. Their ideas were all well thought out and capably presented. The trouble was, each was substantially similar to the strategy that had not worked over the past year. After listening for a few minutes, I suggested, "Maybe what we need is New Year's Eve every night of the year!" You didn't need a Ph.D. to read the team members' reactions. Who is this guy? Is he kidding? (I must admit, in retrospect, the idea was a little weird, even for me.)

Soon, however, the entire tenor of the session changed. Inadvertently, I had done for the team what my boss at Disney had done for me so many times in the past. By making my New Year's Eve statement, I had given the group license to think "out of the box"—and let them know that I believed it was imperative to do so if we were to stay competitive. If the boss thinks that way and reflects this type of thinking in his or her day-to-day actions, then everyone has permission to do the same. Within days, the team was planning a revolution and within weeks they were leading it effectively. Although there were no Sumo wrestlers, soon our guests were dancing in the street, celebrating New Year's Eve every night of the year.

Throughout this period of radical change, I was both leader and student, reminded regularly of the leadership lesson that each of us must embrace if we hope to be successful in the future. Provide people with a supportive environment, allow them to contribute and pursue their aspirations, while ensuring personal accountability, and they will accomplish extraordinary things. Unfortunately, as most of us have learned, creating an environment that facilitates creativity as well as commitment is an incredibly complex undertaking that, in many cases, requires revolutionary changes in organizational practices. As the authors remind us throughout this book, in order to achieve a substantially different performance from our organizations, we must become the architects of a different kind of system that will support these efforts.

I applaud the authors for not suggesting an oversimplified road map to future success. Even though I wish the path were more predictable, I know that they are right and in the end, each of us must customize a method that will work in our organization.

Each of our organizations is as unique as the people who work in it. What the authors do provide, however, is a list of tough questions that challenge us to "rethink our thinking" about what creates organizational success. They suggest a number of practical ideas that can help each of us to make more informed and more effective choices as we attempt to prosper in today's dynamic, global business environment.

As you read on, it will become obvious that the authors have given careful thought to what tomorrow will demand. Each challenge they present illuminates an issue that we can no longer afford to ignore and highlights the need for each of us to become insatiable learners as well as convincing advocates. We must learn to make process management part of everyone's job while we periodically re-engineer each process, and we must use technology to enable every person to productively add value and capture the customer information that may provide us with a glimpse of what might be valued in the future. The authors are the first to admit that these may be daunting tasks, but I believe they are "right on" when they argue that for most of us living in a world of rapidly changing markets, greater competition, and more demanding and sophisticated customers, rapid improvement in these areas is no longer optional.

I also agree with the authors' assertion that people want to commit themselves to a cause that they deem worthy and that each of us is searching for an opportunity to make a substantial contribution. It is the leader's non-negotiable role to build an environment where people can continually learn while contributing to the organizational mission. The journey begins when leaders clearly communicate that every individual's input is valued, honesty is paramount, innovation will be supported, and people can significantly impact the environment in which they work—no matter what their position in the hierarchy.

At the Hard Rock Cafe we have a saying that describes our belief there is strength in the diversity among us—when our efforts are focused on a common task. *Love all, serve all:* I have learned that it is not a slogan but a prerequisite to success in virtually any human endeavor, whether in business, government, or our personal lives. Leadership after all, as the authors remind us, is first and foremost a human endeavor.

ART LEVITT
President
Chief Executive Officer
The Hard Rock Cafe

• • • • • • • • • •

Preface: Leader as *Pragmatist or Visionary?*

Pragmatist or visionary? Most of us are some of each. We go to work, there's a job to be done, and we do it. We may not like the current system, but we understand how it works, how to bend it to our favor. We know how hard we can push before it pushes back, how far afield we can stray before it reins us in. Despite its constraints, we've become efficient and effective. Sure, sometimes things and even people fall through the cracks, but that's the price we pay for practicality, for making do with what we have. Besides, no one ever said that the world was fair or that the system would be perfect.

Still, there's something in us all that wants things to be better than they are. A lot better—for our customers, for our co-workers, for ourselves. There's the visionary in us that tells us that a stronger, fairer, more flexible, more responsive organization lies just over the horizon—all we have to do to get there is to *change*. The problem facing us in recent years, however, is that change is no longer optional. It's imperative.

About this, there is little disagreement. Every pundit, every sign, and every survey tell us that we have to change, that change is the only certainty. We're all struggling with it, trying to understand what needs to be done and how to go about it. There's probably not a leader alive today who hasn't been frustrated by not being able to change fast enough or in the right way.

As it turns out, most of us are better at describing where we want to go than we are at getting there. We've bought into the idea of change but haven't been particularly good at making it happen. We're good at many things, but this business of change is a lot more complicated.

How so? For starters, the marketplace itself is changing so fast that traditional incremental change is often too little too late. Whereas in the past we could take time to reshape our business, today we have to do it "yesterday"—and in some cases the only change that will take us where we need to go is *revolutionary* change. Being managers, not radicals, however, most of us don't have experience with revolutionary change. We're unsure of the first step and even less sure of those that follow. We're simply not that good at what we've never done before.

What we <u>do</u> know is that if revolutionary change is our goal, then the system—and the status quo it represents—will be fighting us each step of the way. We also know that the system will be a formidable adversary. If only we understood it better. If only our skills lay more in changing <u>it</u> than in changing ourselves and others to accommodate it. If only, in approaching major change, the cards weren't stacked against us.

Also complicating change is the fact that it is a moving target. For example, customers have always wanted value for their dollar. Just yesterday the focus of that value was quality. Today it's quality <u>and</u> price <u>and</u> service. Tomorrow it will be giving customers exactly what they want, exactly when they want it. And who's to say what it will be the day after.

Fortunately, there are numerous and notable examples of companies that have been able to change and thrive in a changing environment. In these companies, more often than not, leaders are passionately committed to change, individuals share a common vision, values create a common bond, and the work is considered to be its own best reward. Expectations have been raised and men and women regularly accomplish extraordinary things—as the examples in this book will amply illustrate.

THE FRONT LINE WON'T LIE

How can we know whether our own attempts to improve are working? Most organizations need look no further than the front line. If, as leaders, our personal day-to-day actions reflect our stated commitment and we regularly "walk our talk," then the front line will be our staunchest supporters and change's fiercest constituency.

If, on the other hand, we are not <u>actively</u> working to close the gap between where we are and where we say we want to be, then the front line will be hard on us and more than willing to talk about our organization's shortcomings. And when they do, they'll call it as they see it. <u>The front line won't lie.</u> If they perceive that leadership's commitment to change is weak and its actions hypocritical, front-line workers will become quickly cynical and unabashed in their desire to share their disappointment.

Recently, for example, we called a sporting goods store to find out whether it carried a certain item. When the clerk told us the store did, we asked her how much it cost. "I'm sorry," she said, "but I'm not allowed to quote prices over the phone."

"Seems like a stupid policy," we suggested, "particularly when your radio ads boast about your great customer service."

She was quick to agree. "You better believe it! But then, there are a lot of stupid things going on around here. Want to know a few more?" And before we could stop her, she listed a half-dozen examples of how the company was not delivering on its promise of customer service.

Not long ago, all we wanted from the front line was for them to do what they were told. Today, we rely on the front line to add value, particularly since they are the primary, and often only, point of contact with customers. But when our rhetoric around change outstrips reality, instead of adding value, the front line may just as likely subtract it. Fortunately, by being passionate and sincere in our commitment to remake the organization, we can prevent this from happening. Thinking about change, or talking about change, is not enough. We simply have to <u>do</u> it. The question is, how?

MAKING BETTER CHOICES

We wish we had the answer. We wish that the insights and knowledge we have gained through our contact with hundreds of talented men and women in the dozens of organizations we've had the opportunity to work with over the years would provide us with a solution, a silver bullet that we could pass on to you to facilitate the change process in your organization. Instead, we've found what you probably already know: Each organization is unique, each individual situation is one-of-a-kind, and each of us has to search for our own answers in our own time. Nothing is simple. Precious little is easy. Nothing transfers.

What can simplify and speed this difficult process, however, is having a better understanding of the choices available to us, and being better able to anticipate the intended and unintended effects of our actions. It is our intention in this book to illuminate those choices and their possible outcomes, to plant the seeds for dialogue, to provide a basis for experimentation, and to discuss the issues that confront us as we and those we've worked with perceive them.

Leadership, after all, is primarily about choices—about making the effective ones, to be sure. But, it is also about feeling free in the making of those choices, confident that we are well-informed, and comfortable that the choices we make are in accordance with our assumptions about people, organizations, and the larger world. It is our sincere hope that this book will also serve as a guide to examining your beliefs and helping you apply them to chart a future course that is as humane as it is effective, and as wise as it is profitable.

Ordinarily, a book that claims to focus on customers begins

with a few chapters about what customers want, followed by a few that deal with how to deliver it. This book doesn't. Instead, it begins with a discussion of organizational systems and offers some suggestions about how (and why) to change them. Our reason for doing so is simple. In all too many cases, the efforts of individuals seeking to improve service have been thwarted by systemic practices, procedures, and programs that are either in direct or indirect conflict with the sought for goal of delivering better value. No matter how hard we try, in other words, our present systems too often prevent us from succeeding.

Only when our systems encourage a customer focus can we expect employees to provide one. Only when our systems reward us for delighting our customers, instead of rewarding us for competing against each other, can we have the teamwork and cooperation necessary for exceptional service delivery. And only when our own thinking—along with everyone else's—is consonant with our shared goals can we design workable systems to meet our customers' future needs.

The needs of customers and how to better meet those needs are discussed in the second major part of this book. People—building and retaining a loyal workforce—are the focus of the final part. Our decision to talk about people last is not because they come last in our thinking, but because they are mightily influenced by both the system and the needs of customers—and because people are the final word in providing for those needs. There is little question today that, in a world where added value is the major differentiation between one company and the next, your company is only as good as the people who add that value. They're the ones who provide the vital link between what the system allows and what the customer ultimately gets. While the system governs what we <u>can</u> or <u>cannot</u> do for <u>our</u> customers, it is our people who determine whether we <u>will</u> or <u>will</u> <u>not</u> do it.

We must walk a fine line between pragmatist and visionary; between living with today's choices and creating new choices of our own; between getting the job done and making the job better; between being satisfied by what is and being obsessed with what can be. As leaders, we cannot give up either role. Instead, each day we must continue to walk that line in the face of present-day business realities, relentless change, old system constraints, new system hopes, and our own special and unique view of the world. The first choice we must make, therefore, is the choice to be both pragmatist <u>and</u> visionary.

GARY HEIL
TOM PARKER
RICK TATE

Palo Alto, California
September 1994

America's culture is America's greatest potential strength. Something about American values has enabled ordinary people, assembled haphazardly from around the world, to build the largest, richest, and freest economy in history, and to do so mainly through voluntary actions rather than state direction. The essence of our approach, the true American genius, is a talent for disorder.

—James Fallows, *More Like Us*

Part **1**

Leader as Revolutionary

I hold it that a little rebellion, now and then, is a good thing. . . .

—Thomas Jefferson

1

Leader as Revolutionary

THE CHALLENGE IS CLEAR

What is obscure, we eventually see. What is obvious, usually takes a little longer.

—EDWARD R. MURROW

Let's cut the bull. We all know that we have to be fast, we have to be flexible. If we're big, we have to act small. We have to be more innovative, creative, and productive.

We're living in a world with an overcapacity of everything from crackers to jet engines and the only way to grow for most of us is to grab new customers from our competition while keeping the ones we have. Our products are becoming commodities; quality levels are at their highest ever; and we're having trouble meeting financial analysts' demands because our own projections are being undermined by a fickle, rapidly evolving marketplace. It used to be we could make our numbers by trimming fat and being more efficient. No longer.

Today, there are more quality competitors, and more segmented markets. Smaller companies, capable of providing significantly better levels of value, are aggressively taking over the most profitable niches, walking away with the best customers, while customers everywhere are getting better and better educated. "You are special," they've been told. "You don't have to be one of the masses— you can have it *your* way."

And more and more they're getting it their way, even if they are a relatively small customer by yesterday's standards. Today's buyer has more options and can demand greater value than at any time in history.

Truly, these are exceptional times for American business and its leaders. It's a time when, by some accounts, U.S. companies are introducing two products per hour, twenty-four hours a day, seven days a week. A time when one worker out of ten is actually making something while the other nine are "adding value" to products with the knowledge they have acquired in the distribution process. A time of holy and unholy alliances, where companies compete bitterly for one corner of the market, and work together as partners in another. A time when the world's largest computer company must create its own low-end clone to protect its flank from competitors who have already inflicted serious damage and generated much mayhem.

It is also a time of great uncertainty created by the fragmentation and re-fragmentation of distribution channels. Walk into a Gooding's Supermarket in Florida and there's a Taco Bell. There's also one in your local college dorm . . . or maybe even in the lobby of your own company. In many parts of the country, banks are more nervous about competition from Merrill Lynch and Charles Schwab than they are from their traditional rivals. Long-time distributors are being cut out of the sales process as manufacturers create their own sales forces to deal directly with customers. And video stores count the months until cable companies, regional Bell holding companies, and other telecommunications companies offer movies on demand to households where television sets, telephones, and computers are rapidly becoming one.

One thing *is* certain. With future growth and profitability dependent on keeping existing customers loyal while continually bringing new ones into the fold, every company will be more reliant on its people. The only way we'll win loyal customers is with committed, enthusiastic employees who deliver the added value and build the close relationships that distinguish us from our competitors. And only a highly skilled workforce will be able to continually surprise and delight those they serve. In a time when people are justifiably insecure about their jobs, we must engender employee commitment. In a time when time is short for learning and experimentation, we must find substantially *more* time for both.

To this rapidly changing, time's-up world, we have all brought a great deal of activity. In our quest for that fast, flexible, innovative, customer-focused organization, we have read the books (or at least skimmed them), listened to the speakers, given speeches of our own, or hired a consultant in search of a "better way." Indeed, we are collectively of a mind: Things *do* have to change.

But, if that is the case, if we all prefer this sleek, efficient, customer-focused organization, why aren't we creating it more frequently? Or, more to the point, why do so many of our present practices still reward maintaining the status quo?

THE ISSUE IS LEADERSHIP

People repeatedly overlook a different kind of organization, one that values improvisation rather than forecasting, dwells on opportunities rather than constraints, discovers new actions rather than defends past actions, values arguments more than serenity, and encourages doubt and contradiction rather than belief.

—Karl Wieck

We were on a plane not long ago talking to the president of a well-known training and consulting company. He told us that his company was trying to figure out what products they were going to sell after "Total Quality" had run its course. After some thought, he added, "We think the next issue is LEADERSHIP."

As Yogi Berra said, "It's déjà vu all over again!" *Of course,* the next issue is leadership. It was also the last issue and the issue before that. It's the issue today, it was the issue last week and it will be the issue tomorrow. An organization's leaders are always the ones who must guide the organization into the future. They're the ones who have to set the wheels of change in motion, who must be most persistent in the pursuit of a different kind of organization.

The challenge today is to think about leadership in broader terms. Certainly it's about leading people. It's about inspiration, humanness, and compassion; but it's also about changing organizational structures and systems.

Why, then, haven't more of us created the fast, flexible, customer-focused organization that we all agree is preferable? Because, for the most part, leaders simply have not *chosen to commit* to creating the type of company they so clearly describe in many of their speeches. Instead, faced with short-term accountabilities and a wide range of uncertainties, they tend to do what they do best and what has achieved past success—which is usually what they did yesterday.

What worked yesterday, however, certainly won't work equally as well tomorrow. **We have to make the choice to change.** And when we do, we can't underestimate the commitment it will take. Making this choice will require leaders to abandon their traditional roles as goal setters, motivators, and decision makers. Instead, leaders will focus on helping people (and teams) design processes that will foster learning that can be effectively applied to continuously improving performance. Tomorrow's leaders must become the architects and builders of a very different kind of organization, where a shared vision and shared values—not rules—will provide a sense of order, and where responsibility, not status, will determine one's level of contribution.

If we are serious about gaining the loyalty and commitment of employees instead of just their compliance, we'll have to rethink our assumptions about motivation (as we should have decades ago). To bring about quick and radical change in tomorrow's organizations, our influence will depend less on title and external incentives and more on the power of our ideas, our passion for those ideas, the depth of our commitment, the persistence of our actions, and our ability to learn.

No One Is Exempt!

In tomorrow's organization, there will be no non-leaders. To label a person (or even think of them) as such will be to limit unnecessarily their ability to contribute.

For too long, being a leader has meant occupying a certain box on the company's organizational chart. In the future, the charts and the boxes may not exist in any recognizable form. No one will be exempt. Every person must be willing and able to lead some part of the change effort. Front-line employees will be expected to lead improvement efforts. They will help design and implement the continual re-engineering of delivery processes. They will be called upon to participate in almost every aspect of creating and governing the system in which they work.

For most companies to realize this type of organization will require transformational shifts in strategic goals and leadership practices. It will also require radical changes in organizational capabilities. It may require a "cold-turkey" departure from the practices that defined the old system—*even before alternative practices are "proven" to be effective.* Anything less will only give us more of what we already have.

If these changes sound revolutionary, it is because they are. But are they possible? Yes. Realistic? Definitely! Today, there are a number of leaders who have made the choice, struggled with the uncertainty, and persevered. It *can* be done. And if we're going to live up to what our mission and vision statements proclaim, we *must* make the choice. **We must *choose to change* significantly, and we must do so without a guarantee of success.**

Being a Change Agent Isn't What it Used to Be

We've been given a difficult assignment. As leaders, each of us has been designated a change agent—but the business of change simply isn't what it used to be. It used to be that a change agent's job was to create change <u>in</u> others—to get others to act like the change agent.

Today, as leaders and change agents, we have been asked to help transform the organization while changing the way <u>we</u> think and act. It's no longer, "you becoming more like me"—it's all of us agreeing to continuously change, and to do so without a clear view of the destination and with few, if any, good role models.

CHOOSING REVOLUTION

A non-violent revolution is not a program of seizure of power. It is a program of transformation of relationships, ending in a peaceful transfer of power.

—Mohandas K. Gandhi, "Nonviolence in Peace and War," 1948

Today, it is not change that makes most of us nervous. Rather it is the accelerated pace of change and its unpredictable nature that lead to the uneasiness that we often feel. The Volkswagen of change has turned into a Ferrari. In the past, there may have been some question as to whether revolutionary, transformational, or breakthrough change (substantial change, by any name) was necessary. But as the "champ to chump" cycle gets shorter, as employment becomes more tenuous for everyone—including CEOs—and as Mike Walsh (Tenneco, Union Pacific), "Neutron" Jack Welch (General Electric), and Herb Kelleher (Southwest Airlines) become role models for many, the word *revolution* rolls off our lips a bit more easily.

Experience has taught us that incremental improvement can be effective in creating a better version of what we did yesterday. But we know that doing more of what made us successful yesterday is a dangerous prescription. So it is not surprising that most leaders are calling for more dramatic changes. After all, as a colleague of ours likes to say, "Edison did not set out to improve the candle."

Yet, if we look at the characteristics of successful revolutions, it is also not surprising that so few leaders have actually chosen to make the commitment. Revolutionary changes in organizational capabilities require revolutionary leaders willing to face the unpredictability and pain associated with the radical transformation of any system. To choose the revolutionary route can be risky. For most, this choice will require substantial changes in present practices. To be successful, some may even have to bet their careers—but then, in a revolution, risk comes with the territory. These times are not for the faint-hearted. Caretaker leaders need not apply.

Successful revolutions are:

- **Messy and unpredictable.** No one knows how the revolution will unfold. Maybe the first couple of moves can be predicted. Maybe even the first few retaliatory salvos. After this, however, the revolution becomes a make-it-up-as-you-go-along affair. Not because revolutionaries are poor planners,

but because the relationships among all the entities involved
are just too complex to predict.

Because uncertainty is widely accepted "going in" to the
event, the people leading the effort often have "listening
posts" designed to provide constant feedback so that operations can be adjusted quickly. Also, since the complexity of
the operation is anticipated, leaders are expected to make
mistakes and are judged by the swiftness of their course
changes, not by their ability to predict the unpredictable. In
the words of Bob Allen, Chief Executive Officer of AT&T: "I
really think you have to question the sanity of anybody who
says they know how it's going to come out and what their
particular company is going to look like."

- **Powered by an idea.** The foundation of a revolution is typically a cause that is perceived to be worthy of people's commitment. Without a shared understanding of a compelling
cause, recruits would be difficult to attract. Dissatisfaction
with the present is required. Very few people attempting to
lead a revolution spend much time trying to put a "happy
face" on present performance. When the cause is worthy,
negative information is rarely demotivating.

- **Either fast or they fail.** Speed is crucial. The longer it takes
to reach the objective, the more opportunity the present system has to protect itself and defeat the agents of change. You
don't see many five- to seven-year revolutions these days (at
least not successful ones).

- **Never without casualties.** It's hard to change any system
without some people being disadvantaged by the event. The
nature of any significant change in a socio-technical system
is that some people who thrived in the old system will probably not fare as well in the new one. The leaders of the old
will not necessarily be the best leaders in the new. It would
be very unusual to see significant, effective change in a sys-

tem led by the people who built and prospered in the old. Talking of substantial change without casualties is just that—talking. **To make the choice to change significantly, we must face the uneasiness that comes from causing substantial discomfort for people who were often loyal, committed, hard-working contributors at a different time—in a different system.**

• **Never without resistance.** Allowing partially committed or uncommitted members of the revolution to occupy important positions for any significant period of time can reduce the effort's chance of success significantly. Committed people must occupy important positions from the outset. In successful revolutions, leaders who resist are not allowed to remain in their jobs and are not given the opportunity to undermine the formation of the new system—at least not for long.

Of course, it is asking a great deal to expect leaders to shift their thinking overnight and to embrace the risks inherent in leading a revolution. The characteristics common to successful revolutions are not those found as part of most of today's organizational improvement efforts. Because the skills required to lead a successful revolution have been discouraged in most companies, deciding on revolutionary change is an enormously difficult and potentially dangerous choice to make. But as customers demand more, and as organizations are forced by the marketplace to reshape and reinvent themselves, those who make the choice and are successful in bringing about transformational change will find themselves in ever greater demand. Learning to lead effectively in a rapidly changing competitive environment may involve substantial risk today, but may yield the best (if not the only) form of job security in the future.

Revolution: Choose or Choose Not!

We are reminded of Yoda's response to Luke Skywalker when Skywalker was not sure that he could levitate the spacecraft from the swamp:

"I'll try," Luke said.

"Try?" Yoda said, "Do or do not! There is no try!"

For today's leader, it's choose or choose not! Leadership is about choices and, to date, too few have chosen to take a route that is substantially different from the one they took yesterday. If we "choose not" for much longer, we may awake and find the decision has been made for us.

Part *2*

Leader as System Architect

Put simply, while traditional science focused on analysis, prediction, and control, the new science emphasizes chaos and complexity. Today scientists are developing powerful descriptions of the ways complex systems—from swarms of mosquitoes to computer programs to futures traders in commodities markets—cope effectively with uncertainty and rapid change. And therein lies an opportunity for fruitful dialogue between the world of management and the world of science.

—DAVID H. FREEDMAN, *Harvard Business Review*

2

Leader as System Architect

A system is an assembly of interdependent parts (subsystems) whose interaction determines its survival.

—Douglas McGregor, *The Professional Manager*

It is natural for any system, whether it be human or chemical, to attempt to quell a disturbance when it first appears. But if the disturbance survives these first attempts at suppression and remains lodged within the system, an iterative process begins. The disturbance increases as different parts of the system get hold of it. Finally it becomes so amplified it cannot be ignored.

—Margaret Wheatley, *Leadership and the New Science*

ANTICIPATING ORGANIZATIONAL "WHITE BLOOD CELLS"

For the past half-century, we've found it helpful to think of the organization as an open, organic human system whose survival is determined by the relationships among individuals and groups of individuals who comprise it. In trying to manage revolutionary change within such a system, one of the most critical issues for leaders to understand is the system's propensity to "protect itself." Predictably, when we try to substantially change the performance of a system, the system resists. The system produces the organizational equivalent of "white blood cells" to fight off infection. From all over the organization, people consciously and unconsciously, directly and subtly, protect the sense of order and predictability that characterized the organization yesterday. Traditionally, organizations tend to be the ultimate conservatives. They shy away from the unknown and tend to do what they do best, which is usually what they did yesterday. To be successful, tomorrow's leaders must become the architects of a new system.

An organization's structure is the framework that people create to provide order and predictability in the system. The overall structure is made up of a number of individual substructures, such as company practices, procedures, reward and incentive processes, visions, values, and shared beliefs. The structure of an organization invites certain behaviors and discourages others. Indeed, structure *drives* behavior. Very different people tend to act similarly in an organization. The structure acts to provide a sense of order to the group's behavior. It defines which types of behavior are acceptable and which are not. If people cannot adapt, they tend to find a place (or another organization) where they are more comfortable. In almost every organization, there are large numbers of people who would like to act differently but who feel that it is safer and usually more rewarding to conform to the expectations of the present system. We've often heard people discuss the effects of organizational structure:

"If this were my company, I certainly wouldn't act this way. But in this organization, it's their way or the highway."

"Yes, I'd love to try a new way. But if I did, I would be risking my career. It's just not worth it."

"These are really good ideas, but you've got the wrong person in this session. My boss should be here. She simply doesn't understand and until she does, it's impossible for me to make these changes."

While leaders may respond by saying that these people should take personal responsibility for changing the system, it's naive to think that people will try to make fundamental changes in the organization unless they perceive that the structures of the organization will be changed to support their efforts.

And who can blame them? Most have experienced a litany of change initiatives, have listened to countless warnings outlining the need to change, only to watch the next promotion given to a person who best navigated the old system and who did not live the values espoused—but not embodied—by the organization's leaders. Most people understand all too well that fitting in, finding a way to get things done in the present culture, and being a cooperative team player are rewarded more than experimenting with ways to change the fundamental character of the organization. It would be hard to overestimate the effect of an organization's present structure on the behavior of its individuals.

People find out about expected behaviors in a number of ways. They are implicitly or explicitly taught early on about how to get ahead, what it takes to make more money, who is most likely to get the next promotion and why, and how to stay out of trouble. They learn quickly whether they can talk frankly with the boss without limiting their career, what happens when they fail to live the company's values, and which are the most important rules. Through policies, procedures, leadership styles, shared values, corporate habits, problem-solving methods, and in a hundred other ways, people are told what is expected of them and what consequences they can expect for compliance or non-compliance.

STRUCTURE CAN DRIVE CRAZY BEHAVIOR

In her book *And So It Goes,* TV newswoman Linda Ellerbee tells of her interview with a prostitute for a CBS story. She paid the woman twenty bucks for her trouble and submitted the cost on her expense report. The report came back with a note saying that CBS "did not pay for news stories." She re-submitted the report, explaining that she hadn't paid for the news story but that she had paid for the prostitute's time because "it seemed to me to be the fair thing to do." This time, the expense voucher came back with a note explaining that, though CBS did not pay for news stories, it did pay for dinners. "I caught on," Ellerbee writes. "The third time the voucher was turned in it contained this item: 'Dinner with whore, $20.' I got the money."

Linda Ellerbee, *And So It Goes: Adventures in Publishing* (Berkeley Publishing, New York, 1987).

Significantly, the consequences of non-compliance need not be life-threatening to modify behavior substantially. One of the most mind-boggling examples of how people are affected by structure can be found in an experiment conducted by Stanford University professor Phillip Zimbardo. In the basement of Stanford's Psychology Building, Zimbardo set up a mock prison, populated and staffed by 21 normal, intelligent male college students who, by a flip of a coin, were assigned the role of either prison guard or prison inmate. Zimbardo in *The Social Animal* tells what happened:

> At the end of only six days, we had to close down our mock prison because what we saw was frightening. It was no longer apparent to us or most of the subjects where they ended or their roles began. The majority had indeed become "prisoners" or "guards" no longer able to clearly differentiate between role-playing and self. There were dramatic changes in virtually every aspect of their behavior, thinking, and feeling. In less than a week, the experience of imprisonment undid (temporarily) a lifetime of learning; human values were suspended, self-concepts were challenged, and the ugliest, most base

pathological side of human nature surfaced. We were horrified because we saw some boys ("guards") treat other boys as if they were despicable animals, taking pleasure in cruelty, while other boys ("prisoners") became servile, dehumanized robots who thought only of escape, of their own individual survival, and of their mounting hatred of the guards.

If these students modified their behavior in ways that were inconsistent with their personal values, even when the stakes were low, imagine the homogenizing effect of structure on those who perceive that their livelihood is at stake. The result is typically a high degree of conformity, even among people who prefer to be renegades.

If we want to change organizational performance, we must change the structures that built yesterday's successes. It's nonsensical to perpetuate the same or similar organizational practices and expect substantially different results. We must also design new structures that clearly communicate that a different set of behaviors is not only desirable, but critical, to the group's success. Transformational change or improvements cannot be sustained unless employees perceive that there are radical changes in the structure.

As in all complex endeavors, learning is key to changing an organization's structure. Once we accept that there is no "right" or "best" way, we can begin to improve our ability to work with others to learn about the organization and alter our practices in ways that can result in improved productivity. We must become expert in how our organizational structures reward certain actions and restrict others. We must test key substructures to ensure that they are consistent with our goals. We must seek leverage, identifying the specific structures that, if changed, will create the most substantial changes in performance. We must seek to understand the intended as well as the unintended effects of our present practices. Further, we must be willing to experiment with new ideas without assurances that they will be proven more beneficial than the old.

In most cases, we won't have to look far for a place to begin. The need for dramatic change confronts us daily—like it or not!

INQUIRING MINDS WANT TO KNOW

- Why do we talk constantly about cooperation but perpetuate human resource structures that are designed to create competition among team members?

- Why do we invite people to change in an inherently uncertain environment, but punish their failures via performance appraisals?

- Why do we talk "Total Quality" and "Continuous Process Improvement" but do not develop a shared understanding of the causes of variation?

- Why do we advocate employee involvement but balk when it comes time to trust employees to significantly participate in the management of the processes in which they work?

- Why do we work on solving communication problems but still have front-line people who do not understand the financial performance of the company or the customer's perception of quality?

- Why do we call performance appraisal a "developmental tool" but consistently overlook the fear, internal competition, and perceived unfairness that often accompanies the appraisal process?

- Why do we talk of the need to have interested, committed, loyal employees but continue to advocate leadership development programs that teach the systematic modification of employee behavior through the manipulation of rewards and punishment?

- Why have we advocated the use of so many "improvement tools" without cultivating an effective understanding of the underlying philosophy on which these tools were built and whether they are consistent with our personal beliefs or corporate values?

Combating the Organization's Immune System

Try to change the system—it resists. Push harder, and the system simply produces more "white blood cells" to fight off the infection. It seems the harder we push, the more resistance we encounter. Often, to create change in an organization, it is best to begin by altering the structures of the system to make it uncomfortable for people to perpetuate past practices and to encourage new kinds of performance. By reducing the effectiveness of the system's "immune system," we can significantly enhance our ability to create a very different set of organizational capabilities.

NOTHING TRANSFERS: EVERY SYSTEM IS UNIQUE

All too often, new management innovations are described in terms of "best practices" of so-called leading firms. While interesting, I believe such descriptions can do more harm than good, leading to piecemeal copying and playing catch-up. I do not believe great organizations have ever been built by trying to emulate another, any more than individual greatness is achieved by trying to copy another "great person."

—Peter Senge, *The Fifth Discipline*

Almost every organization that has substantially improved its performance over time has done so in its own way. In cases where we have witnessed a company trying to copy the successful methods of another, the results have been less than desirable, and some of these attempts in large companies have resulted in expensive and ineffective bureaucracies. Only when we stop looking to others for answers, abandon our search for off-the-shelf miracle cures, persistently use tools that promote learning, and engage every group in the organization to find what works best for *us* will we put ourselves on the road to continuous improvement.

While the practices, policies, methods, training programs, or-

---

DANCES WITH TOOLS

I survived two earthquakes, the L.A. riots, the Malibu fires, and TQM.

—Seen on a T-shirt of a student at the University of California, Berkeley

"Total Quality didn't work for us," a manager told us in a recent seminar. "What part of Total Quality did you find problematic?" we asked. "Process Improvement? Employee Involvement? Customer Focus? Systematic Learning?" "No, we agree with the philosophy," he said, "but we didn't find Total Quality any better than the other methods we've tried. It just didn't pay the dividends we were expecting."

How could *it*? *It's* inanimate! *It's* philosophies, methods, and tools that skillful leaders can use to help manage organizational transitions. Like any set of tools, when they are in the hands of a person who doesn't know how to use them or who is uncommitted to the underlying task, success is rare.

Today, our organizational toolboxes are overflowing with methods and tools that many leaders have found effective in helping them to communicate values, order information, communicate roles, and foster learning.

In every case, however, the leaders had to continually customize the methods to the situations they faced. The difference between a management fad and a helpful method is probably not which method is chosen but how much is learned from the initial implementation effort and whether or not that learning is used to improve future efforts.

For those who continue to search for the right tool or right method, the risks are significant.

---

ganizational structures, and assumptions about the nature of success are often quite similar among organizations, differences in people, markets, competitive pressures, and other system elements give every company its own culture, which must be addressed uniquely. Even incremental differences in a system can result in very different reactions to improvement attempts. Nothing transfers!

This is not to say that tools or processes can never be shared from company to company. Rather, the application of methodologies such as Total Quality, re-engineering, continuous improvement, and others must be adapted to address the individual culture of the organization at a specific point in time. More often than not, however, the failure of many change implementation efforts can be traced to a one-size-fits-all approach where "doing quality" or enhancing an improvement methodology in a prescribed way was perceived to be the overarching goal, rather than learning.

EMBRACING THE INESCAPABLE HUMANNESS OF THE SYSTEM

Freud said that all unimportant decisions you make logically, and all the important decisions illogically or emotionally. I believe it . . . In my own case, I trust my emotional decisions quite often more than the logical ones. Why? There is more power behind them to carry them out.

—Bill Caudill, *This I Believe*

The important implication for our purposes, from this rapidly growing body of research knowledge, is that emotional responses, many of which are completely unconscious, are associated with virtually all human behavior. It is clear that attempts to eliminate them by verbal persuasion are futile.

—Douglas McGregor, *The Professional Manager*

The emotions and feelings of the people in an organization greatly affect its capabilities. For better or worse, the complexity (and at times the irrationality) that this adds to the challenge of leadership is unavoidable. It's reflected in statements we hear all the time:

"You have to leave your emotions and passions outside of the room and operate rationally if you want to be successful in this organization."

"I love managing this restaurant. I'd like it more, however, if I didn't have to deal with employee problems all day. . . ."

"This would be a great business if we didn't have to deal with customers who don't always know what they want but feel strongly about the value they deserve."

Although most managers would agree that the people who work for them have strong emotions, many leaders act as if a person can choose to stow their emotions at the front door. Some believe that people can (and should) separate their feelings from their analytical abilities and strive to make purely objective judgments. Still others act as if expressions of emotion in the workplace are inappropriate—providing, euphemistically, "opportunities for improvement"—and that intelligent, educated people can and will be rational and logical in all their business dealings. "Dealing with the facts" and "leaving our emotions out of the discussion" are valued traits in many organizations. The assumption is that to be productive, people should learn to limit their expression of fears, anxieties, anger, and disappointments.

The irrationality of this assumption, the sheer futility of it, should be obvious. Our experience and decades of research make it abundantly clear that people are *always* affected by their emotions, and often significantly so. The more important the issue, the more likely we are to rely upon our emotions in formulating a response. Many emotional responses are unconscious reactions to our environment that we couldn't control even if we wanted to. That's why, instead of expecting people to separate their emotions from their work lives, we must learn to deal effectively with emotions in all our interactions. We really don't have a choice. Every organization is inescapably human.

The desire of some leaders to reduce peoples' emotional reactions often stems from those managers' underdeveloped ability to deal effectively with these reactions. Most of us have simply not been very good at marrying the emotional component of the orga nizational system with the more predictable and certain technical components. Inevitably, the reactions of employees—*and* leaders— are emotional as well as rational. We want all employees to feel like "owners" and approach their work enthusiastically. We want lead ers to be empathetic and caring. Indeed, we <u>do</u> want and need the emotional involvement of each group to do its jobs well. What we have not wanted to acknowledge is the full gamut of our emotions. We seem to prefer that people express only those feelings that serve the organization's needs. But, in reality, allowing people to express their feelings *does* serve the organization's needs.

While the humanness of the system adds complexity, with this complexity comes opportunity. As organizations increasingly rely on people to sustain organizational success, designing a system that builds trust, enhances loyalty, captures enthusiasm, stimulates interest, and deepens commitment may create a hard-to-duplicate source of sustainable competitive advantage. Dealing effectively with people requires, among other things, genuine caring, empa thy, and the ability to mesh organizational objectives with the indi vidual goals of a wide variety of people.

BEYOND NEWTON: LEARNING TO MANAGE THE WHOLE INSTEAD OF MANAGING PARTS

> *. . . An infinitesimal change in initial conditions could have a profound effect on the evolution of the entire system. . . . For all practical pur poses, the behavior of even relatively simple physical systems is funda mentally unpredictable. . . .*
>
> —David H. Freedman, *Harvard Business Review*

Observing hydrogen and oxygen gases reveals little about the na ture of water. Studying water does little to inform us about the qualities of ice. Improving the performance of individuals does not necessarily render the work group more productive, nor do improvements in individual functional departments always result in organizational gains. Understanding the separate parts of a system—be it a single-celled organism, a company, a school system, or the galaxy—does little to help us predict the properties or capabilities of the system as a whole. *It is the relationships among the parts of the system in a particular environment that determine the characteristics of that system at a specific point in time.*

As mentioned earlier, over the past half-century, there has been a growing tendency to describe human systems, such as organizations, within a "systems theory" framework. Yet there is still considerable resistance to thinking systemically in many American corporations. The difficulties inherent in understanding, and effectively dealing with, the complex interrelationships that define an open, organic, constantly adapting system can be daunting to many managers, who are far more at ease with the traditional view of the organization where the focus is on certainty and predictability and on managing individual elements. Understandably, many managers prefer this fairly simple model to explain the complex workings of their organizations.

The model is an old one, dating back to Isaac Newton's 17th-century Laws of Motion and to the principles 18th- and 19th-century scientists used to predict the behavior of complex physical systems. Back then, a system was thought of in machine-like terms. In his 1911 book, *The Principles of Scientific Management,* Frederick Winslow Taylor brought this concept of system-as-machine to the organization. He advised breaking the system down into small parts to arrive at the best procedure for performing a given task. Impressed by the greater efficiencies promised by Taylor's approach, many early 20th-century leaders adopted his theories, and to this day his ideas remain highly influential in shaping the way many companies are organized and the way many leaders think.

These past views of organizational effectiveness aren't wrong; they're just highly limited. As Douglas McGregor said in *The Professional Manager,*

I have argued that the difficulty with many traditional views of reality is not that they are wrong, but that they are partial. This creates a difficulty because what is not explained turns out to be greater than what is.

The knowledge we have gained over the centuries can be very valuable in our future efforts. However, we must remain cognizant that these views represent only a partial, and often oversimplified, explanation of reality. In most cases, traditional models enhance our ability to analyze and improve the performance in part of the system, without giving sufficient consideration to the unintended effects of actions in *other* parts of the system, and without taking into account the interactive qualities of the system's parts. Many managers are aware of the shortcomings inherent in this reductive model, but are hesitant to let go of the "piece part approach" until another equally understandable method is offered. The illusion that we can rationally predict, understand, and control our experiences can be irresistible—especially if we never directly experience the full effect of our actions.

The explosion of scientific knowledge we have witnessed during this century is forcing us to abandon relatively simple explanations of reality for more complex ones. Much of the thinking about physical systems that served as the basis for Taylor's approach has now been superseded. A number of important new theories, including chaos and quantum theory, provide us with new insights. Physical systems can no longer be viewed primarily as predictable and controllable. Instead, they are best characterized by chaos and complexity. Absolute predictability has given way to statistical probability. Newton's "equal and opposite reactions" have given way to infinitesimal changes yielding profound effects. The once-popular view of the physical world as a machine that could be broken down into components that could be understood and controlled is being replaced by a new view of a dynamic organic system that is ever evolving, highly susceptible to external conditions, and seemingly random in its movement.

Of course, it isn't always possible to focus on the entire system when trying to solve problems. Nor should we always try to. Just as scientists sometimes focus on atoms, sometimes molecules, and at other times compounds, depending on what they are investigating, we may choose to focus on different groups and levels of the organization (i.e., individuals, work groups, teams, divisions, functional areas, sales channels, etc.) at different times. Although individuals, work groups, divisions, and business units have characteristics in common, each also has characteristics that are unique. If we can develop better methods for understanding these groups as well as the relationships among them as they exist in the present structure, we may be better able to understand why the behavior in the organization is frequently different from what we think it ought to be.

THE UNIQUE SOUL OF A CORPORATION

There is a little something of the machine in every corporation. Like a machine, a corporation's workings are intricate, each of its components is vital. It is difficult to build and harder still to repair. Yet the organization is also like a human, with strategies that represent its intellect, structures that mimic the body's systems, and people that are at its heart. At its essence, however, the great organization is neither machine nor human, but spirit. The spirit and passion of the organization's founders give it birth, the spirit of its people gives it continued life, and the spirit of a future that everyone in the organization believes in propels it forward.

Look closely at any great organization—your own, perhaps. Then look even closer. Check out the people, their interest, their excitement. Watch its leaders at work. See how skillfully they do their jobs, infecting those around them with enthusiasm. And then compare what you find here to any other company. Chances are, much will be the same. But at the most basic level there will be a difference, for no company is like any other. This uniqueness is the soul of the corporation—elusive, ethereal, special.

While these new theories about systems have a firm hold on current scientific thought, they haven't yet found their way into the mainstream of thinking in most organizations. This is hardly surprising. As beholden as we are to our shareholders, and with billions of dollars at stake, it's certainly easier to embrace a paradigm that promises predictable outcomes than to embrace one whose only given is uncertainty. It's also more comfortable for most leaders to work with the skill sets that have gotten them to where they are than have to adopt a whole new way to lead.

Still, the handwriting is on the wall. Just as scientists must let

---

OUT OF GAS

A large trucking company, Company F, had significantly improved its productivity in delivering gas to its customers—gas stations affiliated with a large oil company. It had lowered costs, and developed a Just in Time method to guarantee a continuous supply of gas to stations. Company F had also developed a sophisticated information system that gave it early warning of unusual circumstances.

Although the customer seemed satisfied with Company F's performance, it awarded next year's contract to a competitor, based on a very small price advantage. The competitor, however, did not make provisions for unscheduled deliveries, nor did it guarantee that gas stations would not run out of gas.

Using the new competitor, gas stations began to run out of gas. Up to 25% of them ran out of gas more than three days before the end of the month and were forced to buy gas from another oil company. In an attempt to win back the contract, representatives from Company F went to the oil company to explain the Just in Time delivery system it had developed and the costs incurred by allowing stations to run out of gas. The purchasing department's reaction was startling. The purchasing agents said that their incentive plan called for a decrease in costs per gallon delivered and they had done their part.

We wouldn't have believed it if we hadn't experienced it.

go of past theory and move on to new levels of understanding, we as leaders must do the same. The time for managing individuals, tasks, and events as if they were unrelated is over. So is the view of the organization as a predictable machine. Understanding only its parts is simply too limiting and counterproductive, and can't possibly provide us with the perspective we'll need to steer our organizations in the direction offering the greatest probability of success. **Maybe the most important benefit of learning to deal with the system as a whole is that it provides a better basis for understanding what really goes on in an organization instead of feeding our natural tendency to see the organization as we believe it ought to be.**

3

The System Challenges

Strategically Planned Unreasonableness: Building a Constituency for Change

People who describe themselves as "reasonable" will always tell you why something can't be done because that's what they understand. The renegades who built this country—our founding fathers—didn't know whether their experiment in a new kind of government, representative of democracy, would work. But they were willing to take the risk and thus, to reap the potential rewards. . . .

—Roger Ailes, *Success*

Reasonable men adapt themselves to their environment; unreasonable men try to adapt their environment to themselves. Thus all progress is the result of the efforts of unreasonable men.

—George Bernard Shaw

UNREASONABLENESS

The best place to look for the basis of organization change is in the future business, and the worst place to look is in the current organization. The present organization, however, may be a good predictor of what will prevent you from developing the kind of organization you will need. Like all creatures, it has a vested interest in continuing to exist.

—S. Davis and B. Davidson, *2020 Vision*

Although there are as many models for goal setting as there are people teaching goal-setting classes, most of us have been taught essentially the same thing: that goals should be specific, measurable, and attainable. In the classroom, these guidelines sound like common sense. In practice, however—especially when considered in conjunction with performance appraisal and compensation practices—setting goals that are specific and attainable can significantly inhibit the effectiveness of change efforts.

Most of us have been there (even if we don't want to admit it). We've sat with our boss and negotiated our goals for the coming year. We wanted them to appear to be "stretch" goals, but we certainly didn't want them to be so ambitious that we couldn't attain them. In fact, we wanted to ensure that there was an excellent chance we would be able to *exceed* them. (After all, in most performance appraisal systems, "fully meets expectations" nets you only a 3 on a 5-point scale.) Having to undergo the same ordeal with his or her boss, our boss was generally sympathetic to our situation, though he or she probably haggled for a little more stretch than we had in mind. In the end, however, chances are we'd compromise

on goals that were somewhat higher than last year's, but still reasonably attainable in the year to come.

The question is, "attainable" in what context? Under the present system? Or under a new system—the sleeker, more flexible,
more responsive one that we should all be working toward? In
most cases, the goals mutually agreed upon between employees
and bosses are those perceived to be achievable in the system in
place at the time the deal was struck. Given the choice of accomplishing the goals in the system we understand or in a new one,
most of us choose the more predictable route.

This is hardly a surprise. Even though many companies talk of
rewarding the mistakes that inevitably result from experimenting
with new methods, performing predictably is usually more career-
enhancing. Setting attainable goals allows us to work in a manner
we understand but may well be an impediment to substantial
change.

The systemic semistagnation encouraged by setting attainable
goals is often exacerbated when linked with most pay-for-performance plans. There is little question that paying for performance
can result in more of a desired behavior. Money motivates. The
problem is, it doesn't usually motivate us to invent a better method
of performance. Rather, it typically motivates us to take the fastest,
most direct, most predictable course to get the money—which, in
most organizations, translates to staying with the old structures.

It is becoming increasingly clear that, under most circumstances, attainable goals—i.e., goals that can *reasonably* be expected
to be accomplished without changing present practices—are an
idea whose utility has passed. Instead, to build a true constituency
for change, the time has come to set goals that are clearly *unreasonable* when measured against the capabilities of yesterday's practices. With reasonable goals come incremental change. With
unreasonable goals, the gap between our resources and our aspirations widens, necessitating that we experiment with more radical
methods, which can lead to more learning and transformational
improvements.

C1

We've Learned Our Lesson

C1

To pave the way for setting unreasonable goals, we must reconsider our accountability and reward practices as they relate to goal attainment. We recently visited a group that last year had set very aggressive goals for itself—significantly higher than those set by similar groups in the organization. By setting such aggressive goals, they essentially committed to a redesign of their process rather than a mere tune-up. The good news was that they were largely successful, and improved considerably more over the year than any other group in the company. The bad news was that they fell just short of meeting the ambitious goal they had targeted twelve months earlier. They were, therefore, excluded from the celebrations held to reward the "successful" groups even though, by any measure, they had outclassed the field. Having learned their lesson, this year they set more moderate goals. However, one member of the group confided, "I liked it better when we were more aggressive, but the price was simply too high."

As the saying goes, to make a Volkswagen go as fast as a Porsche, you can't just push harder on the accelerator—you have to redesign the car. If the changes we seek are substantial, then we must build a critical mass of people within the organization who are willing to commit to unreasonable goals. Instead of meeting goals that were based on a history of hedging our bets, we must reward learning and experimentation. We must avoid practices that increase the rigidity of employees and make it rewarding to redesign the system and abolish unnecessary tasks. Let's ensure that our goals far exceed our resources and the present capabilities of our processes so that innovation is no longer an option. Let's make certain that the system's structures make substantial unreasonable progress the norm.

BUILDING A CONSTITUENCY FOR CHANGE

> *One of the difficulties in bringing about change in an organization is that you must do so through the persons who have been most successful in that organization, no matter how faulty the system or organization is. To such persons, you see, it is the best of all possible organizations, because look who was selected by it and look who succeeded most within it. Yet, these are the very people through whom we must bring about improvements.*
>
> —George Washington

C1

In most cases, substantial change has a small constituency, if it has one at all. Although talk of change is constant in many groups, the actions of most have not lived up to the words. The tendency to underestimate the resistance that will be encountered and to overestimate the cooperation that will be received has led many to take an evolutionary path. This often results in a great deal of activity, but little real change.

The magnitude and sources of the resistance depend, to a large extent, on the past history of the group. In organizations that have preferred balance to novelty and predictability to experimentation, efforts to substantially change will excite significant resistance. However, in companies like PepsiCo, Union Pacific, Microsoft, CNN, and Chase Manhattan PFS, resistance is nowhere near as intense. These organizations exist in a constant state of imbalance and have grown to expect that change is continuous and that to be able to thrive in a changing environment is a condition of employment.

To effectively overcome the natural tendency of the organization to protect its past, we must upset the comfortable balance provided by the existing system. We must learn to create disequilibrium, anticipate resistance, identify its root causes, and begin to alter the conditions that make perpetuating the past more secure and rewarding than renewal. To reduce resistance, we must generate new information and create new processes that effectively

C1

challenge existing practices and the assumptions we considered truths just yesterday. Surprises, disruptions, and confrontations must not be considered career-limiting occurrences, but must be perceived as opportunities for everyone to learn. Only when the system is out of balance can it overcome the natural tendency to resist the efforts of those who could change it.

The order and stability that so many of us have cherished in the past provided us with a reassuring sense of predictability and control. Today, however, we are paying the price. The sense of stability on which so many people depend, the present conditions that so many will not give up easily, only serve to keep real, needed change at arm's length. Creating disequilibrium may seem like an odd thing for a leader to want. But the more the organization expects that change is normal and the better a group's skills at dealing with the complexities inherent in change, the more effective leaders will become at building a constituency to support significant improvement efforts.

CELEBRATED DISCONTENT

> *It requires a strong constitution to withstand repeated attacks of prosperity.*
>
> —J.L. Basford

In organizations where yesterday's achievements are viewed with a feeling of pride at the same time that today's rate of improvement is perceived to be slower than will be required to sustain success in the future, a culture of *celebrated discontent* exists.

A mixture of pride and nervous aspiration, celebrated discontent was very much in evidence on our first trip to Disney World. A Disney manager described to us how critical "cast members" can be when evaluating their performance and how past successes have not dulled the cast's focus on the need for faster improve-

PRIDE AND DISCONTENT

Spend a day with a dozen Microsoft leaders and you can't help but get a sense of the *Celebrated Discontent* that *is* the Microsoft culture. Immediately, if not sooner, you learn that they are proud of what they've accomplished and they're afraid that they are not moving fast enough. Within the hour, the range of emotions runs the gamut:

Discontent. *"We've grown a little too fast. We are much more bureaucratic than we used to be."*

Pride. *"It's an incredible place to work. Every day is a new challenge and the people are brilliant. After working here, it would be tough to work anywhere else."*

Frustration. *"We're just too big to be as fast as we used to be. I liked it better when we were smaller and more focused."*

Focused. *"We will re-define the way information is used in society."*

Caring. *"Our secret is our people. We are committed to helping every individual reach his or her potential."*

Perhaps the most noteworthy are the emotions that you don't see. Faced with the introduction of over 100 new products each year for the next several years, the people responsible for supporting these products openly embraced the challenge:

"Of course, the challenge is unreasonable. That's what makes this place interesting. Life would be boring if things didn't change. Just think, I'm guaranteed new challenges for the next several years. I won't be bored. That's more than most people in organizations can say."

We can see why Microsoft and the people who make up the organization are so good. One simply cannot spend a couple of hours with members of the Microsoft team without learning a ton! Your thinking will be challenged—like it or not!

ment in the future. The manager's impatience for improvement was exceeded only by her enthusiasm for the cast celebration she was about to attend to express appreciation for those members of her team responsible for creating the Disney magic.

We also experienced celebrated discontent on our visit to Honda's manufacturing facility in Marysville, Ohio. The plant associates, who had recently retooled the entire assembly line overnight, were meeting with field service representatives of American Honda. Although both groups were proud of Honda's quality performance, they seemed concerned that they were not improving every aspect of their business fast enough to stay ahead of the competition.

Unfortunately, the ability to focus simultaneously on celebration *and* improvement is rare in most organizations. Many seem to have adopted an either/or mindset—one that focuses on either celebration *or* improvement. The danger of the celebration-only mindset is that it can lead to organizational complacency and a susceptibility to being blindsided by competitors. Conversely, the organization steeped in discontent and focused exclusively on improvement can be demotivating for its people. This can result in a place where nothing that anyone does is good enough. The leader's job is to ensure that there is an abundance of opportunity to celebrate successes while cultivating an impatience with present rates of improvement.

> *If we're going to win the pennant, we've got to start thinking we're not as good as we think we are. . . . It'll be tough convincing these guys of that.*
> —Casey Stengel, Manager, New York Yankees (addressing the 1953 Yankees who were everybody's favorite to win the American League Pennant)

C H A L L E N G E   2

"By What Method?" Learning to Learn

*In times of drastic change, it is the **learners** who inherit the future. The **learned** usually find themselves equipped to live in a world that no longer exists.*

> —Sign hanging on a wall in the office of Jules Trump, CEO of Northern Automotive Corp. (author unknown)

*W*e sat in on a meeting with a management consultant and the management team of a large corporation at a meeting that was held to review the company's annual results. After outlining the many areas in which the company had exceeded its targets, the team proceeded with a comprehensive analysis of why targets had been missed in other areas. Near the end of the meeting, the consultant picked two areas in which the company had far exceeded their projections and asked the team why these areas had been so successful.

The team's reply: " We're not sure. Because we were successful in these areas we spent most of our time trying to improve in the areas where results were lagging."

The consultant suggested, "Sometimes you'll do well because you execute a brilliant strategy effectively. Other times you'll succeed because you're lucky. Isn't it important to know which you were last year . . . and why?"

You could have heard a pin drop. Point made!

Each success only buys an admission ticket to a more difficult problem.

> —Henry Kissinger

C2

A management team's propensity to dissect its failures and celebrate—though pay less attention to—its successes is a common
one. Many of us have learned that spending our time on reducing
failures is not only smart, it's often the first sentence in the company's survival manual. We have also learned that to succeed is
important; to know *why* we succeeded is secondary. Although ex-
pedient, this failure to investigate our successes has made it difficult for many of us to truly learn about our companies and our
markets. Subtly, it has affected our ability to meet the changing
needs of customers, employees, and shareholders.

The way we learn on the job has become second nature for
many of us. A problem arises, we know the result we desire, we
have observed others deal with the issue before, and so we choose
to act in a manner similar to the way that "worked" last time. Our
action again leads to a successful result. We now store this script in
our brain, subject to recall. Having had this experience, we are reasonably assured that if Situation A were to crop up again and we
desire Outcome A, we would only need to apply the same action as
before, Action A. Having succeeded a second and third time, we no
longer even question Action A, nor spend significant amounts of
time analyzing why it was successful or furthering our understanding of its effects on the system. Why would we? Obviously,
we know how to handle Situation A. The result speaks for itself. In
our busy schedules, the Situation A/Action A/Outcome A script
frees us up to think about other things.

Doing this, though, we have learned little about how the system works. Nor do we know what unintended effects Action A
may have had elsewhere in the company. All we really know is
that Action A had the short-term intended effect that we were after.
Had we failed, however, we would have spent considerable time
analyzing why and looking for alternatives that might prove more
successful. Rather than committing a script to memory, we would
have been forced by our failure into a more comprehensive and
profound examination of how and why things did or didn't work.
This examination could have led us to learn more about the sys-

tem, find better ways to deal with the task at hand, and discover a course of action that might be more effective the next time the organization faced a new challenge. **Had we failed more often, in other words, we could have learned more, and could have become a better learner.**

Many leaders simply have not failed often enough to have developed good learning skills. Of course, these people are educated. But, for the most part, they haven't *learned to learn.* It's one thing to learn facts about a given subject and subsequently apply them in certain specific situations. It's quite another to be able to effectively translate our past experiences into a course of action that works when the circumstances are significantly different or when we're functioning in an area where we have little or no experience.

A decade or more ago, when the rate of change was less rapid, learning good scripts from a mentor, applying them, and making them our own may have been enough. The situations we faced tended to be similar, the outcomes we desired were well known and consistent, and our scripts seemed effective. More recently, when the world began to change at a faster pace, we often held sufficient power in the organization to ensure that our scripts resulted in the short-term effects we desired. Unbeknownst to us, our problems started as our scripts continued to prove successful and we began relying on them more and more. As we moved up in the organization, we developed structures that required others to learn our scripts, training programs to teach their effectiveness, and reward and recognition programs to make it personally beneficial to apply them. Having proven scripts saved time; there was no need to keep reinventing the wheel.

Our scripts also made things seem simple and predictable and led us to adopt concepts like "keep it simple, stupid" (KISS). Why not? They seemed to work—and often quite well! But all the while we (and others) were using these scripts, we were gradually developing a learning deficiency. Our desire for predictability and certainty was compromising the ability of many of us to deal effectively with the complexity that surrounded us. And as the world changed, our ability to learn from our experiences diminished.

Today, many organizations have generations of managers who will march through walls if the destination is clear and the script is known. But many have not developed the ability to experiment with complexity and to use their learnings to create new and better scripts. As a result, when their old scripts are no longer working, rather than go back to the drawing board, they search for a different script that might be more successful. But whose? Where to turn next?

Hire a consultant? Find a new tool? How about Total Quality? Maybe if we were organized in teams? Do we need a new leadership model? Benchmarking? Maybe some other company's "best practice" (*that* company's script) will work? We have all been part of improvement efforts where someone else's script was hurriedly adopted as a means for solving a pressing problem. Pick a consultant. If they don't have the answers, you picked the wrong one. Find one with more experience. Total Quality? If it doesn't produce fast results, it must be the wrong tool for our situation.

The reality is that there may be a hundred methods that could work. But no one knows for a fact which one will work in a given organization at a given time. The uniqueness of people and each organization requires a customized solution. There is simply no shortcut, no substitute for experimentation and learning. Sure, we can try to "keep it simple, stupid," but making the task simpler than it is doesn't make sense. We must develop the skills to deal with the complex issues we face.

Seeking the certainty and predictability that *does* exist is fine; but seeking more than there is has a price, and today the price is exorbitant. That we may not be able to trace the cost of doing so to this month's or this year's bottom line makes our quest for certainty and predictability all the more dangerous. These practices can be insidious—tending to diminish our ability a little here and a little there—and almost unnoticeable. But when the time comes for us to call on our skills to learn and manage complexity, we will be forced to dance with the skills we have.

C2

DESPERATELY SEEKING CERTAINTY

Our need to keep things simple can lead to a number of practices that inhibit our ability to improve. Often, our search for certainty and predictability has led to:

1. Oversimplifying cause and effect relationships. Causes and their effects are often separated in time and place. The immediate, observable reaction to any act tells only part of the story. Our tendency to examine only those reactions that are close in time and directly related to the intended effect of our actions can mask other data that is crucial to learning and the effective management of the system. Incentive compensation? It often leads to higher sales levels. But are they the *right kind* of sales? And could an emphasis on individual incentives lead to lower levels of customer service, which is dependent on employee cooperation? Maybe/maybe not—but have we even considered the possibility?

Virtually every action we take has unintended consequences elsewhere in the organization—consequences that are sometimes not manifest for weeks, months, or even years. Therefore, if we measure the effects our actions have only in areas where we expect effects, and only those effects close in time to our initial actions, we will never understand the full ramifications of much of what we do. This is what Peter Senge has referred to as the "core learning deficiency" in most companies. We agree!

2. Reduced experimentation and innovation. If we believe a simple answer exists, there is less need for experimentation and the time-consuming analysis it entails. If there is less experimentation, there is less learning, which results in less innovation. The history of innovation is filled with stories of how failed experiments led to a body of knowledge that, in turn, redefined a product or opened new markets.

C2

3. Reduced information flow and dialogue. If there is a simple answer, there is less need for various kinds of information throughout the organization: i.e., "Because we already have an answer, there's no need to talk with someone in another part of the process about the problem." If issues are kept simple, less dialogue will surround them, and there will be less questioning of present practices and less need for the kinds of information that can lead to higher levels of understanding.

UP 2? DOWN 3?

Not long ago a manager told us, "We really blew them away last month. Customer satisfaction ratings were up 2%! Makes us one of the top three divisions in the company." When we asked him what the margin of error was in last month's results, however, he didn't know, nor did he know whether the process was "in control" or whether this month's performance was within the control limits of the process.

Based on these results, he held a division party to celebrate the great news. As it turned out, that month's margin of error was 2.5%, and the results of all the divisions were statistically indistinguishable. We can only assume that the group was disheartened when the following month's results showed a 3% dip for the division.

4. Underdeveloped measurement skills. If we look at the organization in a simplistic way, there's no need to measure the unintended effects of our actions, learn sampling techniques, understand variation, determine control limits, or devise methods for measuring the effects of our actions in the "soft areas" (i.e., customer loyalty or employee satisfaction).

Incomplete measurement inhibits learning by depriving us of pertinent information.

C2

5. "Flavor of the Month" improvement programs. "If there's an answer, let's find it. Experiment? Hasn't someone else already done the experimentation? Why do I have to reinvent the wheel?"

Our desire to find simple solutions has led many of us on frustrating and often extraordinarily costly searches. It's been common to try a new tool one month and, if it doesn't work, assume it's the tool's fault and adopt another. Imagine trying to assemble a complicated product where substantial assembly is required, then getting frustrated because you can't do it quickly and blaming your screwdriver for the problem. Blaming the tools, discarding them, and looking for the next great idea is among our most destructive tendencies. Instead of looking for the next tool, we would be well advised to learn as much as we can from the system's reaction to our last improvement effort.

6. Increased organizational and personal rigidity. "This is the best method." "This vendor has the best program." "This consultant has the answer." In our desire to be right, to be certain, and to be done with it, we're often attracted to a simple solution, rather than acknowledge that we don't completely understand the problem. This can be especially true in situations where accountability practices make it very difficult to admit that we've made a mistake. Again, if we can't admit that we're confused or uncertain or that we've failed, then we can't use the information we would have learned from our efforts in our renewed quest to succeed.

7. Promoting a risk-adverse environment. When things are simple, there is no reason for mistakes. People begin to believe that mistakes are caused by not following the accepted script. ("We all know it works.") Conforming can become the safe, acceptable behavior and, therefore, improvement attempts are usually limited to the fifth edition of what didn't work yesterday. The result—no real experimentation and, therefore, little if any learning.

PLAN—DO—CHECK—ACT IS A LEARNING MODEL

Sixty years ago I knew everything; now I know nothing; education is a
progressive discovery of our own ignorance.

—Wil Durant

Fortunately, we are not strangers to a methodology that can be effective in helping us deal with complexity—the scientific method. Many of us learned about the scientific method early in high school, if not before. If we haven't conducted experiments ourselves, we've read about scientists who have and we are aware that the results of those experiments have shaped our daily lives. For thousands of years, people have experimented with their environment, debated their findings, and planned how to learn more in the future. The technical complexity of the subject matter has changed significantly, but the basic method has not. From Aristotle to Edison to our most recent Nobel Prize winners in physics, the scientific method has served mankind well.

In the early part of this century, educator John Dewey translated the well-established scientific method into a learning model for use in schools. He postulated that all learning was necessarily connected to action. Test your ideas, act on them, check the results, analyze the information, and capture key learnings that will improve your ability to do it better next time. In business, a similar learning model evolved in a number of forms and under a variety of names. In each case, however, the method was substantially the same:

1. Establish the gap between present performance and the desired state.

2. Review all of the possible causes for the gap.

3. Analyze potential actions that may be used to address these causes.

4. Make a plan to effect the sought-for change (including how the effects of the plan will be measured).

5. Execute the plan (either in a test site or in the entire system).

6. Measure the results of the actions taken and analyze the data—then, return to the first step and start the planning process anew.

Over the last five decades, many more adaptations of this method have been developed—including statistically based methods developed by W. Edwards Deming, J.M. Juran, and others who led the Quality Movement. All are quite similar to the model espoused by Dewey: i.e., first, decide what you're trying to accomplish. Then:

- **Plan.** Lay out a course of action after considering all relevant information, including the potential causation of the gaps that exist between present and desired performance.

- **Do.** Carry out your plan.

- **Check.** Measure the effects of your actions.

- **Act.** Analyze the data, improve the plan, and get ready to act again.

It is this Plan-Do-Check-Act (PDCA) learning process that is at the core of every effective quality improvement effort and is consistent with efforts to create "learning organizations." Peel away the jargon and you have a basic framework for systematic learning that can be used throughout the organization—one that requires that learning be integral to every job and that every person have the skills, tools, and information necessary to improve.

Unfortunately, many organizations have adopted an improvement approach without committing to the idea of system-

atic learning. Too often, the approach has been implemented without a thorough understanding of its underlying philosophy. Instead, many approaches have been applied like recipes, with the instructions carefully followed; but the effectiveness of the effort is not systematically measured, and the resulting information is rarely used to adjust improvement efforts.

We sat in on a meeting not long ago, for example, where a group spent two hours arguing about whether they should adopt a seven- or an eleven-step quality process. We also talked to a senior manager who told us that he didn't believe in quality because he didn't think he could apply seven steps to everything he did. In another company that was four years into their quality improvement effort, we were told that the organization couldn't afford to give their front-line workers a half-hour a week to discuss what they learned and to plan how to improve. In still another, front-line workers received no feedback from which to learn and were still required to sign out when they left their desks for any reason. And we've all seen groups of employees "dunked" in quality training and then returned to their jobs where, because of their narrowly described job descriptions, they did not have the opportunity to use these new-found skills to improve the processes in which they worked.

Even though most leaders tell us they want a stronger customer focus, more effective processes, less rework, better supplier management processes, and significantly more employee involvement, the learning necessary to achieve these goals is simply not a priority in many organizations. People must develop an ability to learn more about how the organization functions today and to use present learnings to help them navigate uncharted waters. Today, complexity is all there is. Methods that grossly oversimplify the challenge may give us the illusion of being in control but seriously undermine our ability to adapt in this era of continual white water.

"By what method?" These three words constituted the opening line in many of Deming's seminars, reminding us that the answer to this question was key to systematic improvement. Today, the options are many. Good learning models abound. We can either pick up a 1950s book on problem solving or pay a company to give us their 1994 version, complete with new jargon.

Any method that is consistently applied, furthers our understanding of present performance, and facilitates our ability to systematically learn from improvement efforts will work when used by a team focused on learning and improvement. The harder part will be to seek out the structures we have built that inhibit learning and to change them *cold turkey*.

We can no longer afford to have employees who don't get feedback on their performance—or when they <u>do</u>, it is accompanied by their supervisor's approval and disapproval. Fear and learning are not readily compatible. We need to ensure that mistakes are learning opportunities and not career-limiting events. We need to look beyond oversimplified cause and effect analysis and increase our understanding of the unintended as well as the intended consequences of our actions—even if they are not close in time and place.

We also need to consider learning a core competency. Although this sounds basic, for many of us it will require that we unlearn many old habits and learn new methods of analysis and new ways of leading. For example, instead of holding people accountable primarily for short-term results, hold them accountable for what they have learned in the last month and how they have used these learnings to benefit all stakeholders. Attach a significant part of every person's accountability to understanding why things improve (or don't), what the major causes of variation are, and how knowledge gained this month should be used in the next.

To be successful in an organization that sincerely values learning, people need time, tools, and support. Becoming an architect of such a system won't be easy for most. History is not on our side. What *is* on our side, however, is people's natural desire to learn. Recent improvements in many manufacturing companies clearly demonstrate the good that can come when we create a sense of urgency and make learning a significant part of individual and group responsibility.

Educate First? Maybe Not!

C2 Do we help people build new skills first and then broaden their responsibilities, or do we first broaden their responsibilities and then require them to learn new skills as a condition of maintaining their position? It often seems preferable to give people more responsibility as they earn it. But, in practice, this alternative is often not the best. We have all seen people being trained to learn skills they weren't sure they would ever need or use. The commitment and enthusiasm of these individuals during the education process is often less than desirable. However, if people understand that learning new skills is part of the continual learning process required by the company, and that these skills will be necessary and helpful in their pursuit of a worthy cause, their reactions will usually be quite different.

In most situations, people learn what they need to learn. When people have a "felt need" for the information, they tend to be more focused. Redesigning the job and accountability practices to require learning can be an effective strategy.

HAVING TO DO IT RIGHT THE FIRST TIME CAN BE A BAD IDEA: LEARNING REQUIRES EXPERIMENTATION

> *I believe that human beings truly seek to live in a more creative orientation. But people don't realize the incredible extent to which traditional organizations are designed to keep people comfortable and to inhibit taking risks. The learning cycle is a continuous process of experimentation. You cannot experiment without taking risks. Despite rhetoric to the contrary, I believe most American businesses are engaged in building "no risk" environments. Even when they break apart old functional bureaucracies, which clearly avoided risk taking, they create decentralized business units where managers stay in one position for two years. Clearly, their eye is on promotion and the only types of risks they will*

*take are ones with a high probability of producing "success" during
their tenure.*

—Ed Simon, President and CEO, Herman Miller

C2

"Why is it that we never seem to have enough time to do it right
but we always seem to make time to do it over?" For many of us
who had pondered this question, Phil Crosby's notion that it was
more efficient, less costly, and in the customer's best interest to
take the time to "Do It Right the First Time" (DIRFT) seemed irresistible—particularly after we learned that the cost of poor quality
in most companies ranged from 20% to 40% of gross revenues.

For many organizations, DIRFT was a helpful reminder of the
need to increase the abilities of employees to systematically improve processes and prevent known problems from recurring.
However, for leaders trying to significantly improve service, compete in time, and build new capabilities within their organizations,
trying to do it right the first time can be more harmful than helpful.
Why? Because doing it right the first time means you may not take
the chance of doing it wrong. This cuts down on failures, on experimentation and, ultimately, on learning. As such, DIRFT can be a
bad idea, especially in changing times.

Instead, we prefer the credo Ralph Stayer (former CEO of Johnsonville Foods) offered while working with us on a quality improvement panel: "Anything worth doing is worth doing poorly."
He went on to say that doing anything for the first time should
be a learning experience, and that no matter how good we are on
our first attempt, we will improve if we focus our efforts on systematically increasing our abilities *and* if we are willing to accept
the discomfort that accompanies most learning experiences. Unfortunately, many leaders shy away from discomfort, are unwilling to
embrace the ambiguity and endure the inevitable mistakes inherent in experimentation, and often respond defensively when they
fail.

As managers, we must reject the notion that there is anyone

C2

DR. IGNORAMUS

"Ignoramus." That's what Dr. Marlys Hearst Witte calls herself. And she's proud of it! She teaches seminars and classes on ignorance to medical students. She awards these scholars a "Doctorate of Medical Ignorance" (DMI) upon graduation.

No, she hasn't lost her mind, but she has raised the issue that must be addressed if any company, organization, institution, or school hopes to continually improve. Without the ability to incessantly and skillfully question present practices, learning and improvement are impossible. Our skills at questioning are so atrophied and have become so inhibited in most organizations that a continuous improvement approach has lost much of its meaning. Without better questions, we can never find the key to that "vast domain of ignorance wherein all knowledge lies."

We must become naive learners, hungry for information, and unwilling to accept present conventional wisdom as true. Just as Dr. Witte has her students read a series of medical journals that have proved to be inaccurate, leaders today must look at commonly accepted practices with a cautious eye. As in medicine, business leaders are finding that much of what we accepted to be gospel in years past is no longer true in a rapidly changing world. It can be disquieting to find out how little we really know. But only then can we earn our Ph.D. in Ignorance.

who can do it right the first time, and embrace the idea that, at times, appearing less than brilliant comes with the territory. Every company's problems and capabilities are unique, and improvement will require a systematic, yet innovative approach to specific issues presented. Managers must learn to learn from their own experiences and from those of others while becoming expert in how organizations differ without allowing these differences to delay improvement efforts. They must embrace ambiguity, rethink past practices, and become evangelical about the need to experiment. They must increase their understanding of present systems, surround themselves with people who can forcefully question present methods, and celebrate innovative attempts to improve—even if these efforts don't succeed immediately.

Managing change, even the simplest change, is exceedingly complex. In most companies, the changes required are substantial. To suggest that there is an "answer," or to build structures that punish mistakes, is to underestimate the challenge and ensure failure. Successful implementations of change require leaders who are excited about learning and about playing a new game, with new rules, in a new, unpredictable environment where there is no detailed road map—and maybe even no road.

C2

C H A L L E N G E   3

Rethinking our Thinking: Building a Foundation for Systematic Improvement

Men are not afraid of things, but of how they view them.

—Epictetus

When we transcend a paradox there is often a quality of obviousness that produces a shock of recognition. No longer held captive by the old way of thinking, we are liberated to see things we have known all along, but couldn't assemble into a useful model for action.

—R.T. Pascale, *Managing on the Edge*

lbert Einstein tells us, "How we think determines what we measure." It also determines how we organize and how we do business. Our thinking, our belief system, our *mindset* determines our priorities, our procedures, our processes, what we expect from people, and the way we deal with them. A distillation of our past thoughts, observations, and experience, our mindset serves as the foundation for the systems we build and perpetuate.

This may sound somewhat theoretical, but it's theory that *works*. If you hope to sustain your success in the future or change your current practices, you must examine the thinking that underlies what you do and how your organization behaves. Before we can create the type of company we desire—the fast, flexible one populated by loyal employees and driven by loyal customers—we must ensure that our mindset will support it. We simply can't, in any event, think one thing and do another, and expect to do either very well.

Our mindset is enormously valuable. It enables us to act. Without it we would have no way to relate yesterday's events and problems to today's, no basis for our predictions, no framework for organizing information, and little confidence in our actions. Without a set of assumptions to guide our actions, every management decision we make, no matter how slight, would take forever. We would have to weigh every variable and ponder every possible outcome. Without a basic set of beliefs to guide us, every decision would be our first.

On the other hand, with a belief system we trust, we can make assumptions about cause and effect, build models to describe how the world works, be confident in our solutions, and generally bring order to the complexities inherent in managing an organization.

The biggest problem with a mindset is that once we have developed one, we tend not to challenge it, particularly when it seems effective. Why should we? If it worked yesterday and works today, it should work tomorrow, right? Not necessarily. Not even probably. In fact, in a rapidly changing environment such as the one we compete in today, leaping to this conclusion is dangerous business. Instead, to ensure that our thinking does not become outdated, we must continuously put our old ideas to the test, to question the efficacy of yesterday's truths—and to do so *before* they fail.

Having a certain mindset can also be problematic for the leader if, when setting new organizational goals and developing new tactics, he or she doesn't go back to question whether the assumptions underlying that mindset are consistent with the company's new direction. If our beliefs are consonant with our new aspirations, chances are that, as we try to change the organization, we'll create structures that will, largely, prompt the desired performance. If, however, our beliefs are not aligned with what we're trying to accomplish, our mindset will become an invisible barrier to improvement. All of us must continually re-examine the way we think.

However, subjecting our mindset to a rigorous re-examination is often easier said than done. Our beliefs are abstractions, hard to pin down and articulate. More than likely, we never committed them to paper, we're rarely in a situation in which we have to defend them, and we seldom have the inclination to question them. In many cases, we don't even know where our beliefs came from or how they originated—they are just an amalgam of our experience over time. Still, they come into play every day, with every decision we make—which, in turn, continues to influence the way people in the organization behave.

C3

In the Name of Involvement

Few leaders need to be convinced that employee involvement is a meaningful goal. Everyone seems to be for it—and why not? We can't imagine anyone arguing that we should treat people like parts of machines or that they should park their brains at the door when they come to work. However, if we learn from experience that it can be risky to trust certain groups, or if we believe that most employees at "that level" are not intelligent and don't make good decisions, it is unlikely that we will act in ways that engender meaningful involvement. If these are our beliefs, we may tend to narrowly define "involvement" and attempt to incrementally alter roles to give the illusion of change. In the name of involvement, we may delegate the ability to make decisions about things that don't really matter or we may design a process to give people the feeling that they are involved, even though we know, and they know, they're not. In most cases, we'd have been better off not trying to pull off this type of charade.

THE SYSTEM PROTECTS ITSELF AGAIN!

> *A long habit of not thinking a thing wrong gives it the superficial appearance of being right.*
>
> —Thomas Paine

Beyond the elusive nature of our beliefs, much of what makes reexamining our thinking so difficult is the reinforcement we receive for holding onto our current assumptions—particularly if we perceive they are serving us well. For example, if a company is successful in its early stages, its leaders receive feedback in the form of sales, profits, and good press to reassure them that their assumptions are correct. Their thinking is reinforced. Those managing the process gain considerable confidence in their approach. As a result, structures are built with these assumptions as their foundation. As the company grows more successful, its leaders will, for the most part, be more reluctant than ever to challenge their thinking. After all, why tamper with the formula that brought them and their organizations to their current levels of success? We've all heard the reactions:

"If our assumptions are so far off, why are we doing so well?"

"The theory's nice, but we have to be practical."

"We focus on results. People who spend time debating theory don't get things done. We simply don't have the time."

For a variety of reasons, many leaders have opted to leave well enough alone, to leave their mindsets unexamined. Where initially our mindset provided the foundation for the structure we built, at some point the system itself became sufficiently powerful to discourage us from even attempting to question our assumptions. Again the "system" protects itself!

It's been said that nothing causes failure as quickly as success. In evolution, as in our personal and organizational lives, success tends to lead us to create more of what made us successful. At some point our success can lead to an excess. What used to be our greatest strength quickly becomes our greatest liability and it's tough for us to see it until failure becomes evident. (Most dramatic changes in organizations come after it's obvious that the failure of the old system is at hand.) It doesn't need to be that way. If we're vigilant in our efforts to question present practices and beliefs, if we bring in diverse opinions to push us outside our comfort zone and continually test the efficacy of our thinking, we may find it easier to devise a strategy and persistently pursue that strategy without the stops and starts that have characterized so many improvement efforts in the past. Commitment requires understanding. Understanding requires learning, and learning requires persistent questioning.

ARTICULATE, QUESTION, AND DEBATE

> *The surest way to get hold of what your present frame blinds you to is to adopt the opposite frame. A person who can live with contradiction and exploit it—who can use conflicting models—can simply see and think more.*
>
> Peter Elbow, *Embracing Contraries*

Examining and updating our thinking will take a combination of guts and forthrightness. The best place to start is by articulating the assumptions we feel are necessary for the future success of our organization. Most probably, this will require that we put our own beliefs to the test by sharing them with others. Until we do, little progress can be made in determining whether our beliefs are serving us well. On the other hand, if we let our beliefs go unarticulated, they can become counterproductive to the organization—difficult to question, difficult to create a dialogue about, difficult to test. This can lead to a perpetuation of those beliefs through generations of employees without our assumptions ever facing the scrutiny they deserve.

CAUTION: Being only human, many of us tend to protect our beliefs (usually unintentionally), rather than genuinely examining them. Indeed, to a greater or lesser degree, we all protect the way we think. Typically this takes the form of:

- Interpreting information in a manner that is consistent with past beliefs.

- Rationalizing conflicting information and discounting the validity of inconsistent data.

- Actively seeking out reinforcing information.

- Hiring people with similar mindsets (because obviously, they are the best qualified).

- Aggressively challenging conflicting views when they are expressed.

- Creating structures where being right is more important than learning.

- Defining our role as advocate of a position instead of a learning partner in the process.

- Punishing mistakes, which makes it more difficult to experiment with different ways of thinking and acting.

- Not developing the skills it takes to question present ways of thinking or to learn from new experiences.

As unproductive as some of these behaviors may seem, in many organizations they are often tacitly, if not openly, rewarded. Our organizations would be very different if, instead of supporting these behaviors, we were held accountable for offering insightful answers to the following questions:

- What have I learned lately?

- In the last six months, what have I changed my mind about?

- When was the last time my assumptions were dead wrong?

- What is different about the way I think this year?

- What about my present mindset do I find myself questioning recently?

- What have I learned this month that makes my actions last month seem less effective?

- Who thinks very differently than I do? What have I learned from them lately?

- How much time have I spent in the last month questioning the way I think and the structures I have designed to support improvement?

Continuously testing the quality of our thinking must become a fundamental part of every improvement process. Inevitably, articulating, sharing, and questioning assumptions will raise issues about what makes for a successful organization. These issues should be discussed among diverse groups to ensure that a wide range of opinions and contrary points of view are heard. We should then take what we learn from these discussions to redesign the way work is done and eliminate any inconsistencies we uncover. If we don't, we'll create a heap of cynicism that will not only destroy enthusiasm but, even more important, undermine trust.

By definition, any discussion of what, why, and how we think will focus more on theory than action. As system architects and leaders responsible for a highly complex structure, we have no choice but to ensure that the foundation we are working from can support what we hope to build.

I stand up on my desk to remind myself that we must constantly look at things in a different way. You see, the world looks very different from up here. Just when you think you know something you have to look at it in another way. Even though it may seem silly or wrong, you must try. When you read, don't just consider what the author thinks; consider what you think. Boys, you must strive to find your own voice because the longer you wait to begin, the less likely you are to find it at all. Thoreau said, "Most men lead lives of quiet desperation." Don't be resigned to that. Break out! Don't just walk off the edge like lemmings, look around you. . . . Dare to strike out and find new ground.

—Robin Williams as Professor Keating, *Dead Poets Society*

C H A L L E N G E   4

Managing the Gap: Sharing a Vision, Values, and Sense of Reality

*If you ask me whether it is easier from the leadership point of view to wait until you're **in extremis,** you know the answer. . . . Does all this change make employees feel insecure? Of course. But anybody who recognizes what is going on in this world and isn't somewhat insecure, I would argue, is not awake. And I think the biggest enemy of progress is happy talk. You need to tell your people that if we do not change, and change fundamentally, we are going out of business. And that will create insecurity. The trick is to turn that insecurity into constructive tension.*

—Mike Walsh, Former CEO, Tenneco

CHANGE MANAGEMENT 101

*T*he first thing we learned in Change Management 101 was that before you can change anything, there has to be common agreement on the gap that exists between where you are today and where you want to be tomorrow. The reason for this is obvious. Providing there is a collective understanding of today's realities and a mutually arrived at and shared vision of where you are headed, your chances of devising an effective strategy for closing

C4

the gap is enhanced. Further contributing to your chance of success is the natural tendency of people to close gaps when they see them, to reduce the tension that exists when there is a disparity between what *is* and *what ought to be*. Add to this construct a shared set of values, and you have the essential foundation for change—an agreed upon starting point, a shared commitment to a goal, and a set of values to guide behavior. Together they can serve as a catalyst for organizational growth and transformation.

We have found few who take issue with the importance of having a shared vision, establishing shared values, and taking an accurate measure of present performance. In most organizations, however, what vision exists is often not a shared one. Ask a dozen individuals where the company is headed and you'll likely get a dozen different answers. And, in those rare instances where people are able to articulate a corporate vision, it is often inconsistent with their own personal vision. The problem around values is that while they are usually clearly stated and understood, they are frequently ignored. Most corporate citizens simply don't practice the values their company espouses. As for accurately measuring present performance, many in the organization are in denial about what's really going on, and dozens of practices exist to keep people, especially bosses, in the dark.

These obstacles notwithstanding, it is everyone's responsibility to manage the gap between our present performance and our goals, and between our stated values and our actions. To this end, we must help engender a shared view of the kind of organization we collectively hope to create, help develop a shared set of core values that can provide order as we constantly adapt to change, and help articulate as accurate a sense of reality as possible. To date, many leaders—from the shop floor manager to the CEO—have underestimated the challenge inherent in successfully managing the gap. In some cases, we haven't developed the behavioral framework necessary to enable employees closest to the customer to make informed decisions. In others, we've allowed people to see the organization (and themselves) as they wished it were rather than as it actually was, reducing the opportunity for learning in the process. And, in company after company, the discontinuity between what leaders say and what they do, between their *talk* and their *walk*, has diminished the trust they need to lead the way to growth and change.

The essential humanness of the organization requires a sense of direction, guidelines that can provide a framework for social order and a sense of reality. We must do as we were taught in Change Management 101; we must constantly focus our efforts on closing the gap between the present and the ideal. It's only a first step—but it's an absolutely critical one.

BUILDING A SHARED VISION

When here is no vision, there you find short-termism, for then there is no reason to compromise today for an unknown tomorrow. . . .

—Charles Handy, *The Age of Paradox*

All my life I've always wanted to be somebody. But I see now I should have been more specific.

—Christy, *In Search of Intelligent Life in the Universe*

Walt Disney, Bill Gates, Tom Watson Sr., Sam Walton—these are some of the names that come to mind when we think of individuals with strong, compelling visions. These men successfully infused their visions into their organizations and watched their companies grow to dominate their markets as few companies ever have. Using today's business vocabulary, we're not sure whether these leaders had a "vision statement." However, people working in the organizations these people founded had a good understanding of the companies they were building. The passion these leaders brought to their work, the types of structures they created, where they spent their time, the types of people who were promoted as the companies grew, the types of dialogues they facilitated, and the consistency of their actions were infectious. Their visions chal-

C4

lenged minds and their passion captured imaginations. Their words were important but only when combined with an obsessive, unrelenting commitment to a worthy cause.

There's more to building a shared vision, however, than having a leader as visionary as Walt Disney or as consistent in his actions as Sam Walton. A shared vision must be commonly understood and worthy of the commitment of everyone in the company. The vision cannot be handed down from on-high. Instead, it must emerge as part of each individual's personal vision of the future. That doesn't mean that each person's view has to be identical for a shared vision to exist; only that everyone's personal vision must be similar to and consistent with the personal visions of others in the organization. Besides, total commitment to someone else's vision is rare. Before most of us are willing to commit to a cause, we have to make it our own. We can be *asked* to commit, but we cannot be *made* to commit—we must *choose* to do so.

We've seen shared visions at work at Microsoft, for example, where it is quickly apparent that those who work there do not feel that they are adopting Bill Gates' vision. Instead, each of the people we met seemed to have built their own vision for the company—though no doubt compatible with the boss' views. In fact, one individual told us flat out, "This is my view, not Bill's. We're definitely on the same team, playing the same game, but each of us sees the world differently and, therefore, has a slightly different view of the future. I'd be surprised if anyone of us is 100% right, but the similarities in our views are striking."

At Disney theme parks, new employees get to share in the company vision from day one. Each new cast member goes through a course called "Traditions One," where they are first provided with a history of the company and an explanation of its goals, then encouraged to come up with ideas on how they might continue that tradition and contribute to realizing those goals. We were enormously impressed with the sessions we sat in on. The discussions were intellectually challenging and emotionally compelling. New Disney cast members aren't read a vision statement.

Instead they are given a look at a dream that they can choose to share.

Unfortunately, companies with a vision that is genuinely shared are still rare—though, in many cases, not for lack of trying. Despite our numerous attempts to build a strong vision that reflects the individual visions of the people in our company, most of us have not had the success of a Disney or a Microsoft. In many cases, we have a vision statement, but there isn't a shared understanding of what that vision means. All too often, the statement was written by committee and reads much like those from other companies. In addition, because our present structures are frequently inconsistent with the priorities espoused in our vision statement, it is common for many of these statements to create more cynicism than commitment among employees. Also leading to the dearth of shared visions in organizations is that, for most leaders, developing such an understanding is simply not a high priority. Even though many say that having a vision is critical, fighting the next fire usually gets the time and the attention.

Certainly one of the key reasons why many of us have been unsuccessful in building a shared vision in our organizations is that we don't have a good method for doing so. Many of our attempts have demonstrated a lack of understanding of the magnitude of the tasks involved. The two-day retreat focused on developing a vision statement may be a first (very small) step in the process. Success, however, will require that we view the process as an ongoing challenge of strategic importance, that we constantly measure our progress, and that we react quickly to ensure that all of our actions (intentional or otherwise) are consistent with the kind of organization we intend to create. Since it is imperative that we gain employee commitment to the vision, we will have to develop new strategies to meaningfully involve employees in the effort— and make their involvement a priority. (If you think you already have, check your calendar. If you've not set aside time to participate in the dialogues required to build a shared sense of purpose, it's not yet a priority.)

C4

A Picture (or a Castle) is Worth a Thousand Words

C4 When Walt Disney was planning the original Disneyland in Anaheim, California, the Fantasyland Castle that was the park's centerpiece was scheduled to be the last structure erected. In support of their decision to build the castle last, the architects and contractors cited logistical and financial advantages. But Walt Disney rejected the building sequence. "I want everyone working on the project to see that castle all day and every day, so they don't forget what it is we're trying to do here."

Characteristics of a Shared Vision

1. A Shared Vision Is Cumulative of Personal Visions

In order to share a vision, you must have a vision of your own. Rarely, however, in the building of a shared vision are people encouraged to develop and discuss their personal visions. Instead, employees are asked to buy into top management's vision. When this happens, you may get compliance—particularly if you pay people enough—but you probably won't get commitment. Rarely, too, will you get employees who are sufficiently interested in and energized by the cause to make the substantial sacrifices that are required to achieve our loftiest aspirations.

2. Effective Visions Are a Function of Information and Dialogue

Because access to information, and sufficient opportunity to discuss its significance, is the foundation of building an effective shared vision, it is easy to see why many individuals have trouble contributing to such a vision. Most employees simply don't have the data they need to do so. And even if they do have access to information, many don't have sufficient training to understand its implications. Employees also tend to have a biased view of the information they *do* have because it is filtered through the lens of their department, division, or functional area. Providing people with the opportunity to see the world through the eyes of others is at the heart of "sharing." Without continuous debate, a common sense of purpose will remain illusory.

C4

3. Effective Visions Describe a Unique Organization

It's hard to commit to a cause that does not address our need to be part of something special. Being merely *one* of the best is not an exciting enough challenge for most. People want to be the very best. They want to be proud of their organization and their own contributions. They want to make a meaningful difference.

We would argue that, in many organizations today, it is difficult for most employees to understand what was intended by the drafters of their company's vision statement. Too often these statements are a long paragraph (or a single sentence that runs as long as a paragraph) that has little meaning to most employees. Read your company's vision statement—does it make you want to sign up?

4. Creating a Shared Vision Is an Ongoing Process

Intellectually, we understand that the development of a vision statement is just the beginning of the process. But it is all too common to see groups go on a two-day retreat, create a vision statement, distribute it throughout the company, and think the process is over. When visions are manufactured in this manner, there is rarely any systematic measure of their effectiveness, no mechanism for challenging them or getting clarification on their meaning, and little structured dialogue about them. Even when there is some discussion, questioning a mandated vision can often be career-limiting. Visions promulgated from on-high suggest that we want change to happen without having to change the way we lead.

5. Participation Is Essential

Clearly, everyone in the organization can't participate in the creation of the vision statement. However, if people cannot challenge, or in some other way affect, the future direction of the company, broad-based commitment to a shared vision will be harder to achieve. In most cases, when there is disagreement or when we're challenged, it will be because there are differences in the information that forms the basis of our differing opinions. There will be times, however, when a challenger has a different (and sometimes fresher) perception than we do because he or she is unburdened by our past experience. In either case, the result of the dialogue that ensues will usually be positive, resulting in more learning and a shared understanding of the challenges we all face.

6. Ensure That The Structure Is Consistent with the Type of Organization You Are Trying to Create

When you ask someone who lives near a busy road or a railroad track how they can stand the noise, the normal response is, "What noise?" They've heard the noise for so long they no longer hear it. By that same token, we can be so used to our organizational practices that we no longer take note of their existence or the implicit messages that many of these practices send. Past practices have resulted in the type of organization we have today. Therefore, if we want to create a credible shared vision of a different type of organization, we must ensure that present practices are in keeping with the new organization we envision.

7. Measure Your Progress and Put the Issue on the Agenda for Periodic Review

If we don't track and evaluate our progress on a regular basis and hold each other accountable for making it happen, creating a corporate vision will remain a back-burner issue. The old saw "You can't manage what you don't measure" rings true here. Without feedback on our progress, systematic learning, and therefore, consistent improvement, is impossible.

8. Get Obsessed and Stay Obsessed

We've never seen a shared vision in an organization where the leader and his or her team were not passionately involved in the effort. Obsession is contagious.

C4

To Play or Not to Play . . . That is the Question

If you *choose* to continue to employ people who cannot or will not *commit* to (i.e., not merely comply with) the shared vision of the critical mass of the company, you undermine your efforts. The process developed for creating a shared sense of purpose should provide every person with a fear-free way of pushing the system and reaching an informed choice of whether or not they want to play in the game. If, however, at some point they choose to play softball when the name of the game is hardball, shouldn't they be relegated to a different diamond? If yours is like most organizations, the league you're playing in is far too competitive to have people out of position for long.

CLOSING THE VALUES GAP

The values gap is the largest single source of cynicism and skepticism in the workplace today.

—Andrall E. Pearson, *Harvard Business Review*

A corporation's values are its life's blood. Without effective communication actively practiced, without the art of scrutiny, those values will disappear in a sea of trivial memos and impertinent reports.

—Max DePree, *Leadership Is an Art*

A company's values are its code of ethics, its behavioral framework. Taken together, they form a statement of what the organization collectively deems as important or valuable—what it stands for. When understood and adopted by employees, values provide a context for action. Values can provide a sense of order without rules, reduce ambiguity without a detailed plan, and bring focus and coherence while allowing individual expression and self-determination.

Most organizations have a published set of values. They are usually well written and widely communicated . . . and are a significant source of frustration. Why? Because it is the rare company today where people practice the values their organization preaches. Just listen to the grumbling at coffee breaks, read between the lines at the next employee meeting, or read the verbatims on the employee survey—the gap between our professed values and our values in practice is significant:

- If respecting the individual is a core value, why do we promote so many people who are technical experts but have lousy people skills? And why do we tolerate managers who get results but are frequently disrespectful to people in their work group?

- If we value cooperation and teamwork, why have we designed so many structures that reward people for competing more than cooperating?

- If every employee is encouraged to seek excellence, then why do we still have so many uninteresting, narrowly defined jobs? Why is training the first thing to be cut when money is tight?

- If providing the best possible service to customers is a core value, then why do we make so many rules that make it hard for employees to meet customers' needs?

- If we have adopted a Total Quality approach, why are so few senior managers actively involved in the effort?

. . . and the list goes on. Our failure to measure the extent to which we live our espoused values has made it easy for many to overlook how often we do not "walk the talk." The result has been lower levels of trust, greater confusion and frustration, and less sense of community among employees in many organizations. People genuinely want their company to stand for something. And when it does, it increases people's feelings that their organization is special.

C4

The first step in closing the gap as it relates to values is to *choose* to get serious about doing so. Look at the values you've published. Just how committed are you about acting within this framework? If a person purposely acts in a manner inconsistent with these values, what is the likely consequence? Dismissal? Coach and counsel? For most, it's an easy decision when an employee steals from the company. But what if one of your core values is "respect" and a long-time supervisor disrespects an employee in front of the work group? When this supervisor keeps his or her job after acting disrespectfully, what is the message sent to others in the organization about the importance of core values?

We know, it's tough to be truly tough on values. But we wonder if we haven't let the pendulum swing too far in the "give 'em another chance" direction. If there isn't significant accountability for the clear and deliberate abuse of values, then there are no values. On the other hand, when you *do* take action, when people who don't live the values are asked to leave, there is usually little, if any, mourning.

Those companies that take a tough stand on having their people live their values are often the most successful and have the strongest cultures. The stories of how Walt Disney was intolerant of those whose actions did not reflect the "Disney Way" are still told. Often, there wasn't a second chance for a significant digression. At Nordstrom, you're trusted to live the company values. If you breach that trust, you usually don't get the opportunity to do so again.

If we're not going to live our values, we would be better off not listing them. The only thing worse than not having a set of guidelines to provide order to behavior within the system is to have a visible set of values that are situationally enforced or largely ignored. In these cases, employees are reminded daily of how little leaders in the company can be trusted to keep their word. Values must be

C4

every organization's North Star—an ever visible guide that employees can look to to tell whether they are acting in ways that promote the organizational good. To be effective, values must be:

1. Profound enough to touch the hearts and minds of all employees, yet simple enough to be readily understood.

2. Concrete enough to provide a useful framework for decision making.

3. Pragmatic enough and sufficiently consistent with organizational structures so as to be reinforced in normal day-to-day activities.

4. Communicated over time in every aspect of the business.

5. Reinforced through accountability.

STORIES HELP DEFINE VALUES

Great teachers have always used stories to help people learn. When used effectively, stories about the behavior of the organization and its people allow the listener to visualize the event and provide a context for the information. They encourage an individual interpretation of the subject matter and can help people understand information through the lens of their past experiences. Every person can (and usually will) "get" a different message, which makes a story meaningful to a diverse audience. When used effectively, stories can point out deficiencies or things an employee must change without engendering defensiveness.

As information design guru Richard Saul Wurman says, "If the Bible were a list of rules, it would have been out of print centuries ago." The stories that tend to have the greatest impact are those that are dramatic, consistent with our past beliefs, include enough detail for the listener to encourage understanding, and are about events which are perceived to be important. They tend to make the abstract concrete, they name names, define places, and create a convincing and powerful reality. Research shows that the types of stories most often told in the organization concern:

C4

- Breaking the rules.

- The boss is human.

- Anyone can accomplish great things.

- People getting fired or laid off.

- How people get promoted.

- Management's reaction to mistakes.

- Where the boss spends his or her time.

Not surprisingly, these stories deal with the themes that are the concerns of virtually every employee: equality versus inequality, security versus insecurity, control versus lack of control, and trust versus lack of trust. They are about sincerity and sense of purpose. They can be entertaining, colorful, graphic, revealing. Above all, a story can be a powerful teacher and revealer of the fears, beliefs, and aspirations of the workforce. We must listen carefully to the stories that are told in our organizations and we must learn to learn from them. The stories people tell reflect accurately the values "in practice." We ourselves must also become better story tellers, because stories can be such valuable communication and teaching tools. As leaders, our actions create stories daily, intentionally or unintentionally. We must learn to create the stories that communicate the messages that are consistent with the values we espouse. We must be sure to consistently walk our talk and we must look for those dramatic, unexpected opportunities to make a statement.

A Suggested Vision and Values Building Process

1. Augment your management team with representatives from other levels in the organization. Through dialogue, build a picture

C4

> **TEST-DRIVING YOUR VISION**
>
> We've all been in the meeting where one person makes a suggestion
> that we think is ill-advised. But after debating the issue for an hour or
> so, evaluating different alternatives, and listening to multiple points
> of view, we end up with solid agreement on a course of action that is
> substantially similar to the proposal offered at the beginning of the
> meeting. Most of us would never have agreed without having
> the benefit of hearing differing points of view or without having the
> opportunity to kick the tires and take the idea for a test drive. This
> experience is similar to the dialogue that must be part of an effective
> visioning process.

of the type of organization that you would like to create to meet tomorrow's challenges. Let this be the first draft of your vision and
values statement (which can be later used to stimulate further discussion throughout the company).

We've found it helpful for each person to begin this initial
working session with a statement of their personal vision and values, and not to endorse the draft until they understand it and believe it is worthy of their commitment.

2. Ensure that the draft that evolves from this session describes
how the company will relate to shareholders, customers, and
employees. Ensure also that the draft is in sufficient detail so people can understand not only what *is* part of the vision, but what *is
not*.

3. After the first draft is completed, members of the management team should share it with their direct reports or a larger
group. People should come to this meeting prepared to compare
their personal visions and values with the initial draft. Are there
more than semantic differences? Are there statements made in the
draft that don't belong? Can the group commit to the draft? What

changes would be required before the group could get excited by the challenges contained in the vision and values draft?

4. Comments and criticisms of the draft should be addressed, with changes made at the management level, then communicated back to the group.

C4

5. This process should be repeated throughout the organization, with challenges to the draft allowed to sift up the chain of command (if there is one) and with reactions and changes as a result of these challenges discussed as they arise.

6. Build a feedback loop to test the effectiveness of the overall process, to ensure that the feedback emerging from these dialogues is unbiased, and to keep skeptics at bay. Keep in mind that any process you adopt for building a shared vision will only be an approximation of the more effective one that can result from feedback. There are no substitutes for systematic learning and persistence.

7. Expect and encourage minor differences in personal visions. When personal visions differ significantly, check information-sharing practices to make certain that people have the information they need to make informed decisions; then check training practices to ensure that people have the ability to understand the significance of this information.

8. Once a broad base of people that commit to a shared vision and values statement, ask them to define their individual roles in building the organization and to devise a feedback mechanism they can use to measure their progress. Each person must then be given the responsibility to evaluate his or her progress over time, communicate key learnings, and build the skills necessary to meet future challenges.

Sign Up or Sign Out

C4   In some organizations, values are now communicated to each employee, who must choose to sign up—that is, agree to live these values. Many of the sets of values we've seen lately are more specific than the more generic types of value statements that were common just several years ago. The "Team Pledge" shown here is a good example of a specific set of values that can be used to stimulate discussion and provide a sense of order, continuity, and accountability to the work environment.

9. Assign a team to evaluate progress and to make recommendations about present methods. This assignment of responsibility may make it more difficult for busy leaders to push their efforts onto the back-burner. It is crucial to build in accountability for the management team.

CREATING A SHARED SENSE OF REALITY

Why do we persist in playing this elaborate, unrealistic game? Why do we pretend that reality is what we know it is not? There are undoubtedly many reasons, but one of the important ones, I believe, is the anxiety that man experiences when he cannot perceive order and predictability in his world.

—Douglas McGregor, *The Professional Manager*

He who would determine the true from the false must have an adequate idea of what is true and false.

—Benedict Spinoza

It's difficult to see reality, period! No matter how empathetic we are (or think we are) as leaders, no matter how open, the organizational deck is stacked against us. When we are liked, people often color the information they give us because they don't want to dis-

Team Pledge

I hereby make a freely-chosen decision to be an integral part of Carlson Travel Group as a valued member of the team.

As a team member of this company upon which many co-workers, friends and their families depend for their futures, I hereby pledge my word to them and to my fellow teammates that:

- I am unequivocally and indisputably on the team, and should this commitment change, I will show respect for myself and my teammates by leaving the team with honesty, alacrity, and professionalism.

- I will, through my daily efforts, work for the good of the team above all else, never seeking to gain personal profit or success at the expense of the team.

- I will conduct my daily business with honesty, integrity, candor, and dignity, knowing that my actions reflect not only on myself but my co-workers.

- I will, each day, put aside past issues and petty concerns and refuse to engage in the promotion of discontent.

- I will work to build a workplace known for its trust and honesty.

- I will show respect for and expect respect from all co-workers regardless of gender, race, age, disability or religion, and will never allow issues of diversity to become weapons of intolerance.

- I will offer my counsel to the team, but when it cannot be accepted will support the team's final decision and neither publicly nor privately work against it.

- I will take responsibility for honestly communicating to my teammates when I believe they are close to being out of bounds, and hereby ask them to do the same for me.

- I will trust those who have likewise given their word to do these things, but will never use another's failure to honor their pledge as a reason to break my own.

To these tenets I pledge to remain true.

_____

Team Member

_____

Witness

_____

Travis Tanner

Carlson Travel Group, Inc.^{SM}

AMAYS The Travel Agents	**Carlson** Travel Network®	*P. LAWSON TRAVEL*	**Carlson** Travel Academy®
United Kingdom	North America, Europe, Asia	Canada	North America

C4

appoint us, they don't want to complain, they don't want to seem like nitpickers. If they fear our reaction (either because of our past actions or our position), very little information about the less than positive aspects of the current situation is volunteered. Most of us have felt the pressure to not be "too negative," or to ensure that bad news is balanced with enough positive information—even if this requires coloring or recasting reality. The expression "*You* tell the boss" didn't evolve because people were reluctant to be rewarded, but because they didn't want to experience the boss' reaction.

In most organizations, people are biased toward seeing things as they wished things *were,* not as things actually *are.* The choice to avoid the truth is not always a conscious one, and is often quite subtle. Just look at the number of ways people in your organization are implicitly (and sometimes even explicitly) rewarded for making things sound better than they are or telling their bosses what they think their bosses want to hear. Bad news doesn't travel "up" quickly in most organizations, but it should. By selectively modifying reality, we falsely diminish people's understanding of "the gap" and therefore rob the organization of the sense of urgency and creative tension that will be required to focus and sustain improvement efforts.

◀ Developing a shared sense of reality must be a strategic issue. It is exceedingly difficult to change reality if you don't see it, or if there is no agreement on what "real" is. We must recognize the effect present structures have on our willingness and ability to see reality and we must search out and eliminate those practices that make it safer or more rewarding to do anything but "tell it like it is."

To be successful, we will need to develop a method to ensure that a direct, straightforward picture of the present situation is communicated throughout our organization. A number of companies are currently experimenting with different methods to accomplish this but too few are doing it in a manner that is likely to further every person's understanding of reality in key areas. Many of today's attempts have been characterized as "internal quality audits" and have been developed to provide information about the breadth and depth of Total Quality deployment. Many of these efforts are still evolving and a small but growing number are already providing management teams with a much more accurate sense of reality.

C4

In too many assessments, however, companies have focused on the scores, ratings, and awards that they have made part of the system assessment process instead of on the quality of the information being generated. Some companies have started paying division or business unit leaders based on assessment results. Do we really think this provides an incentive for people in that group to communicate an accurate sense of reality? Isn't there a strong likelihood that these incentives will result in the very practices the assessment was designed to overcome?

When effectively implemented, periodic system assessments can be a powerful change tool. The results (if they describe a well-rounded view of reality) can provide a mirror for the management team to ascertain if their attempts to steer the organization in a given direction are working. When the information from these assessments is shared and discussed throughout the organization, a shared sense of reality results. Successes can be celebrated and course corrections in our implementation efforts can be made.

In the future, we suspect that periodic system assessments to capture an accurate picture of reality will be common. The positive potential of these tools is simply too great to ignore. To gain the maximum benefit from these efforts, however, companies will have to ensure that the information emerging from their assessments is understood and widely shared, and that next steps in the change or improvement process are widely discussed. When used effectively, system assessments can offer a snapshot of today's performance in key areas, facilitate a shared understanding of the "gap," and provide an opportunity for employees at every level to discuss issues and further their understanding of the type of organization that will be required in the future.

Still, there will be resistance. Making information visible that in the past has been purposely or inadvertently suppressed, can be threatening to many, especially in an environment where facts have not always been perceived as friendly. The resistance can take many forms: "Is this really necessary?" "Can we afford this process?" "This is too time-consuming and I'm too busy." "If you ask me, I'm not convinced that this information is correct." "I can't believe that we're that bad. If we were, we would have known it." Only sixty years ago, managers were resisting the necessity of financial audits. Now, they have learned to use these audits to help bring a shared sense of the financial reality to all stakeholders. The resistance we encounter today to organizational assessments seems predictable. Major changes in structure will always be resisted. We must choose to make seeing what is a priority.

C H A L L E N G E 5

Information: Changing the "Need to Know" to the "Right to Know"

An individual without information cannot take responsibility: an individual who is given information cannot help but take responsibility.

—Jan Carlzon, former CEO, Scandinavian Airlines

Of all the skills of leadership, listening is one of the most valuable—and one of the least understood. Most captains of industry listen only sometimes, and they remain ordinary leaders. But a few, the great ones, never stop listening. They are hear-aholics, ever alert, bending their ears while they work and while they play, while they eat and while they sleep. They listen to advisers, to customers, to inner voices, to enemies, to the wind. That's how they get word before anyone else of unseen problems and opportunities.

—*Fortune*

*I*t is no accident that at the same time one group of revolutionary forces storms the palace, another attempts to take control of the government communication center. It's not by chance that, prior to the actual revolution, the airwaves crackle with broadcasts unsanctioned by the regime in power and the most sought-after tool is the printing press. Nor is it happenstance that, in most major cities around the world today, there are armed guards in the lobbies of the buildings housing television and radio stations. There is little question that whoever controls the flow of information has enormous power, primarily because of the power of information, in and of itself.

C5

Not only is this true of the larger world, but also of our own organizations, where information can change mindsets as well as lead to a shared vision, common values, enhanced learning, improved service, greater productivity, and the successful integration of technology. Even more than capital, information is the organization's sustenance, the nourishment it requires to grow and transform itself. This being the case, whether you just want to shake things up a little or develop a whole new culture, looking at the way people in your organization receive, analyze, and act on information should be at the very top of your "To Do" list.

The question is, if information can be such a powerful and positive force, why then are most organizations so miserly with it? Why, for example, do so few employees know what kind of organization management is trying to create? How many customers were lost last year, and why? What the financial performance of the company is? We believe the reason that so many in the organization know so little is quite straightforward: many leaders simply underestimate the transformational power of information and its ability to radically improve performance.

In many companies, in fact, far more attention is paid to using information as a means of perpetuating status, protecting positions in the hierarchy, and enforcing past practices, than as a means to promote growth and change and to expand the potential of the workforce. Virtually all individuals we've spoken within organizations tell us that they are capable of accomplishing more than they presently are. Information—particularly in the form of <u>immediate, comprehensive</u> and <u>understandable</u> feedback on performance—is the means for tapping into this wellspring of underutilized and often underappreciated talent. We've seen it borne out in organization after organization: information—and feedback, in particular—is the true breakfast of champions.

THE RIGHT TO KNOW

Secrecy cloaks the infectious madness that causes people to participate in their own destruction.

—Earl Shorris, *Scenes from Corporate Life*

Given the growth and improvement that information can bring about in the organization as well as in the individual, we must learn to manage it more effectively than we have in the past. In many companies, this requires that we begin by abandoning the traditional need-to-know information strategy that derives from the managerial notion that "I know what information you need, and therefore I'm the best person to give it to you," and that results in information being meted out on a limited basis and controlled by relatively few individuals. In place of this hierarchical rationing system should be one predicated on the *right to know,* where access to a wide range of information is not a privilege bestowed at the boss' whim, but guaranteed to all workers to enable them to be knowledgeable participants in the work process and to ensure that they can do the best job possible.

All too frequently, our need-to-know mentality has resulted in large parts of the organization being dramatically underinformed—and often precisely those individuals dealing with customers or working in other parts of the delivery process, who need as much information as possible to respond to customer questions and demands or improve the efficiency of the process. On the other hand, with a right-to-know mentality at work in your organization, people will be able to respond to the questions customers are asking, or be confident in their ability to find the information they need to provide those responses.

In making the transition from a need-to-know to a right-to-know strategy, we must first confront the essential paradox of information management: i.e., we can't manage information, but we must. We *must* manage information because of its enormous value and potential benefit, because it can take so many forms, and because it originates from so many different sources. We *can't* manage it because doing so inevitably means getting in the way of the information itself—interfering with its getting to the people who need it, slowing the process, filtering the data, and generally contaminating the feedback loop. For example, many performance evaluation systems require that supervisors interpret performance data instead of letting front-line employees receive the data directly, "hot off the press." Other reasons why we can't manage information are its pervasiveness, its sheer quantity, and the fact that there is absolutely no telling what people will or can do with it once they have it.

Still, with information multiplying and the demand on knowledge workers increasing, we have little choice but to improve the way most of us do manage information, targeting a right-to-know system as our ultimate goal. The alternative is to stay with the information system we have—and, in most cases, that's simply not good enough. Even the best companies have hardly scratched the surface in their efforts to discover the benefits of a truly informed workforce.

As complex as managing information on a right-to-know basis can be, the strategy that governs it is relatively straightforward:

- Put as much information into the hands of as many people as possible.

- Give people access to any and all information that will enable them to do a better job.

- Make people responsible for getting the information they need.

- Ensure that information is in a format that people can understand.

- Broaden job responsibilities so that people can act on what they learn.

Only information that could compromise the success of the organization should be withheld. Besides, it's probably safe to say that far more companies have been undermined by rumor and innuendo than by critical information falling into the hands of the wrong individuals. Keep in mind, too, that the need for information in social systems is so great that, in the absence of information, people will make it up—and **what they contrive will usually create far more problems than what really is.**

C5

What You See Is Not Always What You Get

We all differ in what we know, but in infinite ignorance, we are all equal

—Sir Karl Popper

Of the many reasons to employ a right-to-know information strategy, perhaps the most compelling reason is that if you don't, your organization will eventually not have the information it needs to understand its customers—or even its own processes—nor will it be able to anticipate where the market is headed. There are two principles at play here. The first concerns the variety of people necessary for gathering and processing information. The second concerns the number of people involved in the effort. To be successful, organizations need to give serious consideration to both.

A principle governing variety is the well-known Cybernetics Law of Requisite Variety, which states that, *for a system to adapt to its external environment, it requires internal variety.* The less variety inside, the less well the system is able to deal with the variety on the outside. Applying this law to the organization, if we want to be able to continue to understand what is going on outside our system (with our customers, our competitors, and the marketplace), we'll need a wide variety of people on the inside of the company listening and absorbing the information that is being generated. This is particularly crucial at the organization's periphery, in those areas that are generally not our main focus and where most of our interaction with the outside world takes place. The less variety among the people involved in this process, the less diversity of thought, and the greater the chance of organizational failure. Not only must your company reflect the diversity and the changes of the outside world, it must be open to and equipped to receive the diverse information from that world in order to regenerate and reinvent itself over time.

As a corollary, **internal** variety is also necessary as a means to improve the *internal* environment. The less variety there is among the individuals examining our own processes, the more limited our view of those processes, and the less likely it is that new ideas and innovations will emerge.

Another principle influencing whether our organization will know what it needs to about itself and the outside world states that *no matter what we observe, we exclude more than we see.* This is partially the case because we are limited by how <u>much</u> we can observe: put us in a room with a dozen people and we won't be able to focus on them all. More than likely, in fact, we'll only be able to give our full attention to one or two, meaning that we'll miss much of what is going on with the others. If we're genuinely interested in what they say or do, therefore, we have no choice but to put more observers in the room.

Also limiting our powers of observation is the unique lens through which each of us views the world. For example, if we witness an argument between two people, we may only remember the gist of the argument, but forget what precipitated it or what the arguers were wearing. Or we may recall only what one person looked like and said and forget about the second person's looks and point of view entirely. Another observer, on the other hand, may only remember the second person.

This is hardly a surprising phenomenon, because what we see or remember is heavily influenced by what we think and/or the tools we use to measure. Therefore, what we see or learn in a given situation will, more often than not, be limited to what we can conceive of or envision going into it. For this reason, the fewer people we have gathering, processing, and acting upon information and the less informed they are, the less complete our data will be.

C5

Putting only a few people in charge of gathering and analyzing information, therefore, no matter how smart or perceptive they are, is simply not enough. On the other hand, the more information gatherers you have, the more you'll learn, the better the chance that you will also have the variety of people you need. The days when only managers could think, observe, analyze, and then plan, organize, and control the work of others are dead—or *should* be. Instead, we must put everyone's intelligence, talents, and powers of observation to work.

Information and Communication

Drowning problems in an ocean of information is not the same as solving them.

—Ray E. Brown

Just about every leader we talk to tells us that the single largest problem faced by his or her organization is *communication*. The fact that poor communication is also the number one complaint voiced by front-line employees suggests that these leaders' concerns are on target. The message, whatever it is or wherever it's coming from, is not getting through.

Typically, whenever we come up against a communication problem, we tend to try to solve it as an isolated event. We assume, in communications jargon, that somehow our *message* has not been appropriately *encoded* so that our *audience* can correctly *decode* it. In focusing on this single issue, however, we often ignore the larger issues: that our communication problem is really a problem with the way the organization handles information and that we're spending too much time worrying about encoding and decoding and not enough time focusing on making information available in its unfiltered form to all those who really need it. Why, for example, don't we tell employees how much our electric bill is, instead of putting up signs to turn off the lights when they leave the room? Or why don't we tell them how our competitors are more effective than we are, instead of trying to put a happy face on our deficiencies? As long as we keep looking at our communication problems in isolation, we'll only solve <u>those</u> problems (if that), and rarely address the more pressing information-handling problem that generally underlies them.

Sometimes an organization's information problem stems from leaders who simply want to be heard and obeyed and who refuse to think of communication as a two-way process. Far more common, however, are leaders who are genuinely committed to communicating but who enjoy limited success, either because they don't believe that employees need to know a great deal, or because the information that flows through the corporation isn't readily understandable.

Leaders tell us, for example, that they want employees to have a better understanding of the business, so they publish ROA/ROI and dozens of other figures in their internal releases. Some leaders may even highlight these numbers in a video that is made available to every employee. The problem is, without training or education to explain what the figures mean, many employees can't interpret the information, nor can they apply it to their day-to-day work. In these instances, the information was disseminated, but not well communicated.

Some people may think that this failure to communicate is caused by the message not being correctly tailored to the audience: i.e., that the information hasn't been made sufficiently simple for most people to understand. We take a different approach, and suggest erring on the side of complexity rather than on making things too simple. While it isn't necessary for everyone to understand every bit of arcane information that is generated by the organization, the greater an individual's depth of understanding is of that information, the more effectively he or she will be able to use it to delight customers, improve processes, and generally do a better job. We feel, therefore, that every effort should be made to bring organizational audiences <u>up</u> to the level of the information—i.e., to educate them—rather than bringing the information <u>down</u> to the current knowledge level of the audience. Interestingly, if you ask many employees whether they want more information—and in some cases, whether they want more education in order to deal with more information—they'll say, no. We have found, however, that once they get that information and understand it, they appreciate having it and use it effectively—often far more so than their managers had anticipated. One caution, however: once employees have access to information, once you have made it obvious that you trust them and respect their intelligence, they'll never again be satisfied with a job that prevents them from putting their newfound knowledge to work.

With organizations increasingly implementing client/server computing (where a data repository or *server* may be accessed by any legitimate user or *client* on the network) and adding an ever-increasing number of nodes to the network, the means to provide more people with more and better information is gradually falling into place. Giving everyone in the company access to the network along with the option of being able to choose their own information rather than having it chosen for them can also be a major step in opening up the organization to the diversity of ideas and insights it needs to thrive.

Just How Informed Are We?

> The meanings of words are <u>not</u> in the words, they are in us.
>
> —S. I. Hayakawa

To be well informed, people need to know far more about the organization than their predecessors did. At a minimum, in addition to thoroughly understanding the processes, they should have *some* knowledge of the company's customers, competitors, and suppliers, as well as a basic understanding of the company's finances and

C5

its reputation in the community. Just how informed are we? Here are a few questions to consider:

C5

- About our **customers,** how many of them are loyal? Will they buy from us again? Recommend us to others? Why do we lose the customers we lose? Keep the ones we keep? What are their expectations? Their priorities? Are they changing? Why? How do we know? Is our data reliable?

- As for the **competition,** who are they? Are they changing? How are we better than they are? How are they better than we are? Is there data to support our opinions? Does it reveal any trends? Who will our competitors be tomorrow?

- **Suppliers** are like close relatives: they sometimes know us better than we know ourselves. How do they view the quality of our work? Are we easy to deal with? Difficult? Why? Are we giving them the information they need? Are we providing feedback on their performance? How do they want us to change?

- Our job is inextricably tied to the **financial performance** of our organization. Do we know if our company is profitable? More profitable this year than last? How about the cost of the service our group provides? How does it compare to the amount spent by our competitors?

- Finally, how about **the company as a whole?** Is it well thought of in the outside world? Considered a good employer? Environmentally sensitive? Do its people share a set of values? Understand its strategic plan? Does it give back to the community as much as it takes?

Of course, it's unreasonable to expect everyone to be well versed in each of these areas. But, contrary to Alexander Pope's admonition, "A little learning is a dangerous thing . . . ," for many people, even knowing the answers to just a few of these questions can result in greater insight, interest, and improved performance.

C H A L L E N G E   6

Capturing the Advantages of Diversity:
Learning to Love the Weird

*. . . When I listened most closely I could hear the unheard. . . . To hear
the unheard is a necessary discipline to be a good ruler. For only when a
ruler has learned to listen closely to the people's hearts, hearing their
feelings uncommunicated, pains unexpressed, and complaints not spoken of, can he hope to inspire confidence in his people, understand when
something is wrong, and meet the true needs of his citizens. The demise
of states comes when leaders listen only to superficial words and do not
penetrate deeply into the soul of the people to hear their true opinions,
feelings, and desires.*

—C. W. Kim and Renee A. Mauborgne, *Harvard Business Review*

*T*hrough design and necessity, almost every workforce in
America is more diverse today than it was just a decade ago. Few
companies, however, are capturing the benefits inherent in this
diversity. Most corporate cultures suppress nonconformity in employees, no matter what their ethnicity, gender, or experience.
Until we develop practices that encourage diversity of thought and
action, employees who would present different points of view will
suppress these views and be homogenized into the prevailing culture. The successful organization of the future must incorporate diversity into its internal processes by rewarding the expression of
internal differences. The management of diversity must become a
strategic issue.

LEARNING TO LOVE THE WEIRD

C6

I used to think that anyone doing anything "weird" was "weird." I suddenly realized that anyone doing anything "weird" wasn't "weird" at all, and that it was the people saying they were "weird" that were "weird."

—Paul McCartney, Leadership philosopher and sometime musician

Too many companies have systematically eliminated "weird" from their organizations. To be "weird"—that is, to have and express opinions that question present practices and systems or espouse a different set of beliefs—has rarely been perceived as career-enhancing. Even companies that have worked hard to hire a diverse workforce do not typically change practices and systems to capture the advantages of such diversity.

Much of our managerial behavior has been predicated on the assumption that a manager's job is to rationally order the behavior of employees. In many cases, conformity and providing answers have been rewarded more than creativity and asking questions. Many leaders have surrounded themselves with people who think and act as they do. Often, the lack of tension and conflict within a group has been mistaken as an indicator of agreement and effective decision making while disagreement and contention have been perceived to be the outcomes of ineffective leadership. These assumptions must be challenged.

The successful organization of the future will incorporate diversity into its internal processes by encouraging the expression of internal differences. A company's options are expanded as different points of view are expressed. Diversity of experience, education, race, gender, expertise, and opinion can aid any organization in attempting to understand customers, competitors, and suppliers, anticipate future trends, and effectively provide a challenging workplace for employees. As we mentioned earlier, if the requisite level of diversity does not exist or is not effectively managed within the organization, the organization will be unable to adapt to a rapidly changing external environment.

Yes, the level of diversity within most organizations is growing. However, capturing the advantages of a diverse workforce will remain illusory until we come to grips with the reasons why diversity has been undervalued and ineffectively managed in the past. We must find new ways to visibly and symbolically communicate that individual differences are valued. Whatever the solutions, the effort must begin with a redefinition of the manager's role. Leaders must view their jobs as maintaining a constructive level of debate within their organizations. They must reward questions that lead to experimentation conducted in search of improvements that will translate into increased customer value.

QUESTIONING: A GOOD FIRST STEP

> *Be patient toward all that is unsolved in your heart and try to love the questions themselves like locked rooms or books that are written in a foreign tongue. The point is to live everything. Live the questions now. Perhaps you will then gradually, without noticing it, live your way some distant day into the answers.*
>
> —Rainer Maria Rilke

Although encouraging questions is not likely to solve problems without further action, it's hard to think of a more effective first step. Questioning is the essential activity to begin and foster a culture of continuous improvement. Without incessant questioning of present practices, there can be no search for new, innovative ideas that can lead to substantial improvement. Although most leaders agree with the need to continually question, many have been slow to reward critical thought and promote individuals who strongly question present organizational habits and mindsets.

"Don't bring me a question without a proposed solution." This old

admonition is at the heart of the problem. It demonstrates a preoccupation with answers and effectively limits questions within an
organization. Children learn because they question everything.
Students are rewarded for questioning effectively because we understand that gaining knowledge is impossible without a "questioning" frame of mind. Unfortunately, employees are continually
reminded *not* to question and are rewarded for conformity. The
dearth of questions in many organizations reduces employees'
ability to learn and, therefore, restricts a company's ability to
change and compete.

Diversity is the fuel of the questioning process. Each person's
view represents a facet of reality; when encouraged, the realities of
different employees challenge one another and raise questions.
The more diverse the workforce, the more questions can be expected. Without the perceived ability to express differences safely,
systematic questioning and significant levels of debate cannot be
sustained. As a consequence, a culture where success is defined by
continuous improvement will remain unreachable for most.

Wanted: Disagreeing and Sometimes Disagreeable People Willing to Question Everything!

**Too often, much of the discussion around diversity suggests that
managing it effectively is leading the group in ways that reduce
internal conflict and discomfort. Although empathetic leadership and more sensitivity to the differences among us would
benefit most groups, we must not surrender our ability to challenge the issues that stand in the way of improvement. To capture the advantages of our diversity, we need more disagreeing,
and at times, disagreeable people who are confident in their abilities to push the organization outside of its comfort zone. Recruiting a diverse workforce and then encouraging employees to
act as a homogeneous group, where the tendency to agree inter-
feres with critical thought, is not success. It is merely a waste of
human talent.**

EIGHT IDEAS FOR CAPTURING THE ADVANTAGES OF DIVERSITY

The results of numerous service quality assessments we've conducted in the last six years tell volumes about the problems that are created when management practices value order more than creative thought. While no company or person has found the answer to these problems, the following eight ideas can be helpful in continuing the effort to capture the advantages of diversity.

1. Reward people who continually question present practices. Traditionally, those with answers have been rewarded more than those with questions, even if the suggested course of action did not address the root cause of a problem or inadvertently created additional variance in the process. People who continually question present practices are often perceived as non-team players or are perceived as employees who lack the creativity to generate solutions.

Most organizations need more questioning, more experimentation, and more innovative attempts to redefine the way work is done. Rewarding people who continually challenge conventional wisdom will foster experimentation and create a perception that a different point of view is valued. An award ceremony for the group who most effectively challenged present practices would be refreshing.

2. Promote weirdness. Merely tolerating the weird—those in the organization who think and act differently—is not enough. Until being different is perceived to be career-enhancing, organizations will never capture the full benefits of a diverse workforce.

"Promoting the best qualified" often results in promoting someone "similar to me" for most managers. Leaders tend to judge candidates based on a subjective assessment of how they meet the criteria that the leader considers important, as well as the candidates' ability to do the job as it presently exists. The applicant who is different, won't fit in easily, is skeptical of present practices, and is difficult to manage may well be the "most qualified" candidate to move the organization further down the track of continuous improvement.

C6

● **3. Analyze the business from a competitor's point of view.** Challenge a group to devise a plan to put their own organization "out of business" by coming up with a unique way to add substantially more value for customers. This exercise forces the group to think differently and allows each member to use talents not called for in normal operations. Incorporating "outsiders" in the process can further broaden the diversity of thought within the planning group.

● **4. Reward experimentation: love the .500 hitter.** An individual's preoccupation with avoiding failure restricts the ability to innovate and experiment. It focuses employees' attention on the less risky task of managing the status quo. The need for diverse thinking is reduced, and people with different views are valued less.

Organizations need to learn to love their .500 hitters—those who are willing to experiment—with the understanding that if half of these individuals' improvement attempts are successful, they're doing well. As we said before, innovation invites some failure. Without the ability to fail there will be less questioning, less experimentation, less learning and, therefore, no transformational improvement.

● **5. Redouble education efforts! Ensure inconsistencies!** Education within the diverse organization exposes people to different ideas that stretch present paradigms and lead to a continual questioning of accepted practices. Education can help reframe issues in ways that help individuals and groups better learn from their experiences. It is helpful to select educators who hold very different views from those in the organization and who offer a different perspective from other educators. By exposing everyone to inconsistent, even controversial views, discussion will ensue, and the diversity that exists in the company can be tapped. Beware of the management team that censors, controls, or overly directs the content of the educational process.

C6

THE POWER OF WHY

Reduce cycle time, reduce costs, improve service, involve employees, and improve quality—the goals are familiar. Like so many managers, the leadership team at Northern Telecom's Morrisville, North Carolina, customer service facility faced the challenge of where to begin. They chose to start by encouraging every person to ask "Why?" If there wasn't a good answer, they'd change present practice. If there was a good answer, they'd explain. If they weren't sure, they'd find out and then respond.

After initial skepticism, the questions began to multiply. Soon every group questioned the way work was done, the roles of supervisors, present organizational structures, and the effectiveness of accountability and reward practices. The unique perspective expressed by each person and group set the agenda for improvement activities and served to transform the mindset of the leadership team guiding the effort. The result: a 55% increase in productivity, an 83% reduction in defective shipments, and a reduction in shipping times from weeks to hours in less than 30 months.

Encouraging questioning throughout the organization can "jump start" the continuous improvement process.

● **6. Empower everyone.** Empowering people to better serve customers and continually improve internal processes will help capture creative ideas that have often been overlooked. When every employee is actively involved in gathering customer information, measuring performance quality, helping design delivery processes, identifying mistakes, experimenting with improvement ideas, eliminating bureaucracy, and customizing the customer's experience, there are more opportunities to contribute and more need for each employee to bring his or her unique perspective to the job.

C6

● **7. Invite outsiders in; push insiders out.** By involving our suppliers and customers in the design of delivery processes, the company gains new ideas and perspectives. Customers, suppliers, and consultants can challenge assumptions and help people think differently. In addition to bringing their special expertise to a project, outsiders often identify obvious things that insiders have overlooked.

Sending insiders to visit customers, suppliers, or other companies that can provide information critical to the improvement process also increases the diversity of thought within an organization. Exposure to different views increases the knowledge level of the organization, stimulates experimentation, and facilitates debate. Systematically inviting outsiders in and pushing insiders out sends a very strong signal that diversity of opinion, continuous learning, and consistent improvement are valued. The symbolism of these actions may be as important as the information gathered in these endeavors.

● **8. Redefine success.** If leaders can be successful merely by avoiding failures, resolving conflict, maintaining order, and efficiently managing present practices, they may perceive that it is not necessary, or even desirable, for them to encourage the aggressive questioning or the expression of divergent views that might lead to a redefinition of the way work is done. If only incremental improvement is desired, constant discussion and the resulting disagreements can be perceived as unnecessarily distracting attention that could be focused on "getting the work out."

In today's competitive environment, merely avoiding failures and maintaining order seem to be a prescription for corporate suicide. Successful management of the status quo ensures a shorter life cycle for the business and invites competition. Rapid, continuous improvement and innovation must be a prerequisite to success at every level in the organization. Debate and conflict must not only be acceptable but invited. "What have you changed lately?" must become a more popular question. When change and transformational improvement become prerequisites to individual success, diversity of opinion will be valued; without diversity and the willingness to express and act on differing opinions, change—especially substantial change—is impossible.

C6

PAUL MacCREADY'S "WEIRD" ELECTRIC CAR

Key Learning: Bring oddballs together, and watch how they'll find astounding solutions by redefining the problem. . . .

Creating an electric car that will move people from point A to point B efficiently, quickly, and with style has stumped car makers for decades. There's no shortage of car designs, but no amount of brains or capital has conquered the stagnant and inefficient state of battery technology—until Paul MacCready, inventor, engineer, and breakthrough thinker, hooked up with General Motors. Together they unveiled what may become the solution to building a car that's fast, sexy, and electric.

The answer came from facing the battery problem head on: instead of creating better batteries to run cars designed like today's gas-powered versions, MacCready and team designed a dramatically different car to run on today's battery technology. He skinned the cat from the opposite end.

To get there, MacCready pulled together an entire team of oddballs: people from various disciplines, unaccustomed to working together. The diversity of backgrounds, styles, and training caused them to look at old problems in new ways. For example, they thought about the ways traditional car designs wasted horsepower. They supposed this and supposed that. They tested ideas. They learned that cars would run with less drag if traditional designs were turned around: make the front fat and the back tapered so the car would part the air, then hug it and utilize it. *(cont.)*

C6

For the problem of weight, they turned to the airplane industry. They cut holes in panels in hidden places, shaving a millimeter here and an ounce there. They saved over 200 pounds. Dozens of other unconventional ideas kept coming—like using an AC motor instead of DC, thus capturing and then reusing heat from the brakes for energy. These ideas sprang, in part, from smart people with vision. But mostly, they came from cross-boundary teamwork that allowed differences to work for the team rather than against it.

Reprinted with permission from Pacific Bell Corporation,
Management Telesis Division.

C H A L L E N G E 7

Competitively Disadvantaged: Building Cooperation Instead of Internal Competition

We act competitively because we are taught to do so, because everyone around us does so, because it never occurs to us not to do so, and because success in our culture seems to demand that we do so.

—Alfie Kohn, *No Contest*

Are they (the people in your company) thinking more about customers or employees? About competitors in the marketplace or competitors in the hallways? About products or protocol?

Davis and Davidson, *20/20 Vision*

$\mathcal{T}$eamwork. We're all for it! Many of us have taken part in expensive team-building exercises where we've climbed rope ladders, built boats, gone on challenging photo safaris, faced mythical enemies, and solved mysteries. Over and over, we've been told we have to learn to work together more effectively. And for good reason. Today's world is too complex for any one person to manage the value proposition alone. This is particularly the case in companies where individuals from different functional areas, departments, and physical locations have to work in harmony to meet the unique needs of their customers. If we hope to succeed, there is, in fact, no real alternative for many of us *but* to work as a team, to *cooperate.*

Unfortunately, it is this alternative that most organizations are least well equipped to implement. We are simply not prepared to cooperate—culturally, structurally, or philosophically. We are, after all, a nation that makes heroes of individuals who distinguish themselves competitively. From corporate raiders to rock stars, from baseball's Most Valuable Player to the most famous heart surgeon, we've focused on individual winners. Looking out for #1 is not only expected, but rewarded.

Nowhere is winning (and losing) more a part of everyday life than in our organizations. Here, the thrill of victory or the agony of defeat is relived by many on an almost daily basis. Unfortunately, the primary field of battle may not be in the marketplace, but in our hallways. The arena where the most intense competition in business is often waged is *within* the corporation itself, among its employees. The costs of unnecessary internal competition are prohibitive in most organizations.

We talk about being part of a team but, instead of cooperating in a system that encourages teamwork, we are pitted against one another to compete and win as individuals. As much as we claim we want cooperation, most of our structures don't reward it, our corporate culture doesn't support it, and our leaders are reluctant to embrace it—though it is often in the best interests of the organization to do so. Our people return from their team-building weekends and, within a few days' (hours'?) time, they're often back to building their empires at the expense of the other person and with the hope of a superior (i.e., winning) performance appraisal, higher merit pay, the next promotion, or more job security. To meet today's demands we need to be pulling together, yet the internal competition endemic to our system is undermining our efforts.

In Spite of the System

We're not saying that cooperation doesn't exist in most organizations. In fact, cooperation <u>can</u> and often <u>does</u> prevail. People frequently act on their more noble instincts and help one another. Indeed, it is nothing less than amazing that, given the systemic promotion of competition and the resistance to cooperation, there is as much pulling together as there is. It seems that individuals are genuinely driven to do the "right thing"—contributing to the overall good of the organization—rather than feathering their own nest. But the cards in many organizations are essentially stacked against it. There are simply too many barriers to acting decently and cooperatively and, conversely, too many rewards for acting otherwise. If our structure required teamwork, most people would readily cooperate without a library of team-building exercises. The task itself would create a cause to rally around.

AVOIDING A SCARCITY MENTALITY

Old-culture Americans . . . find it difficult to enjoy anything they themselves have unless they can be sure that there are people to whom this pleasure is denied. . . . Since the society rests on scarcity assumptions, involvement in it has always meant competitive involvement.

—Philip Slater, *The Pursuit of Loneliness*

It has been a while in coming, but the jury has mostly decided in the case of Cooperation vs. Competition within the organization. While a few arguments may be made for internal competition being effective over the short term to gain a certain sought-for result or to encourage the performance of simple tasks, the overwhelming body of current research points to the fact that <u>it's cooperation, not internal competition, that promotes higher achievement.</u> A number of these studies also indicate that the com-

C7

petitive environments in which people are the least productive are those where rewards are limited, and where winning by a few necessitates losing by many. In environments where wins are in short supply and losses are the rule, not the exception, a scarcity mentality develops. Unfortunately, it is environments such as these that are the most prevalent in many organizations.

We've all seen how a scarcity mentality plays itself out in the larger world. Individuals or small groups scramble for whatever is in scarce supply. Whenever they find what it is they are looking for, they hoard it and do whatever else is necessary to protect it. The fear that the scarcity will persist robs them of the inclination to share what they need. Often, values are perverted, and the individual forsakes a larger sense of community.

Divisionary Divisions

We'd been involved with a company that had come a long way in improving the level of service and internal cooperation until it decided to give a Division of the Year award to the division that was most progressive in customer service. Within days of the announcement of the award, cooperation among divisions began to disappear. People started hoarding information and refusing to share resources. It was no longer "we." Instead, it became "us" and "them." Getting the highest score, not improving service to customers, became the most important goal.

The organization whose employees must compete for a limited number of wins or rewards—whether it's membership in the President's Circle or the prize for Employee of the Month—tends to create a scarcity mentality of its own, complete with the same scrambling, the same hoarding, the same subversion of potential values, and the same failure to consider the greater good. The principal difference in the type of scarcity that exists in world markets—shortages of food or medicine, for example—and that which exists in the corporation is that the former is real while the latter is artificially created. Organizational structures such as forced distribution performance appraisal or programs such as sales and service contests get people to compete against one another—a few people win at the expense of others. Ironically, what is scarce and often bitterly fought for in the corporation is not even necessarily something that has real value in the outside world—the boss' praise, for example.

If a scarcity mentality exists in an organization and if employees compete for a limited number of wins, the chances are good that many people will be more focused on the competition and the reward than on their work. In any event, it is far less likely that they'll cooperate with one another any more than they have to, and far more likely that much of their energy will be consumed in the campaign for whatever individual rewards are available.

Of course, this wasn't our intent when we first put these various limited-win structures into place. On the contrary, we had hoped the competition would spur better performance and stimulate creativity. Originally, the goal may have been to increase sales, so we implemented a commission structure, then organized a Quota Club for our top performers. Or, if the goal was to improve service, we decided to "pay for performance," limiting the number of dollars available in any department. The competitive culture that these incentives, elite clubs, compensation structures, and other limited-win programs have spawned, however, often has a negative, less visible effect on performance. The structures that invite internal competition are undermining the cooperation and teamwork that we all desperately need to add value and create loyal customers. Because most of us grew up in competitive environments, we tend not to see what should be obvious to us by now: instead of adding value, internal competition, particularly when coupled with a scarcity of wins, has become a significant value subtracter in most organizations.

Publish or Perish?

C7 On a recent flight, we spoke to a well-known research scientist who, not long before, had synthesized a drug that eased the suffering of AIDS patients. He told us that developments in his field were considerably slowed by decisions surrounding whose names would appear, and in what order, in the medical journal articles. He suggested that new drugs would get to market faster if the researchers' names were eliminated altogether, but that would be difficult because publication credits are a key indicator of personal success.

The question is, <u>Why</u> do we do it? Why do we limit the number of people who can win? Are there great payoffs for the distinctions we make? What are the potential downside risks? Here are eight, for starters. There are many, many more.

1. Internal competition drives out creativity and innovation. Individuals competing against one another must be playing the same, or similar, game so that the appropriate comparisons can be made and the winners selected. Spawned by competition, this need for similarity makes it more difficult for the individual competitor to experiment and try new methods. The result can be significantly lower levels of creativity and innovation.

2. Internal competition <u>inhibits dialogue</u>. Add the concept of winning and losing to a dialogue and you get a debate. In an internally competitive environment, individuals become less interested in sharing and thinking about new or conflicting information and become more concerned with scoring points or pressing their case, right or wrong. After all, in a competition, winning is the name of the game.

3. Internal competition impacts relationships negatively. Though many of us naturally expect the best from people, when we know we are competing—whether for a promotion, to curry favor with the boss, or to get a bonus—it is difficult for us to build trust, work as a team member, or create an honest relationship. This is especially so when wins are limited, and your victory is made possible by the failure of others. In any event, competition makes people suspicious of one another, and often results in greater anxiety in workers, who constantly feel they have to watch their backs.

4. Internal competition lowers product and service quality. As different individuals and different departments compete among themselves while trying to get products and services out as quickly and profitably as possible, the temptation can be to cut corners, particularly if the problems created in doing so won't come back to haunt the company for years, long after the individuals involved have moved on.

5. Internal competition destroys focus. Winning and improvement are very different goals. When we focus on besting others, we are not necessarily focusing on improving the present system. In fact, there is significant evidence demonstrating that winning can actually result in lower levels of performance. When people compete with a focus on winning, they often take the fastest, most reliable, most predictable route to winning, which is rarely the most effective route to continually improving the method of work!

6. Internal competitiveness reduces efficiency. When individuals are less innovative, less creative, less trusting, or more combative, it costs the company in a variety of ways. For example, when people compete with one another, they tend to work independently, often duplicating the efforts of others, solving problems that have already been solved, generating data for projects for which perfectly good data already exists.

C7

7. Internal competition demotivates the non-winners. The theory was that if people competed and the winners were rewarded, they would feel appreciated and all those who didn't win would strive to do so in the future. In most cases, however, it hasn't worked out that way. Far too many artless and incomplete reward systems result in the selection of "winners" whose performance was not any better, and was sometimes objectively worse, than that of some of the "losers." Predictably, this can be demotivating to those who "lost." Precisely how demotivating is hard to tell, because we usually evaluate the motivational effectiveness (or ineffectiveness) of our efforts by tracking the reaction of the winners rather than that of the non-winners. Instead, we simply assume that non-winners are generally satisfied, and that they'll try harder next time. In fact, the opposite often occurs. Once people are labeled non-winners or feel the deck is stacked against them, they sometimes stop trying altogether—and who can blame them?

8. Internal competition lessens self-esteem. When some people lose (or at least are labeled non-winners) in the competition, they begin to question their ability to succeed in this (and maybe any other) system. After all, they worked hard, tried their best, and came up short. Losing is more common than winning because of the way the system has been designed: i.e., to make sure that most people don't win. The long-term effect of constantly coming up short can be significant. Less confident people simply don't learn or experiment as effectively as those who are confident.

Having read this far, if you still think that the same argument can be made *for* competition that Winston Churchill made for democracy (i.e., that democracy is the worst form of government . . . except for all the others), please reconsider. Current research suggests otherwise. Internal competition, particularly when wins are limited and cooperation is required, has hidden costs we've only begun to realize.

66 studies found that cooperation promotes higher achievement than competition, 8 found the reverse, and 36 found no statistically significant difference. Cooperation promoted higher achievement than independent work in 108 studies, while 6 found the reverse and 42 found no difference. The superiority of cooperation held for all subject areas and all age groups.

—Alfie Kohn, *No Contest*

C7

BUILDING COOPERATION

Fortunately, there are a number of ways to break the hold that internal competition may have on our organizations:

- **Increase the interactions between individuals and groups.** The faceless person in another office performing another function can easily be ignored. It's far harder not to cooperate with people you know, especially if your interaction with them is frequent and you have to cooperate to get the job done.

- **Ensure that everyone has the opportunity to win.** This doesn't mean rewarding non-performers. However, when a number of people seek the same goal and the number of wins is artificially limited, competition will result. If everyone can win, one person's success doesn't necessitate another's failure.

- **Establish cooperation and respect as core values.** As long as internal cooperation is perceived to be optional and internal competition is tolerated, little will change. Elevating cooperation to a core value will ensure that climbing someone else's back to get ahead will be career-limiting. Take a few minutes to analyze whether cooperation is career-enhancing in your organization. How do you know whether people are cooperating effectively or not? Do you understand the effects of the structures that promote competition? Do your human resource practices encourage teamwork or individual excellence? What happens to people in the organization who play politics at the expense of others?

- **Recognize teamwork, appreciate cooperation, improve recognition abilities**. The more symbolically, visibly, and frequently we demonstrate appreciation for teamwork and interdepartmental cooperation, the more of it we'll get.

- **Educate everyone about the entire process.** If people understand how their performance affects others, they will be less likely to act in ways that negatively impact others or the company. Most people want to do the right thing and, given a choice, will make a good decision unless it is personally punishing. Providing information about the process enables each person to make an informed choice.

- **Beware of quick rotations.** A focus on short-term results often leads to a less cooperative environment. If a person has only a short time in which to impress the boss or make an impact, the long-term benefits of cooperation can be perceived to be less important. This is especially true if a person will be rotated before he or she will experience the negative effects of non-cooperation. Clearly, in the fast-paced world in which we compete, most jobs don't last long and quick job rotations are necessarily the rule. In these cases, it's even more important to ensure that internal competition is limited and that accountability for cooperation is significant. If part of everyone's evaluation included an analysis of what a person or group has done to further teamwork, most organizations would be very different. Whom have you helped lately? From whom have you learned? Whom have you taught? What group has influenced your thinking the most? Which people, outside your group, have been the most instrumental in helping you succeed?

- **Involve everyone in at least one cross functional improve ment effort.** Mandating that people must work beyond the boundaries of their own department or functional area will not only result in more talent being applied to complicated process issues, but will result in a greater appreciation of how the entire process works to benefit the customer. One of the most important reasons for mandating participation may be symbolic, showing people that cooperation is not optional and that everyone will actively participate. People should also be held accountable for their participation. There's no greater waste of time than to be a mandated team member on a team that accomplishes very little.

- **Consider teams as the primary unit of responsibility. Design in interdependence.** It hardly makes sense for several members on the team to be able to win when the team as a whole loses and when the customer is shortchanged. If a task requires teamwork, ensure that teamwork is required of everyone. Make the team responsible and accountable. Beware: As some organizations have begun to organize in teams, many have been unwilling to completely abandon the old structure, keeping team members accountable as *individuals* to their former functional department. The result is usually a group that does not function as a team but as individuals representing an area of expertise, each with veto power over most decisions. Frustration levels tend to be high as people are torn between functional responsibilities and group commitments. If we want teams to act like teams, we must make them cohesive units, with a real task and knee-knocking team accountability. Going halfway can be very costly.

C7

C H A L L E N G E   8

Winning with Teamwork

We must all hang together, or assuredly we shall all hang separately.

—Benjamin Franklin upon signing
the Declaration of Independence

Teamwork doesn't happen automatically, and it doesn't result just from the exhortation of a single leader. It results from members paying attention to how they are working together, identifying issues that block teamwork and working them through, and consciously developing patterns of working together that all members find challenging and satisfying. Team members have to talk to each other about how they are working as a team; they have to process their group actions. This calls for a collective self-awareness, openness, and maturity that are still not widely found in very many teams in our culture.

—Peter Vaill, *Managing as a Performing Art*

*W*henever we've seen examples of a cooperative culture at work, we have been both impressed and moved—impressed because the team approach generally seems to work (and far better than we had ever dared assume); and moved because, in the absence of internal competition, everyone's actions appear more noble, team goals are put ahead of individual goals, relationships seem deeper, and mutual trust is evident.

Indeed, if the situation is right and the price is not too high, people will cooperate . . . and gladly so. People will behave in ways that are consistent with the teamwork we so desperately need. While we may be culturally biased toward competition, most of us have an even stronger need to be part of something larger than ourselves.

The concept of working in teams is not new, of course. Teams have been around for thousands of years. Tribal societies were teams in action—individuals working together in the accomplishment of common goals for the greater good. But, somewhere along the way it was the individual, not the team that became the basic building block of most organizations. Still today, many of our organizations revolve largely around individual accountability, individual compensation, individual roles and job descriptions, and work groups managed by supervisors responsible for the performance of the individuals that make up these groups.

C8

It's time to question the assumptions that lie at the foundation of these practices, however. The world is just too complicated and our organizations are too diverse to continue to focus primarily on the individual rather than group expertise, nor can we afford the cost of the internal competition that individualism as practiced in most organizations spawns. We can also ill-afford to continue to act as if functions don't need to cooperate and can be managed as piece parts. Individual and functional isolationism is simply too costly and too slow. The genuine interdependencies that exist in today's organization mitigate against it and our customers will not stand for it. There is little question that the way for most of us to win today is no longer in competitive isolation, but by bringing together the expertise necessary to build value.

Without people acting in concert, little gets done effectively. It takes teams—whether we call them that or not—to see a situation from a number of different perspectives and make informed, well-rounded decisions. Teams are the foundation for learning. It is the dialogue, debate, questioning, and confrontation that occurs within a team that allows people to see the world from differing perspectives. Working in teams can also have positive motivational effects. When team members share a common vision and enjoy regular contact with their co-workers, they generally receive faster, more accurate feedback, have more control over their work environment and enjoy a more varied and interesting job experience. With teams there can also be more opportunity for self-manage-

ment and effective mentoring without playing to the boss and unnecessary internal competition is often reduced.

In addition, the complexity of managing teams forces leaders
to think and act more systemically. This complexity tends to challenge the thinking of supervisors, who must evolve a new set of assumptions and practices to manage effectively. And since team
members often take on many of the responsibilities now held by
supervisors, fewer may be needed. For example, managing forty
individuals is proving difficult (if not impossible) for many supervisors today. Yet it is entirely conceivable that the same supervisor
could effectively manage ninety-six individuals were they organized into a half-dozen or more teams.

ALL THAT JAZZ

A number of those who have written about teams have used the
metaphor of a jazz combo or orchestra. In these examples, individual
musicians—many with very different talents and playing different
instruments—play "as one." Teamwork is not optional, but a
prerequisite to successful performance. They are led by a leader who
coordinates rather than controls who points the way but does not
define it. The individual musicians not only know how to play, they
know how to play *together*. Finally, driving each musician's
performance is a vision of a given piece that is shared by others. The
result is a group performance that is significantly more satisfying
than the sum of its individual parts.

Genuinely embracing teamwork rather than just talking about
it won't be easy, however, for a number of reasons—not the least of
which being that we are organizations of individuals and proud of
it! We also know comparatively little about working in teams. Our
structures have not been designed to give us that experience, and
we are still in our infancy in the quest for understanding when and
how to form teams and how to facilitate the best results.

It's not that we haven't experimented with teams. From team-building retreats to self-directed team experiments, almost every organization has dabbled in ways to capture the benefits of individuals working together toward a common goal. Outside the factory, however, the results of our efforts remain mixed. In many cases, we seem to be trying to work in teams while maintaining existing structures that focus on individual performance—without seriously questioning the assumptions and beliefs that created these practices. Often the costs have been significant. Ineffective attempts to utilize teams have resulted in wasted time, lower productivity, and reduced levels of trust in many groups.

In the future, many of us will organize in teams not because it furthers employee involvement, but because it is the most efficient way to customize and deliver value in an era where specialization, speed of delivery, and rapid learning are keys to organizational success. There are no recipes for development and management of effective teams. In the end, every leader will have to choose the method that best fits the unique characteristics of his or her organization, the current business climate, and the team members' personal skills and style. In forming a team, however, it may be useful to keep in mind that successful teams usually have:

- **A shared commitment to clearly defined objectives.** While overall team objectives may be broadly stated, the entire team must have a concise understanding of why the team exists and what its specific goals are.

- **Interdependence as an integral element of team design.** An effective team succeeds or fails as a group, with the success of the team requiring a coordinated effort.

- **A compelling purpose that evokes commitment.** This purpose usually evolves in response to challenges from management, customers, or suppliers. However, the team must also understand the *importance* of this purpose. A combination of shared purpose and specific goals is essential.

C8

- **A methodology that facilitates learning.** Too often, teams underperform or fail because they don't have methods for solving problems, analyzing causation, measuring progress, and sharing information.

- **A combination of the right skills and abilities.** Team members are often selected for their position in the organization or for personal or political reasons. This can be problematic. In assembling a team, consider technical skills, knowledge of specific processes, access to information, ability to sustain relationships, understanding of corporate goals, etc.

- **Mutual accountability as a core value.** Team members must be willing to hold each other accountable. Accomplishing performance goals must be more important than agreement for agreement's sake.

- **Trust from the outset.** Trust must be assumed initially and deepened over time. If we aren't willing to trust others <u>first</u>, we ourselves will never be trusted.

- **A supportive organizational structure.** For teams to thrive, the company's structure should be modified to reduce internal competition and make it career-enhancing for people to subordinate their personal desires in favor of team goals.

- **The challenge to overstretch the present system.** Challenging the team to stretch for objectives that may or may not be attainable under the current system can be team-building, energizing, and highly motivational, provided that failure is not punished.

- **Diversity of thought.** A heterogeneous group, the team can bring a variety of thought to the solution of problems. Teams function most effectively when individual team members contribute their own unique approach to problem solving.

- **Quick starters.** Effective teams set shorter rather than longer deadlines. Initial floundering is inevitable but too much delay can reduce commitment and any sense of urgency the team feels. We often underestimate what can be accomplished in a short period of time.

C8

- **Clear values and rules of behavior established early on.** Every group or social system needs boundaries to provide order to group efforts. Successful teams start by defining a set of expectations or shared values concerning attendance, distractions, loyalty, honesty, respect, willingness to challenge, information sharing, roles, etc.

- **Significant time to spend as a team.** Team dialogue is a must. The amount and quality of learning and improvement that occur in a team environment correlate directly with the amount of time team members can spend together. You can never anticipate just when the best learning will take place.

- **Regular, structured, honest feedback.** Structuring the opportunity to dialogue is easy compared to the challenge of ensuring that the group is committed to seeing reality and providing honest feedback.

No Floaters!

We observed a twelve-person group assembling a side of an automobile at the Honda plant at Marysville, Ohio. Their policy: no floaters! When a team member did not come to work, the eleven remaining members were supposed to do the work of twelve people. There was very little absenteeism.

"Don't you ever want to take a Friday or a Monday off?" we asked one of the associates. "Yep, I sure would. But they'd kill me."

"Who's they? The supervisors?"

"Nope. My teammates," he replied. "They wouldn't put up with it. Besides, it would be unfair to them to have to do my work as well as theirs. I just couldn't do that to them."

Even though we've been studying individual motivation for

decades, we have few answers. It seems that we know even less about the effect of group responsibility on individual and team performance. Maybe that's why we've been slow to experiment with team accountability—especially with management jobs.

C8

MANAGEMENT TEAMS?

> *It helps to remember that a group dominated by a leader will never exceed the talents of the leader.*
>
> —Max DePree, *Leadership Jazz*

Although the characteristics of effective teams seem similar at every level in an organization, management teams are more difficult to form and manage effectively. Management teams usually form because of organizational structure and are usually more interested in protecting self-interest than accomplishing goals. Most problems encountered in management teams are caused at the time of formation. Some common failings include:

1. **All direct reports must be on the team.** This becomes a team looking for an issue! It comes together as a result of historical organizational design , rather than in response to the need for a group to solve pressing problems.

2. **The team's goals are the organization's goals.** This results in goals that are often too broad to be effectively addressed by a team.

3. **Goals of the team members are not aligned.** The talk is of acting as a team but performance is still managed individually. Accountability for team performance is often secondary to a manager's individual goals that relate to performance in a part of the organization.

4. **Systems support competitive behaviors more than cooperation.** Present systems often limit the number of team

members who can win—get bonuses, raises, performance appraisal marks, etc. Internal competition results in diminished levels of trust. People who want to cooperate will hesitate if cooperation is punished.

C8

5. **People are selected by position and not their potential to contribute.**

6. **Status differences lessen the willingness of members to challenge ideas and thinking.**

7. **Everyone must be involved in every decision or people feel left out.** Being a team member can become a symbol of success. The problem is that since the team's goals are often the organization's goals, involving everyone in everything is inefficient.

8. **Managing the boss' perception is the primary goal of some managers.**

9. **The illusion of agreement is often the implicit goal of the group or "groupthink." Those who confront others are often considered "non-team players."**

10. **Systematic feedback on team effectiveness does not exist.**

TOOLS MUST NOT BE CONFUSED WITH GOALS.

A manager told us that he thought that his company was doing a pretty darn good job at employee involvement. "How do you know?" we asked.

"Well, we have 86 employee teams," he told us. Later, we asked one of the employees what his team was doing. "Not much," he said. "I've been on this team for two years, and we haven't done dip."

"So why do you stay on the team?" we asked.

"Well, everyone has got to be on a team here. If you're not, you're in real trouble."

C8

PRONOUN-CIATION

Listening to the language used in conversations among team members can often provide insights into the level of teamwork that exists in an organization. The use of pronouns can be revealing, providing insight into the assumptions and beliefs of the team members:

Some people say:
<u>I</u> listened for their input.
<u>I</u> ensured that it was done.
<u>I</u> was responsible for them.
<u>I'm</u> proud of my team.

Others say:
<u>We</u> made it happen.
<u>We</u> discussed the issues.
<u>We</u> were successful.
<u>We're</u> proud of our accomplishments.

Some people say:
<u>My</u> team was successful.
<u>My</u> responsibilities were met.
<u>My</u> objectives were clear.

Others say:
<u>Our</u> team was responsive.
<u>Our</u> responsibilities were met.
<u>Our</u> objectives were clear.

Some people say:
<u>They</u> report to me.
<u>They</u> asked me for approval.
<u>They</u> did it without me.

Others say:
The other team asked <u>us</u> for help.
They included <u>us</u> as part of their problem-solving group.

There is little doubt that the use of pronouns reveals a particular mindset. The only thing worse than saying "I", "I", "I" is to say "we" when you really mean "I." You can't fool people for long. It's best not to try!

C H A L L E N G E 9

Performance Appraisal or Development: The Need to Choose

The performance of anybody is the result of a combination of many forces—the person himself, the people that he works with, the job, the material that he works on, his equipment, his customer, his management, his supervision, environmental conditions (noise, confusion, poor food in the company's cafeteria). These forces will produce unbelievably large differences between people. In fact, apparent differences between people arise almost entirely from the action of the system that they work in, not from people themselves. A man not promoted is unable to understand why his performance is lower than someone else's. No wonder; his rating was the result of a lottery. Unfortunately, he takes his rating seriously.

—W. Edwards Deming, *Out of the Crisis*

*T*hroughout this book, we've talked about structures whose unintended effects often undermine teamwork, inhibit experimentation and learning, encourage mediocrity, and stifle creativity and innovation. Nowhere are these effects more readily apparent than in the performance appraisal process practiced by so many organizations today. Not surprisingly, since performance appraisal is often used to determine compensation, promotion, and job security, it's the process that generates the most controversy among employees at all levels.

About performance appraisal, there are currently many more questions than answers. Are performance appraisal methods fair? Accurate? What are the effects of a forced distribution process?

Should compensation be tied to appraisal results? Is past perfor- mance a valid indicator of future performance, particularly when the job changes significantly? Will positive feedback from an ap- praisal lead to higher levels of performance? Are the methods used to measure the effectiveness of performance appraisal themselves effective?

Of all the questions raised by performance appraisal systems, the single most compelling, we feel, is whether their primary pur- pose is evaluative or developmental: i.e., are they a grading tool or a learning tool? The answer in most organizations is, *both*—skew- ing, however, in a vast majority of cases, in the direction of evalua- tion. This leads to a second question . . . and a third: can a single system perform twin functions? And, as currently designed, is the performance appraisal process particularly effective at doing ei- ther? Our experience suggests that, in most cases, the answer to both these questions is no.

With the best of intentions, leaders in almost every organiza- tion have tried to develop systems that provide fair, honest feed- back to help employees learn, while providing information managers need to differentiate among performance levels and re- ward individuals or teams accordingly. When learning and evalua- tion are combined into one system, however, a single overarching problem inevitably arises: the problem of the boss as both evalua- tor and coach.

In order to really learn and develop, people must be able to share weaknesses as well as strengths and must view information about present performance as hopeful and non-threatening. How- ever, in a process where one individual is both evaluator and coach, can we really assume that employees will be truly candid in discussing their weaknesses? Probably not.

PERFORMANCE EVALUATION:
DISTINGUISHING THE INDISTINGUISHABLE

C9

In forced distribution evaluation processes, the frustration of try-ing to differentiate individuals where no major differences exist has led many a manager to take imaginative steps. It was from a supervisor that we first learned of the "knockout criteria" he claimed to use in performance appraisal.

"What do you mean, `knockout criteria'?" we asked.

"You know, like did the guy I'm evaluating smile when he walked into my office?" The supervisor smiled himself as he said it.

"Did he know he was supposed to smile?" we asked, still not cer-tain about the knockout criteria concept, but beginning to catch on.

"Of course not. If I told everyone that, then they'd all smile, and I'd have to come up with other criteria."

Of course, he was kidding—but his point was serious: any method that attempts to distinguish among indistinguishable per-formances doesn't make much sense.

As an evaluative tool, performance appraisal is generally used to rate performance, skills, and experience for compensation pur-poses, serve as a basis for rewards and recognition, and provide a foundation for promotion practices. Often, too, performance evalu-ations are meant to motivate employees to perform better in the hope of getting a better evaluation (or for fear of getting a negative one) next time.

The problem, almost everyone in the organization will agree, is that the information generated in most performance evaluation systems is incomplete at best and can frequently be misleading. Also, aside from one or two top performers or one or two poor per-formers, it is exceedingly difficult to differentiate among individ-ual performances. In many cases, too, the erroneous assumption is made that the performance of an individual can be isolated from

that of the system. Or, it is assumed that the system affects everyone in the same way. As a result, very few in the organization genuinely favor the evaluation process or consider it a fair or accurate
representation of their performance.

Widespread disapproval of performance appraisal is nothing
new. Many a manager has experienced the frustration of facing the
explicit or implicit requirement to differentiate high performers
from average performers from low performers, even if there is no
rational basis for such distinctions. The task is often made even
more difficult by the lack of measurements and observations available to make an assessment. Because of implicit or explicit forced
distribution systems, most of those appraised will be disappointed
or frustrated with the results—usually only 30–35% are allowed to
get "winning" marks. Often, too, since everyone knows that what
gets put down in a person's file may damn him or her forever—
and since managers hate confronting poor performers almost as
much as public speaking—the evaluator is rarely forthright in his
appraisal if any negatives are involved.

3 Out of 5 Is Good Work—Not!

We had the opportunity to discuss a performance appraisal meeting with a manager who had just been told that she had earned a
3 rating out of a possible 5 (as compared to her peers). She told us
that after she was given her "rating," an extensive, in-depth discussion about her strengths and weaknesses followed. But she
remembered little if any of what was said. From the instant she
had been labeled a 3, she said her eyes glazed over and she
became angry. All she could think about was that damning 3,
how unfair it was, and how it would submarine her career. "But
doesn't a 3 represent fully meets expectations in your system?"
we asked. "Yeah, I guess," she said, "but labeling a 3, fully meets
expectations, doesn't fool me or make me feel anything but average."

Even if the information gathered in performance evaluations was accurate, its negative, unintended effects would still be reason to seriously question the viability and value of its use. Chief among these effects is the fact that competition is inherent in most performance evaluation systems and that appraisals weigh individuals against each other and force them to compete for a limited number of wins. Performance appraisal, therefore, can result in many of the same problems that arise from competition, including:

C9

- A scarcity mentality that inhibits cooperation and teamwork
- Stifled creativity and innovation
- Reduced efficiencies and compromised product and service quality
- Inhibited dialogue
- Demoralized "losers" and destroyed self-esteem
- Compromised relationships

In addition, used as an evaluation tool:

1. Performance appraisal can shift the focus of the employee from the customer to the boss. When your future depends on one individual's perception of you, managing that person's perception becomes key. As much rhetoric as there is in organizations today about teamwork and customer focus, with performance appraisal in the balance, the boss becomes the number one focus—particularly because instances where a boss can measure an employee's ability or performance are so infrequent. While this may serve to reaffirm the boss' status in the organization ("I give out the numbers") and his or her need for control ("If you're going to hold me accountable for their work, I want to write their appraisals"), it does little in the way of increasing cooperation, and even less for enhancing the value that can be delivered to customers. We've all been to meetings where the primary concern of most people in the

room was to please the boss—even if it meant <u>di</u>spleasing the customer somewhere down the line.

Bossism

**An officer of a Fortune 500 company proudly told us that she had
cleared her calendar to make time for her team, her first priority.
However, she also carried a beeper with her wherever she
went—even to on-site meetings—with a standing order to her
secretary: "Don't call me unless my boss calls."**

Her team was her first priority—second only to her boss.

2. Performance appraisal can encourage mediocrity. Whenever evaluation is part of the process and the results of the evaluation can affect your career, the tendency is to negotiate for goals
you know you can easily meet, rather than ones that require experimentation or new processes where the possibility of mistakes or
failures are greater. And woe be to us if we negotiate for true
stretch goals and succeed. Since then, more than likely, next year's
goals will be set substantially higher—often without an analysis
of whether the goal is even achievable. Since the price of failure is
often high, better to be realistic in our negotiations, set goals
that *appear* to be a stretch but aren't really. In this way, while
the absolute level of our performance may be mediocre (i.e., substantially similar to that of others) it can still serve us well in our
careers.

**3. Performance appraisal can reduce and pervert information
flow**. If you're reluctant to talk about things gone wrong, problem
areas, or experiments that may fail for fear that the information
will be used against you in your performance evaluation, all that is
left to talk about are the positives. This results in a rose-colored
glasses view of the organization that leaves bosses at every level
with progressively more distorted pictures of reality.

They're Clean, but Do They Work?

We watched with interest at a utility yard of a corporate division
one day as workers polished trucks in anticipation of the visit of
a vice-president. To ensure timely customer deliveries, the division was in dire need of new trucks, but division honchos were
even more concerned with making points with the VP who
wrote the division manager's appraisal and determined raises
and promotions—hence the elaborate effort to make the old
trucks look good. When the VP finally arrived, he looked around
and said, "I don't see why you need all this money for new
trucks when the old fleet looks great."

Ultimately, the inaccurate state of affairs communicated by the
shiny old trucks delayed the purchase of new ones by more than
a year.

C9

4. **Performance appraisal can create a short-term focus.** Because of high job turnover and rapid rotation rates, managers are
usually most concerned with performance improvements that can
be demonstrated during their tenure. Also, because the duration of
an evaluation is typically no more than a year, the tendency of
many being evaluated is to tailor their performance to that same
time period, rather than thinking of their jobs as a continuous,
evolving endeavor. And because memories are short, appraisals
done in December may ignore the successes of March or April and
focus on the "failures" of October and November.

5. **Performance appraisal can undermine organizational vision and values.** A manager can talk about a vision, can paint it
clearly, write the most eloquent vision statement, then cause nothing but confusion if the achievements of the people promoted and
rewarded do not reflect that vision. Such promotion and rewards
are often the case, however, because the measures that provide the
basis of many performance appraisals do not describe performance adequately. Too often, evaluations are based on what is easy

C9

to measure or has been traditionally measured, whether the person made the boss look good, or whether the person is perceived as a team player (i.e., one who doesn't rock the boat or whose ideas aren't thought to be too "weird"). When a person is promoted because of an outstanding evaluation, many will try to emulate that person's behavior. If there is a disjunction between that behavior and the one articulated in the vision, there is little question which behavior will be mimicked.

6. Performance appraisal can destroy trust. Simply put, to base someone's future on forced rationalizations and "knockout criteria" is embarrassing for the manager who has to do it and unfair to the employee to whom it is done. Sure, it may be possible to differentiate between your highest and lowest performer. But what about all those in between, particularly those you don't have frequent contact with? And how do you differentiate among those whose efforts you support and those you don't? For the individuals on the receiving end who garner anything but the highest rating, the first response is usually frustration (if not anger) followed by disappointment, and ultimately by a lack of trust in the organization (and, by extension, its leaders) that underwrites what is perceived to be an inaccurate, unfair evaluation process.

CONTAMINATING THE FEEDBACK (LEARNING) LOOP

Ideally, performance appraisal as a developmental tool provides feedback and the opportunity to discuss present performance. It identifies problems and provides a forum for resolving them, and serves as a basis for the creation of a plan that lets people grow and systematically take on greater responsibility. In practice, however, performance appraisal, when used as a developmental tool, tends to inhibit learning and slow development by inserting an administrative procedure between the individual and his or her performance results, thereby contaminating the information feedback loop.

The feedback loop is that phase of the continuous process improvement process where information about present performance is provided to individuals and groups so that they can learn and improve. The fact that feedback is fundamental to rapid improvement and organizational learning is irrefutable. Timely feedback is as important to the employee striving to meet his or her goals as it is to the missile whose course must be altered in flight as revised target data is received. Therefore, when feedback to the employee is delayed, filtered, or otherwise perverted, improvement slows and learning suffers.

In many organizations, supervisors are responsible for measuring performance. Feedback from the process goes first to the supervisor who then decides what aspects of the data will be communicated to the worker and how that data will be presented. This introduces a number of significant variables and impediments into the feedback process, including the supervisor's interpretation of the data and the amount of time that elapses between when the data is available and when it is passed on to the worker. Compounding the problem is the fact that, more often than not, the supervisor is also the worker's evaluator, interjecting an element of fear into what should really be a learning process.

Another major variable is the supervisor's method of presenting the data. Taken by itself, data carries no real emotional charge. Introducing another individual into the equation can turn this information transfer into an emotion-charged event, which may thwart rapid and effective learning.

Re-engineer a better performance management system that doesn't undermine an individual's or a team's ability or willingness to learn, but facilitates more learning. For example, instead of basing performance appraisal primarily on past performance data, wouldn't it make more sense to base the appraisal on what the individual does with that performance information—how he or she uses it to become more productive and improve the process? With this type of appraisal, a person's willingness and ability to think and effectively react to information in real time is what is measured. In such a system, a person's ability to use information wisely becomes more important than short-term performance data. Getting a better report card takes a back seat to learning.

In a knowledge-based economy, better thinking, more effective decision making, and an understanding of reality are critical. It makes little sense, therefore, to interfere with employees trying to achieve these goals by slowing and contaminating the information they need to learn, and by evaluating short-term results that are often more attributable to the process itself than to the individual.

Here are ten guidelines for re-engineering a better performance management system:

1. Determine whether you intend the system to be evaluative or developmental. It's extremely difficult to have both. If you don't decide, you'll usually end up with a little of both, like it or not. Compromise systems usually don't do either job effectively and often create many negative unintended effects that inhibit our efforts to become more productive.

2. Reduce any *perceived* threats in the system. Face it, if information contained in an appraisal is in any way critical of performance or illuminates mistakes or variations to a boss or supervisor, it is threatening. If people feel threatened, they will act accordingly.

3. Develop "self" control—get feedback to the person who will use it first. One way to cut down on fear in the appraisal process is to give the person being evaluated the chance to deal with the data before giving it to the boss. Then, have the boss see the data in the context of the employee's analysis.

4. Ensure that everyone can win. Avoid any practice that will limit the number of people who feel they are succeeding. Being rated a 3 (out of 5) rarely feels good. This is especially true if the person being evaluated knows that there isn't a significant differ ence between his or her performance and others who were graded higher. Putting a behavioral indicator in front of the 3 such as "fully meets expectations" doesn't help. Although conferring these ratings provides organizations with a sense of administrative certainty, we believe that most leaders will soon realize how damaging these practices can be to employee morale and performance. If you doubt this is the case, make a list of the advantages and disadvantages of limiting the number of wins in your organization. Your careful analysis, we're convinced, will bear out our point.

C9

5. Eliminate explicit or implicit forced distribution. Who is smart enough to decide ahead of time how many people will perform at a given level? In small groups in particular, why do we persist in advocating the idea of normal distribution? After all, we try to hire the best and we rely on the performance of the critical mass. So, why have a system that alienates the many to reward the few? One unfortunate answer might be to divide people into categories to accommodate the compensation system. Keep in mind, though, that the only thing worse than not getting a raise is not getting a raise <u>and</u> getting a lousy evaluation.

6. Avoid unnecessary or meaningless distinctions. Don't distinguish among performance where no real distinction can be made. Any time you attempt to artificially categorize performance, trust is diminished and the perception of unfairness permeates the system. Forcing people into structured categories often says more about an organization's expectations of its leaders than it does about the performance of the employees who are being evaluated: i.e., by asking supervisors to make these meaningless distinctions, aren't we really implying that they won't confront poor performance unless we force them to?

7. Evaluate people on their willingness and demonstrated ability to learn. As we said earlier, evaluating short-term process results can inhibit learning and is often more an indicator of the effectiveness (or ineffectiveness) of the process than of individual performance. A far better measure of performance is how well an individual applies his or her learnings to better the process. The key to improvement—of one's own performance or of the larger process—is learning. As in any endeavor, if you concentrate on consistently improving your performance, the score will take care of itself. It's amazing how many people know their score, but don't have the discipline, tools, time, or information to systematically improve.

8. Give each person the responsibility for demonstrating the value that they create for the organization. Shouldn't all employees understand specifically what the company has invested in them? Ask each employee to demonstrate how they have added value to the organization and to show how this translates to a return on that investment (for example, through process improvement, product delivery, customer loyalty, innovating product and distribution systems, or increasing the knowledge base of the company). Then use this information to create a dialogue about priorities for the coming months and years. This is a good start toward creating a developmental performance management system that can systematically develop meaningful participation and encourage people to get rid of low or no value-added activities.

9. Every system should require a complete analysis of learnings and areas for improvement. There is always variation to reduce or another hill for the individual to climb. Having people identify these opportunities can facilitate learning and help reduce fear in the system. When it becomes okay to have shortcomings and when people feel that they can get help in these areas, learning can be significantly accelerated.

It seems silly that so many systems recognize the necessity for identifying opportunities for improvement but place that responsibility with the boss. If only the boss knows best, chances are the system is badly broken. If the employee had access to the information that reveals problem areas or, better yet, felt that it was career-enhancing (rather than career-limiting) to point out opportunities for improvement, the ability to learn in the system would be greatly increased.

C9

10. Get rid of any job descriptions that are not redesigned frequently. Why do we use static job descriptions when we desire fast, transformational change, and employees who are constantly learning, innovating new work methods, and taking on new responsibilities? If we must have job descriptions, maybe we ought to track how fast and how often these descriptions change.

Part 3

Leader as Customer Advocate

*To effectively build loyalty today, it's not enough for leaders to be committed to delivering value to customers; they must be **obsessed** with anticipating what the customers will value in the future. Waiting for the customers to realize the "need" for something is a recipe for failure.*

—JOSE SALIBI NETO,
Managing Director, HSM Cultura , Brazil

4

Leader as Customer Advocate

LEADING FOR LOYALTY: EXCEEDING THE CUSTOMER'S RATIONAL, EMOTIONAL, AND RAPIDLY CHANGING DEFINITION OF VALUE

There is only one boss: the customer. And he can fire everybody in the company, from the chairman on down, simply by spending his money somewhere else.

—Sam Walton, founder, Wal-Mart Stores

It's not a secret anymore. For most companies, *customer loyalty* is the key to future profitability and growth. Corporate newsletters, national periodicals, and most executive speeches are peppered with a litany of examples demonstrating the relationship between customer loyalty and profitability. In almost every market we've learned that retained customers:

- Are less expensive to serve because they know their role in the process.

- Tend to lower marketing costs.

- Often purchase more over time.

- Are open to purchasing new and different products as they are offered.

- Will refer new customers.

It may be "just common sense" that retained customers are profitable customers. But, for many companies, awareness of just how much sense it makes is a rather recent realization. It is only lately that attempts have been made to determine how profitable it can be to improve customer loyalty. In one such study, it was determined that a 5% increase in customer loyalty can result in increases in profitability that range from 25% in some industries to as much as 125% in others. From credit card companies to health clubs (where 50% annual customer attrition is not uncommon), and from chemical manufacturers to automobile dealerships, the eye-popping results of these studies and others have created a desire to become "customer-focused," that is long overdue.

And most of these studies do not include the effect of a delighted customer's willingness to buy related products or to tell the world how great the company is. Nor do they factor in the negative effect of a dissatisfied customer, who is usually more than willing to spread the word about an unsatisfying experience.

If we conservatively assume that 1 out of every 8 loyal customers gives us a referral, and 1 out of every 8 frustrated customers blemishes our reputation to the point that it prevents a sale, the importance of customer loyalty and the danger of frustrated customers become readily apparent. As we begin to understand the revenue stream that a loyal customer represents, we are more likely to make significant investments to improve customer retention and more likely to become interested in the quality and depth of our relationships with customers. Changes in present practices that yesterday seemed impractical, too expensive, or not "that" important, begin to take on a new level of significance.

In almost every market, customers are beginning to receive greater value. To increase customer loyalty, a growing number of companies are improving their ability to add value at a rapid pace. Pick up a newspaper or magazine and you're likely to read about yet another company that has re-defined value in a particular market. Customers are being educated to expect—no, *demand*—more. And it seems that no matter how unrealistic customers' expectations become, someone is willing to serve them, educating them to expect even more. The power has shifted. Today the customer really is "in control."

This is especially true for companies whose customers are large corporations that wield increasing influence over the markets in which they do business. Companies such as Wal-Mart, Home Depot, and Toys R Us are exerting so much power and control over their suppliers that they are fundamentally changing the way many do business. Today, it is common for large companies to require their vendors to price and bar-code products, develop customized packaging, or pay penalties for late or incomplete orders (just one day late and one item incomplete can result in a 10% reduction in payment for the entire invoice), and even change organizational structures. Efforts to improve the efficiency of the entire distribution process have become almost a religion. Manufacturers and distributors have learned that changes are not optional but are a prerequisite to customer retention and, therefore, to corporate survival. Increasingly accepted among Fortune 500 companies, this trend toward a customer-driven marketplace is quickly proliferating.

Today, the Customer Revolution is spreading beyond the largest, most powerful customers. Even small customers in many markets are being taught to expect a customized response. And once they experience radically better value, what was a satisfying experience yesterday is no longer quite as satisfying.

> ## PROGRESSIVE-LY WAITING FOR AN ACCIDENT . . .
>
> Imagine being involved in a minor car accident and your insurance adjuster is on the scene before the police! This type of rapid response is exactly what Progressive Insurance Company of Mayfield, Ohio, is attempting to make the industry standard. . . .
>
> Progressive's goal is to have its adjusters reach the scene of an accident within minutes after being notified of it. Photos of the damage can then be taken and transmitted by fax to main computers in the company's headquarters, where repair costs are calculated and an estimate is prepared and returned to the adjuster. If it makes good business sense, the adjuster can cut a check to the client on the spot and arrange for the client's transportation. Science fiction? Not today! Progressive is making it happen in a number of cities.
>
> Efforts like these have enabled Progressive to continually improve its customer retention rates while lowering its cost of operation. In recent years, Progressive has shared these success rates with its predominately "high risk" customer base by reducing rates.

BEYOND SATISFACTION

> *The difference is not one of skill or education or experience. It's a matter of values. To be customer-oriented is not to be self-oriented.*
>
> —Max Depree, *Leadership Jazz*

The owner of a vehicle repair facility told us recently that he had just lost a customer that represented 30% of his company's revenue. He said that he had worked on the relationship, had consistently solicited feedback and improvement suggestions, and had invested considerable sums in ensuring that this customer received good service. He wondered whether any customer was loyal these days. "After all," he told us, "I still can't imagine what we did wrong. "

Maybe his team didn't do anything wrong. Maybe they just

TABLE 1.

	Customer Rating	Intend to Repurchase (%)	Willing to Recommend (%)
Completely satisfied	5	90	96
Somewhat satisfied	4	56	71
Neither satisfied nor dissatisfied	3	12	19
Somewhat dissatisfied	2	3	10
Very dissatisfied	1	7	7

didn't do anything "right enough." Maybe they didn't give this customer a compelling reason to resist the temptations inevitably faced by every customer in an era where there are too many competitors and too few customers, an era in which many companies are fighting to survive, one customer at a time. Maybe providing merely good service, or good value, is no longer enough to guarantee that a customer will re-purchase and send new customers your way.

In case after case, we have found that a moderately satisfied customer is not necessarily a *loyal* customer, who is willing to become what Scott D. Cook, Chairman of Intuit Software, calls an "apostle." Developing apostles—customers who are willing to spread the word and help convert the uninitiated—requires something more than satisfaction. To become loyal, customers must get something that is unique, something that makes them feel special. They want to have trusting relationships with companies that are flexible enough to address their specific needs. It's no wonder, then, that so many companies have begun to talk of the need to focus on *exceeding*, rather than merely meeting, expectations—*delighting*, not simply satisfying, their customers.

As the example data in Table 1 indicates, when customers give a company a 5 out of 5 score ("Completely Satisfied"), a very high percentage say they intend to re-purchase and are willing to recommend the company's product or service to others. However, customers who give the company a 4 out of 5 rating ("Somewhat Satisfied"), say they are less willing to re-purchase or recommend the company to others. These customers may be satisfied, but certainly not loyal. Companies have found that a customer who rates the company 5 out of 5 is twice as likely to re-purchase than the customer who rates their experience a 4 out of 5.

Still, most companies, including those applying for quality awards, combine the 4's and 5's and refer to these combined groups as "satisfied" customers. This practice unfortunately communicates to all employees that there is no significant difference between the two ratings. So why do so many continue this practice when it is so clearly misleading and reduces the sense of urgency to improve relationships with those customers who are not yet loyal? Could it be that we know that to design structures to delight customers will require that we think and manage very differently, and we're just not ready? Or do we think the good old days of easy growth are coming back, so we don't have to change as quickly? Maybe we are afraid of what it might cost us and, when push comes to shove, rhetoric notwithstanding, our real strategy is to cut costs, cut costs, cut costs.

The first step to building customer loyalty is to *choose* to do so. Considering the expectations we have created in customers, the challenge of winning their loyalty is hugely more difficult than it was a couple of years ago. For most organizations, meeting the challenge will require wholesale changes in the way we design processes and organize work environments. We must try to continually adapt to our customers' ever-changing definition of value—which at times can be a more emotional than rational one.

THE CHANGING DEFINITION OF VALUE

The future ain't what it used to be.

—Yogi Berra

Loyalty is a function of the customer's subjective perception of value. Today, customers have more choices and are more educated about their alternatives than at any time in our history. Customers—both large corporations and individual consumers— weigh the quality of the product, the quality of service, the degree of choice, and the price in their individual computations of value. Also entering into their computations are intangibles—those *essentially human reactions* that often defy rational analysis. The emotional nature of customers is a major factor that is often overlooked when we consider the customer's perception of value. To a large extent, it is often the human connections we make with customers that turn them from a merely satisfied customer into an apostle (from a 4 out of 5 to a 5 out of 5).

Certainly, the old saying, "If you build a better mouse trap, the customer will beat a path to your door," needs updating. As the quality of products has universally improved and we've developed the ability to clone even the most complex products, competitive advantage based solely on product quality has been difficult to sustain. The emphasis has shifted to service quality, which is more difficult to achieve and tough to imitate. Service quality typically has a greater human component, is inherently more intangible, and requires greater cooperation among disparate groups. However, once achieved, for these reasons it may be very sustainable. Therefore, the new strategy has become, "Build a better path, and people will buy (and maybe even re-purchase) your high-quality, competitively priced, but no longer unique mousetrap."

Consider the challenges we must face in building this path. We've been told for a decade that customers consider "responsibility" and "responsiveness" key factors in making buying decisions, yet these words seem to get re-defined weekly, if not daily. Customers want things that work, services that add the value promised, and more and more they want *what* they want *when* they want it. They have grown increasingly intolerant of even short delays.

Consider also speed and flexibility. Just how fast and flexible will we have to be to delight customers in the future? It's anyone's guess, but it seems certain that, by today's standards, our speed will be mind-boggling. Half-hour mortgage approval is already replacing the thirty-day process. Overnight delivery is giving way to same-day delivery in many time-sensitive markets. Remember how impressed we were with Federal Express' "Track and Trace" system that enabled us to call in for information about the exact location of a package—24 hours a day? How much faster (and more convenient) can it get? Today, instead of calling, you merely hit a key on *your* computer. On-line information is rapidly replacing many publications as we get more addicted to "real-time" information. How about custom-made shoes assembled in the back of the shoe store and delivered in less than 10 minutes? At least one athletic shoe company says that such a system is imminent. No wonder we're intolerant when faced with the slightest of delays, frustrated by a maze of automated voice mail systems.

Reliable? The standard is near perfection. If you are not reliable, *very* reliable, you're in big trouble. Delivering what you have promised when you promised it is the minimum level of service expected today. Maybe that is why we are witnessing an unprecedented increase in the number of guarantees. (After all, how do you prove you're reliable if nothing goes wrong?) From restaurant meals to new cars, from long-distance service to the delivery of appliances, guarantees are proliferating. And many of today's guarantees no longer require fourteen copies of verification, patience while the company tries to fix the problem on multiple occasions, or other such hassles that cause customers to avoid making a claim because the remedy is perceived to be worse than the disease.

The guarantee of the future is a subjective guarantee of complete satisfaction rather than a guarantee that the product meet some objective list of characteristics. Instead of preparing to defend themselves from customers who might take undue advantage, companies increasingly are making a visible and meaningful commitment to their customers. They have decided it's worse for the customer to decide not to re-purchase than it is to have a customer make a claim

---

GUARANTEED FOR LIFE

I do not consider a sale complete until goods are worn out and the customer is still satisfied.

We will thank anyone to return goods that are not perfectly satisfactory.

Should the person reading this notice know of anyone who is not satisfied with our goods, I will consider it a favor to be notified.

Above all things we wish to avoid a dissatisfied customer.

—1912 L.L. Bean Circular

*No wonder there is no hassle for returns at L.L. Bean . . . it's a simple decision for service providers when products are guaranteed to the subjective satisfaction of the customer for the life of the product. **There is no fine print!***

---

against the warranty. Better to forsake some short-term revenue in order to ensure that they have the opportunity to retain the revenue stream. As more and more companies find out that most customers are honest and do not take unfair advantage, these guarantees will become more common. In the future, guaranteeing the satisfaction of customers may be a prerequisite for doing business. If the parade is coming, wouldn't it be better to lead it than to spend the same money to play catch-up and get little credit from customers for the effort?

VALUE: THE EMOTIONAL COMPONENT

Service is just a day-in, day-out, ongoing, never-ending, unremitting, persevering, compassionate type of activity.

—Leon Gorman, L.L. Bean

In a recent interview, we asked a woman to name the company to which she was most loyal and tell us why she felt the way she did. She told us that she was most loyal to JC Penney. When we questioned her on specifics, she replied that she considered the quality of their products to be good (although, because she was loyal, she did less comparison shopping than she might have). She said she believed that the prices were fair and the service was adequate. Selection? Adequate to meet her demands. She told us that it might not be rational, and she might not be able to completely explain her feelings, but that she trusted this company and that it had "always been there for her." "Besides," she said, "my mother liked JC Penney, and I like my mother."

The fact that her loyalty had such a strong emotional component should not have been a surprise. But, for some reason, we had never seen it quite so clearly. For the better part of two decades, we had been studying the issue, trying to develop a rational model that would explain the relationship between a company's value proposition and customer loyalty. We learned to explain customer preferences but it always seemed that something was missing. Even though we had seen the emotional side of loyalty as it is played out between a captain and crew, husband and wife, and boy and dog, we had systematically undervalued the emotional component in a customer's decision to re-purchase. The decision to be loyal to JC Penney may not have been completely rational. It was, however, a predictable human response, the type of response that is an essential part of every purchasing decision.

We've all been there. When we think of the four or five companies to which *we* are most loyal and why, the emotional component of loyalty is obvious. Many of us have been loyal to restaurants that have average food because the host remembers our name or found us a table on Saturday night when "none were available." We've been loyal to dry cleaners who don't press our clothes better or charge less, but stayed open for ten minutes after closing one night because we asked. We've been loyal to companies that make mistakes, but then take responsibility for those mistakes and fix the problem quickly, without argument. *All other things being equal, we choose to do business with people we like or those who show that they care about us.*

Good Guys Win More Often

Research conducted by Roper Research Worldwide indicates that customers like companies that support good causes. When choosing products of equal price and quality, 78% would choose a product made by a company that contributes to medical research, education, or other worthy causes. Two-thirds would switch brands to a manufacturer that supported a cause they deemed worthy, and one-third said they were more influenced by a company's social activism than by its advertising.

At times, loyalty is difficult to explain. Ask a customer what you can do to build their loyalty in the future and they often can't put it in words. But they will tell you that they "know it when they see it," or, maybe more appropriately, "when they *feel* it!" Certainly, a customer's loyalty is predicated on product quality, choice, price, and service. But it is also based on relationships, trust, and commitment. It is both rational and irrational. We have been told for a decade that "perception is all there is." We've heard the words and listened to the stories, but we must now come to grips with the fact that perception is an inescapably human endeavor in which customers see the world through emotional as well as intellectual lenses. We must map a strategy that is rational but that also anticipates the quirky, subjective, fickle, and emotional nature of human beings—our customers.

The Not-So-Lonely Maytag Story

At a talk we gave in Oakland, California, we mentioned that several appliance manufacturers had made great strides in quality and could now compete with Maytag. A man in the audience

loudly disagreed. "Maytag is the best," he said. He went on to say that although his wife overloads it, he kicks it, and it's been moved seven times, his Maytag washing machine has worked without a hitch for 20 years. For the sake of argument, we countered that the statistics showed another company was manufacturing machines of comparable quality for a lower price. The man challenged us again. "Have you ever owned a Maytag?" We had to answer no, but we continued to try to convince him. We then asked the 400-person audience who they believed. They were unanimous in their response. We didn't get a single vote. The man had personal experience and he wasn't bashful about sharing it.

Most customers will not choose to do business with us if we do not offer a very good product, or if our product is not delivered in a customer-friendly manner, at a competitive price. This level of value, however, is becoming commonplace. Today, in order to turn the "somewhat satisfied" 4-out-of-5 customer into a "loyal" 5-out-of-5 customer, we must make an emotional connection that leaves the customer more *delighted* than satisfied. For most organizations, this will necessitate significant changes in strategy, skill sets, and practices.

5

The Customer Advocate Challenges

CHALLENGE 10

Making Flexibility a Source of Competitive Advantage: One Size Does Not Fit All or Even a Few

Whether you sell $100-million planes or 79-cent pens, your buyers have changed enormously in the past few years. Their demands are lengthening; their patience is shrinking. Epochal shifts in the global economy have given them a sultan's power to command exactly what they want, the way they want it, when they want it, at a price that will make you weep. You'll either provide it or vaporize.

—"Meet the New Customer," *Fortune,* Autumn/Winter 1993

$\mathcal{R}$ecently we were present at a conversation between representatives of a sporting goods manufacturer and one of its suppliers, a large chemical company. When the supplier asked for a list of priorities for the coming year, an executive representing the sporting goods manufacturer responded, "We don't know what we need. If we did, this meeting would have been over hours ago. What we need is for you to help us figure out how to improve our business, show us how you can assist us in the process, and then deliver what we need when we need it." Clearly, these customers were expecting more than a shipment of chemicals or fast response to existing requirements. They expected their supplier to anticipate future business needs and then find a way to customize a solution. Just another day for most suppliers to large customers.

But how about those who serve the medium-sized customer or the individual consumer? Is it possible to efficiently customize products and services to match their individual needs, wants, and desires? In most cases, the answer is a resounding *yes*. A combination of technology and better distribution methods is enhancing companies' abilities to customize delivery to meet customers' individual needs for a variety of products and services—from bicycles to computers, from credit cards to food service, and from greeting cards to financial services. Customers are learning that they can "have it their way." We are entering an era where one size no longer fits all—or even a few. Today, one size fits one.

Stop in to an American Greetings card store and you can design your own card and print your personalized message in minutes. Personal computer companies will configure a machine "your way" and deliver it to you in two days. At least one credit card company is preparing a "design your own" credit card. You decide: Do you want airline miles and product discounts or do you want a card with no annual fees? Do you want the benefits that come with a card with a high interest rate or do you want a lower interest rate and fewer bells and whistles? What do you want on the face of the card. "Save The Whales" or your favorite ball team's logo? Remember when overnight delivery meant over*night* delivery? Now it can be same day, next day before 10 or before 3 or the day after—you decide. Or maybe you'll walk into a Starbuck's coffee store as we did the other day and observe a person ordering a short, half-decaf, half-caf, non-fat (milk), no whip (whipped cream), mocha, coffee. The smiling response—*No problem!* The message in each case is similar. The customer is in control. The challenge is to find a way to standardize some parts of the process while efficiently customizing in those areas that the customer will appreciate and consider worth paying for.

This strategy simply attempts to take advantage of the basic human need to feel special and important. In any relationship that we care about, we want to be recognized as individuals. We want to know that our family, friends, and associates care about us. And we want the same thing from companies with which we choose to do business. We want to know they will be there in good times and bad. We constantly "read" the actions of others and draw conclusions about their motivations and feelings. As in all relationships, it is the little things *and* the big things that are important. Consistently demonstrating that you care—in a hundred ways—is fundamental to building loyalty and commitment in your home as well as in your business.

Although customized products are impressive, the flexibility required to make a "personal" connection with the customer does not necessarily require an instantaneously manufactured product. Often, the customization that is most appreciated by customers is the personal treatment they receive as part of the sales and delivery processes. Most customer requests are not unreasonable, but do require that the person serving the customer have the autonomy to efficiently react and to offer the support customers need. It's the front-line employees who must execute the plan to deliver the basic product in a customized manner. It's up to them to take advantage of the many opportunities to add value, no matter how insignificant it seems at the time. In most cases, the essence of customization is to build a process where knowledgeable people are able to ensure that our products and services address specific customer needs and are delivered in a way that demonstrates our caring and commitment.

TOWARD A NEW DEFINITION OF QUALITY

To date, most quality improvement efforts have focused primarily on systematically reducing variation, eliminating rework, and reducing cycle time (the time it takes to produce and deliver the product or service). Effective implementations have enabled many companies to better attract and more efficiently serve customers. Significant gains in reliability, responsiveness, and productivity are evident in a wide range of organizations. Now, the best companies are taking quality improvement to the next level. They are learning to manage the inevitable tension that evolves from a process that is designed to be both reliable and continuously customized.

Although necessary, our commitment to reducing undesirable variation in the delivery process has often resulted in a preoccupation with the elimination of mistakes that result in customer dissatisfaction. We now know, however, that eliminating dissatisfied customers does not necessarily result in substantial increases in customer loyalty. Delighting customers to the point of loyalty requires additional skills and a different approach. It will require that we focus as much on innovation, customization, and flexibility as we have on the elimination of problems. It will require that we do more than meet customer requirements or anticipate next year's needs. To be successful, we will have to serve, entertain, customize, resell, build relationships, and make a hundred on-the-spot decisions that communicate our willingness to flexibly serve. It will require that we give our employees instantaneous access to specific customer information and the ability and autonomy to use that information productively.

Because no two customers or situations will be identical, every

IT'S NOT OPTIONAL

C10

An executive of a large decentralized manufacturer (with 150+ business units) was approached by a large retailing customer. "We think your decentralized structure is great. You're quick, innovative and responsive, but the 100+ invoices we get from your different business units and the checks we write to each of these groups are something we can't afford. How about if we give you one P.O. and one check per month and you figure it out?"

The manufacturing executive replied, "We can't do it quickly. We have different product codes. Each business unit is different. We'll work with you but it will take time: for all practical purposes, we really are separate companies—we're that decentralized."

The retailer interrupted with what is becoming a familiar refrain. "Was there something I said that led you to believe that this is optional?"

The manufacturer quickly reorganized and formed a team to "rep" the products of the 150+ business units and make the entire process seamless to its customers. It turned out to be cheaper for all concerned. The executive told us, "We've got to learn to listen to demanding customers. If that customer had been a $300 not a $300 *million* customer, we wouldn't have been as flexible—and we would have missed a great opportunity. We have got to change and become more flexible—it's a matter of survival."

We must learn to listen to our most demanding customers. They may see opportunities that we haven't considered.

attempt to serve will be something of an experiment. It will be imperative that all service providers develop the ability to learn from their experience so that they can more effectively and more efficiently address their customers' individual needs. The traditional management practice of spending the majority of time "managing by exception" (focusing on problems) will have to give way to a more balanced approach. Every person must become passionately involved in finding a way to increase the number of customers willing to give us the 5-out-of-5 score (if not a 6-out-of-5). It won't come easy. Most organizations have decades of experience in designing control systems, communicating standard operating procedures, training people to do things the same way, and designing feedback systems that communicate the extent to which an employee did things according to plan. Maintaining the discipline of systematic learning and rigorous process improvement while designing the front-end of the process to be flexible so that the people who serve the customer can do whatever is necessary to build loyalty will require that we augment our past methods and embrace the idea that flexibility and consistency are simultaneously achievable.

C10

C H A L L E N G E   1 1

Making "Delighting" Customers Company Policy

*Our number one goal is to provide outstanding customer service. . . .
Nordstrom Rules: Rule #1: Use your good judgment in all situations.
There will be no additional rules.*

—From the one-page Nordstrom Employee Handbook

*W*e were recently intrigued by an article in the *San Francisco Chronicle* that argued that perhaps we should authorize capital punishment for any individual who utters the words "Company Policy." At first blush, the idea seemed a bit extreme. However, the more we thought about it, the more merit the idea seemed to have. After all, there are probably no other two words in the English language that get in the way of delighting customers more than "Company Policy." And because delighting customers is critical to the very *life* of the company, it follows that any practice denying us from doing so may be considered a capital crime—witness the commission of a few familiar felonies:

"I'd like to ring you up on this register, but I can't. It's just Company Policy."

"I know the product doesn't work, but we don't give refunds, only store credit. It's Company Policy."

"I'd like to help you, but I need a manager's approval. It's Company Policy."

C11

Have you noticed that when people use the words "Company Policy," it is rarely in a way that is beneficial to customers. Instead, the words are usually invoked by an individual in the company to make his or her life easier, to improve internal efficiency, or in an attempt to make certain that the customer can't take advantage of the system.

But where does this "policy" originate? Is it written down? Sometimes, but more often than not, even after significant investigation, we've been unable to find its source. *Many times, in fact, Company Policy is just an understanding, mysteriously passed from one generation of employees to another, to give a person or group a reason for <u>not</u> doing things differently.* But nothing is more frustrating for customers than to be told that common sense cannot be applied in a given situation, because Company Policy dictates otherwise.

The next time you hear the words "Company Policy"—investigate. You'll probably discover that the Company Policy was written to protect the organization from the tiny percentage of customers who might take advantage of the system. Unfortunately, this unnecessarily restricts or punishes the huge percentage of customers who are absolutely critical to the company's success.

Here's a thought: Wouldn't it be a lot better if your organization issued an edict that the words "Company Policy" could only be used in a positive context? For example:

> "I'd be happy to get that order out for you today. It's Company Policy that we do everything we can to give you great service."

> "Sure, you can return that gift without a sales slip or the original packaging. It's Company Policy that we trust our customers."

Why not make it company policy to delight customers? Why don't we make it very difficult for any of us to say no to any reasonable (or maybe even unreasonable) customer request?

> "Five separate invoices? Sure thing. It's Company Policy that our customers can have it their way."

Unfortunately, Company Policy is seldom used in this context. For many it continues to serve as an excuse for not doing something for customers or employees. That being the case, maybe the expression *should* be outlawed.

DESIGNING TO DELIGHT

Too much of a great thing is wonderful!
—Mae West

If we adopt a strategy that makes delighting customers company policy, can we go too far? Absolutely! If we improve in areas that the customer doesn't value, we can waste time, effort, and money. If we try to be everything to everybody, we'll probably end up being nothing to anyone. We need to develop the ability to put our efforts where our customers will most appreciate them—under standing full well that no two customers will see our efforts in the same way. Still, to constantly delight customers, we must improve our ability to:

1. Act in Real Time

Customers are impatient and growing more so. They've been educated by an increasing number of companies that anything short of immediate delivery of products, services, and information is too slow. Hotels, like car rental companies, are doing away with traditional check-in procedures. Grocery stores are demanding that their suppliers manage the distribution process so that little or no inventory is required and so that product is always available. Want to check your bank account balance at midnight? In some areas, 24-hour phone banking has been a reality for years. Time is quickly becoming a very valuable currency.

If you had but a single shot at delighting customers, what would it be? We think reducing cycle time while monitoring reliability would be a good choice. Doing so will require you to monitor

C11

the time (which may be a better indicator of costs than budget numbers) that every step in the process takes, with an eye toward simplification. A simpler process is usually a more reliable and efficient one. Creating a companywide passion for acting quickly helps eliminate internal politics and bureaucracy while it communicates to customers that their requests are worthy of immediate attention.

2. Seize Opportunities to Demonstrate Flexibility

In the past, the customer who wanted something done his way was often perceived as a difficult customer, and sometimes one that was too expensive to serve. We missed the point then, and many companies still don't seem to get what today's customer knows to be obvious: When we *don't* do things their way (i.e., give them what they want), it's pretty hard to earn a 5 on the loyalty scale. However, loyalty is often created when we go out of our way to demonstrate to customers that we value their business. If we can develop a culture in which everyone understands the importance of productivity, yet still relentlessly pursues every opportunity to show how far the company is willing to go to ensure that *every* customer gets more than they bargained for, we win!

3. Provide Novelty and Entertainment, Not Just Usefulness and Comfort

Customers want to be entertained. They want things that are hard to get—and they are being inundated with new opportunities daily. Visit Nike Town in Chicago. Is it a store, a museum, or an entertainment facility? Is the Hard Rock Cafe selling food, T-shirts, or a Rock and Roll experience? How about the Harley Davidson Cafe and Planet Hollywood? Walk into a Warner Brothers or the Disney stores in the mall. Where do your eyes wander first? To the large video screen, to the animations, or to the clothing? Or how about the Buena Vista Holiday Inn outside Disney World? There, children have their own check-in, restaurant, and art contests and they can make an appointment to get personally "tucked-in" by the resident life oined Disney character. There's also free day care (yes, free) and myriad entertainment options. It's hard to tell whether the place is a hotel or an attraction. If you want to decide for yourself, make your reservations early. Needless to say, it sells out quickly.

C11

The challenge is to learn what we can from businesses like these and apply it to our own, perhaps more conservative enterprises. Many already have. The Texas street fair that Banc One held to attract new customers, and Home Depot "do it yourself" classes are just the beginning. What's possible is only limited by our creativity.

4. Provide Added-Value Information as Part of Every Product and Service

Keeping our customers informed at every key step in the sales cycle—from ordering to billing—gives them a sense of greater control over the process and makes them feel more like partners in an ongoing (loyal) relationship. Federal Express' "Track and Trace" system, for example, enables the company to put its customers' minds at ease, and provides critical answers in the small percentage of cases where there are problems. Are they selling package delivery, information, peace of mind, or all of the above? Creative billing can give birth to a host of new products in many markets. MCI's "Friends and Family" is an immensely successful product derived from the capabilities of a world-class billing system. When we recently called a catalog company to order a gift for a colleague, the order taker asked, "Are you sure that's what you want to send him?" "Why, isn't it a quality product?" "Of course," she replied, "but you sent him that last year." Phew! Added-value information saved our bacon!

What's the number one reason lawyers get sued for malpractice? Client neglect. A call with a little information may be the best insurance policy. In most cases, however, whether we're lawyers or manufacturers, we're usually too preoccupied with our internal problems to effectively manage the perception of our customers—especially when they're not standing in front of us.

5. Build Relationships at Every Level in the Customer's Organization

C11

Our large customers are really a number of customers—many with widely disparate needs and priorities—working under the same company name. The purchasing department's agenda is often quite different from operations' or marketing's. The telecommunication manager's goals can be at odds with those of his or her internal clients. We must, therefore, develop a process for attending to each of our relationships in the client company. Our customer information systems must track the needs of each group so that our sales and service teams can customize their approach at any given time. As in managing any complex system, we can only successfully work with the whole if we take into consideration the complex relationships among the parts.

6. Put the Customer in Control Instead of Creating a Structure to Control Customers

The beauty of self-service is that the customer controls the timing and focus of delivery. Automatic Teller Machines, Federal Express' desktop tracking system, on-line mortgage application, and the fully automated gas pump, all put the locus of control in the customer's hands. When you set an appointment time with the Department of Motor Vehicles or for service at your specialty retailer, you're controlling the timing of the interaction. In contrast, staying home half the day waiting for the technician from the power company or for the refrigerator to be delivered can be maddening. We've always wanted what we want when we want it. It's now becoming *possible*.

When you hear the words, "It's company policy," beware. These can be code words for "We'll give it to you *our* way. It's not our policy to give *you* control." But more and more consumers want a major say-so in the processes that affect them. Providing customers with greater control is rapidly becoming a valuable core competency in many markets.

7. Anticipate the Customer's Future Needs

Customers may know what they want today, but they rarely know what they will want in the future. For example, for years customers told us that they had no need for overnight delivery and fax machines. Now they can't do business without them. At the point where everybody agrees on what is needed, it is often too late for the company seeking an edge. Instead, we must become so in tune with our customers' businesses that we can help them anticipate their future needs, and in the process help create tomorrow's trends. A little naiveté can be a good thing in the service of this goal. It may be to our advantage not to know (or at least not to believe) what the industry thinks can't be done and to have the perspective to see the big picture without being blinded by the day-to-day details of the business. Make no mistake, this is a skill that must be developed and will require practices that make it possible for people to become knowledgeable in a given market.

8. Guarantee Everything

. . . And make it a guarantee that meets the subjective satisfaction of the end user. Sound dangerous? It is. Not because too many of your customers will take unfair advantage of it, but because you may not be as good as you think you are. Case in point: One of our colleagues who owned a few restaurants tried to imitate the Cooker restaurant chain's "complete satisfaction—or don't pay" guarantee and he nearly went broke in a week. His problem was that he had mistakenly assumed that the absence of complaints in his restaurants meant that his customers were satisfied. The good news? Watching the losses mount induced him to take immediate improvement measures. Changes that otherwise might have taken months to implement quickly became today's priorities.

As companies improve reliability, guarantees are surfacing everywhere. Even those providing services where success is subjective—advertising agencies, for example—are beginning to guarantee their work. Are we going to lead the parade or follow? Will the second company to offer an exceptional guarantee in a given

C11

market get anywhere nearly as much credit and good press as the first? If we were forced to guarantee our work tomorrow, would we be able to do so?

9. Refuse to Be Satisfied with Satisfaction

If everyone in the organization is thinking "delight" rather than satisfaction, flexibility inevitably follows. It's just too hard to delight someone if you're delivering a one-size-fits-all product or service. Words like "delight"—or "entertain," "thrill," "fascinate," and "bewitch"—can seem a bit like overkill when applied to the customer relationship. But thinking in these terms may lead us to develop the types of practices that build loyalty. Thinking in terms of satisfaction rarely results in service levels that make people feel special and appreciated.

10. Above All, Care

It doesn't take long for customers to question whether the people who are attempting to serve them genuinely care about them or just smile to get the order. All of us have been frustrated from time to time by a company that acted as if they were doing us a favor by doing business with us. In most of these cases, it is difficult for us to tell whether it's the employees who don't care or whether the systems in which they work make it difficult, if not impossible, for them to show that they care. Whichever it is, a single unpleasant interaction can destroy much of the goodwill built through a long list of pleasant ones.

Buttons and Banners

We walked into a bank recently where a large "WE CARE" banner hung on the wall. Every employee wore an "I CARE" button and the bank's new brochures heralded their individualized service. We had always been cognizant of the mediocre service normally delivered by this bank but, after looking at the signs and

the buttons, the indifferent treatment we received left us much more dissatisfied. Merely saying you care is not caring. If you're not going to delight customers (or even be helpful), it's probably not a good idea to say that you will.

C11

We asked about the buttons. "They represent our new service improvement effort," we were told. One employee told us they wanted to improve their service but hadn't really started yet, didn't know when they would begin and, at any rate, every employee was told that they would wear the buttons—like it or not.

RING AROUND THE ROSIE

It was 11 P.M. on a Friday evening and we were riding on a Disney bus with at least twenty families returning from an evening performance of a Disney attraction. The bus was well lit, making it nearly impossible to see anything through the windows. This might not have been a problem except that Jerry, the bus driver, was giving us a tour of the Disney property (knowing full well that we couldn't see a thing). At first most of us thought that Jerry didn't understand the situation. It soon became apparent, however, that the joke was on us. He was just another part of the show. He single-handedly turned a bus full of tired families into the audience of a four-wheeled comedy act.

When he pulled up to the parking lot that was supposed to mark the end of our bus ride, he wasn't done. Instead of stopping, he broke all the rules by driving the bus in circles in the parking lot, leading all of us in a chorus of "ring around the rosie." As the guests left the bus smiling, each stopped to thank Jerry—not for the ride but for the entertainment.

Scripted? No way. Jerry said that he is not sure that his boss would approve but they told him that he was "on stage" and "in the entertainment business," so why not? Spontaneous, sincere, funny, caring, polite—no matter what they paid Jerry that evening, it wasn't enough!

Ultimately, every aspect of business is inescapably human. Caring and being cared about is one of the most basic human needs. As customers, the only thing we dislike more than someone who doesn't care, is someone who pretends to care but clearly doesn't. We believe that most people share that feeling and can spot a bad actor a mile away.

C11

C H A L L E N G E   1 2

Becoming Customer-Focused: Re-engineering the Process from the Customer's Point of View

Join me in testing the view that most companies are functioning at only 40, 50, or 60 percent of their capacity, and that the much higher levels of performance reached in emergencies—when a major new customer might be brought in, when a new product must be developed in record time, when a natural disaster strikes, when the employees walk out—are actually much closer to true, sustainable potentials than are the "normal" levels of performance.

If you consider that those crisis performance levels are spontaneously generated with a minimum of formal organization and technological or management systems innovations, you can begin to imagine how much might be possible if the crisis-motivated forces were combined with sophisticated, managed improvement.

—Robert H. Schaffer, *The Breakthrough Strategy*

*L*ast year when the California Attorney General filed claims against a well-known automobile repair facility, the case received widespread media attention inside and outside California. Allegedly, this company defrauded customers in eleven out of the fifteen instances in which the state had "shopped" its auto repair facilities. How could this happen in a company with a long-time history of serving its customers? At least part of the reason for this alleged abuse of customer trust appeared to be a compensation plan that challenged employees to sell a certain number of products and repair services each month. As a result, if you went in to one of these facilities for an oil change close to the end of the month and the garage hadn't sold enough brake jobs, you might be told you needed one—even if you didn't.

If what happened at this company is surprising, it shouldn't be. Putting pressure on employees to move merchandise, whether through incentives, quotas, or other organizational pressures, has been a normal practice for decades in many businesses. Of course, that doesn't mean that every sale in companies where these practices are in use constitutes fraud. But in more than a few instances it does mean that customers are sold something that, for one reason or the next, is not in their best interest. If a financial product is not selling, for example, many companies will raise the sales commission on it to stimulate sales. Make the commission high enough or the "challenge" to the salesperson demanding enough, and you can sell almost anything. We've seen it in industry after industry, from telecommunications to computers, and from apparel to automobiles. Make your numbers! That's the fastest way to get ahead. If a product's sales are not meeting budget, run a sales contest, increase the commissions, or re-define the compensation plan to require a certain volume of sales for each particular category.

We're not suggesting that most companies are out to bilk their customers. Far from it. It's been our experience that most companies genuinely want to serve and provide value for their customers. They want to do the right thing. Often standing in the way of doing so, however, are practices that reward exactly the opposite, and sometimes actually punish employees for doing the best by their customers. The pressures on workers to act contrary to their customers' best interests are often implicit and ingrained in the organizational system—which everyone agrees must change, but in many organizations never quite does. Some of these pressures originate from the unintended negative effects of practices that were designed with the best of intentions—i.e., incentive systems or sales quotas that attempt to align employee success to the success of the organization. Unfortunately, when we view the effects of some of these practices on the entire delivery chain (and their effect on customers, in particular)—these practices are often revealed as being significantly less than desirable.

The truth is that most processes were designed, and are still managed, for the good of the people managing the processes, not for the good of the customer. Even though "Customer Focus" is the song sung at every meeting and in most corporate communications, internal efficiency, adhering to policy, managing our time effectively, and meeting department goals still dominate our design and improvement efforts. The "internal" (i.e., non-customer) focus of many organizations is so strong, in fact, that it is difficult for some employees to even *imagine* just how different things could be.

This is especially true in companies where the design of processes makes it difficult for employees to satisfy, much less delight, customers. Most processes have been designed for internal efficiency and to ensure that neither employees nor customers take advantage of the company. The desire to avoid the small mistakes of the past has given birth to hundreds of rules and procedures that were supposed to prevent such occurrences. The by-product of many of these rules has been the disempowering of many employees, who would simply like to make common-sense decisions in order to better serve customers.

We say we're customer-focused, but are we really? Examples to the contrary abound:

- **Automobile dealerships.** The hardest part about purchasing a car in most dealerships is not deciding which model to buy, but getting the deal done. We've all endured that seemingly interminable time when the sales manager and our "salesperson" collude to figure out how to get that last $100 from us. A few months later and a few thousand miles down the road, we return to the dealership to get our car serviced. Who do we pick it up from? The mechanic who worked on it? The service manager who knows about the work that was done? Our salesperson? Nope! The cashier—who usually doesn't know which end of the car was worked on. The cashier's job: collect the money.

- **Medical clinics.** Like the airlines, many medical clinics and doctor's offices overbook. Doing so ensures a filled waiting room so that the medical staff can take people at their own speed and not be inconvenienced by the occasional no-show or late arrival.

- **Financial institutions.** We've all waited in lines and we understand that some waiting is inevitable. Nothing makes us more angry, however, than to be in a line and see other employees who could help but are preoccupied with other mysterious work. We remember waiting in a long line at a bank when a customer asked a gentleman in a suit doing paperwork at his desk if he would open another teller window. He said he couldn't because he was the loan officer. We polled those waiting in the line behind us to see if anyone needed a loan—no one did. The loan officer was neither amused nor impressed. Neither were we.

- **Airlines.** Have a special need or problem? Why is it so difficult for airline employees to use common sense and help us instead of citing "company policy"? Call and get a fare quote ... if you don't like it, call again and get a different one. Even the employees don't understand the fare structures despite one of the most sophisticated information systems known to man! Suffice it to say that most people who serve us on airlines have too little information and too little autonomy, and are as frustrated as we are.

- **Retailers.** Check out most return policies. Do you get the feeling that they are designed to impress customers who have made the choice to buy from the company? Or are these policies designed to protect the company from the 2 or 3 percent who might take advantage of the policy?

Most companies have been successful at improving service. Few, however, have made the revolutionary changes in thinking, practices, and designs that will be required to consistently delight customers. *Incrementally improving a process which was never designed to impress customers rarely results in building substantially higher levels of customer loyalty.*

C12

To build and retain loyalty requires nothing less than continually re-engineering delivery processes with the customer's needs foremost in mind. Re-engineering has the advantage of allowing the group to question the assumptions that have formed the foundation of present practices. Which practices add value? Which don't? Is this really what the customer prefers? Are these the skills required? Wouldn't it be more effective if we were organized in teams? How can we make information more available? Also, by including customers and outsiders in the re-engineering effort, past beliefs will more likely be challenged and updated as part of the improvement process. Effectively implemented, delivery process re-engineering can result in higher levels of both customer and employee loyalty as well as increased internal productivity—provided that we also re-engineer the way we manage the new process. Re-engineering will yield significantly less impressive results if we don't increase the effectiveness and flexibility of our methods for managing day-to-day activities.

Yet even if we are successful in designing a truly customer-focused process today, over time we will make decisions that will swing the pendulum back to a more internally focused process. While unfortunate, this is to be expected—*particularly if we are successful.* That's because with success come more customers. And with more customers, there's more stress on the system. To reduce this stress, compromises are often made that unintentionally divert our attention from the customer. While any one change in the process may not seem significant, cumulatively, these changes can result in a process that is considerably less customer-focused. As employees sense this drift back, they often interpret these changes as a lessening of the company's commitment to its customers. This, in turn, may lead employees to become cynical about the company's stated vision and diminish their shared sense of purpose. For this reason, every re-engineered process must be continually monitored and adjusted to ensure an ongoing customer focus.

C12

HOW ABOUT THE INTERNAL CUSTOMER?

Although we used to advocate thinking of the groups we serve inside the company as "internal customers," we have found that some organizations have not benefited from the internal customer concept. While for many, thinking in these terms has helped to increase customer awareness, trying to improve service to the "internal customer" has *not* proved helpful when it:

Reinforced the belief that the process can be effectively managed by improving the performance of "parts of the process." It is the relationship among the parts that determines the success of the process.

Resulted in non-value-added activities being given priority because they were demanded by an "internal customer."

Gave some managers a sense that substantial process improvement was the likely result of serving internal customers, without assigning accountability for macro process improvement and developing an understanding of the causes of variation in the process.

Instead of thinking in terms of internal customers, we might be better off if we viewed each person or internal group in the company as a "partner" whose responsibility is to build a process that can deliver significant value to the company's (external) customers.

C H A L L E N G E 1 3

Making Continuous Process Improvement Everyone's Job

In knowledge and service work, partnership with the responsible worker is the only way to improve productivity. Nothing else works at all.

Peter Drucker, *Post-Capitalist Society*

*C*ontinuously improving important processes is fundamental to sustaining long-term success. Who could disagree? Like motherhood, baseball and apple pie, process improvement is something everybody favors. It lies at the heart of every quality improvement effort, and today's preoccupation with re-engineering speaks to our desire to not only improve the process, but to do so quickly. Before Dr. Deming died in 1994, thousands of people gathered each week to hear him speak of the need to "improve constantly and forever the system of production and service." But, for all the study and dialogue on the issue, good examples of companies that have made systematic process improvement a part of the fabric of their business are few and far between, especially in the service sector.

Most companies today measure customer satisfaction and are working to ensure that the customer's voice is fully integrated into the organization's accountability practices. Most managers can articulate last month's customer satisfaction rating to the nearest tenth of a percent. Ask these same managers to identify the major causes of variation in the delivery process, however, and a large

C13

majority of them will look at you as if you were speaking a different language. Or ask them what the margin of error was in the latest satisfaction score. How about control limits? "Don't know" or "What do you mean?" are the most common responses we've heard to these questions. It seems that many companies are more preoccupied with the scorecard of yesterday's performance than they are with improving tomorrow's.

Further revealing the lack of focus on process improvement are the conversations that ensue when you ask people in most organizations to describe their jobs. Rarely do they tell you about their role in the process or how their responsibilities support the corporate mission. Most simply describe the list of tasks that they perform daily. Next, ask a group involved in one part of a process about the responsibilities of those in other parts. The answer you'll likely get will be a short one. Traditionally, employees have been taught to mind their own jobs and let others focus on theirs—despite the fact that many of these people must cooperate to be successful.

Finally, try to find the person whose responsibility it is to set process improvement priorities. Usually there's no one with direct responsibility for effectively managing the entire process. Instead, in many cases it is assumed that the leaders of different groups will naturally cooperate to ensure that process improvement efforts will be coordinated—though it is rare that the goals of these disparate groups are aligned. And we've all been to the showdown where one group points the finger at another group. It's no wonder that, for many organizations, process improvement has been slow in coming.

There may be no shortage of dialogue about improving processes, but the evidence is clear: few leaders outside the factory have put the issue on their daily calendars, and fewer still have developed the skills necessary to facilitate a systematic approach. If we are committed to the continuous improvement of key processes, our commitment to our commitment is suspect.

Organizational structures have been designed to promote personal accountability and functional performance. Changing the process in ways that might affect another group often proves difficult. Many processes fall under the aegis of a number of functional areas and, in many cases, it seems that each of these groups have *de facto* veto power over any improvement suggestions. As one manager told us, "I feel like my job is Design and Defend. I help design the processes and then defend them until my dying day."

One of the key reasons we haven't come farther than we have is that traditional training programs don't provide most employees with the tools and skills required to devise a systematic approach to improving processes. And, other than scientists and industrial engineers, most employees don't have much experience doing causal analysis, designing data-gathering techniques, sampling, or doing statistical analysis. But, instead of teaching these skills, many training efforts focus on developing the abilities of managers to effectively control and motivate the people in their groups so that they will consistently do *more* of the designed task rather than finding a way to do it differently or better.

We sat with a management group last year that was reviewing the customer complaints they had received over the past seven days. The management team was upset. They had received four more complaints in Week #3 of this month than they had in Week #3 of last month, and their customer satisfaction rating was trending at 3% below the prior month's. At the beginning of the meeting, the head of the group spoke of the sense of urgency she felt and how quick action must be taken to reverse this negative trend. It was noted that every time the group put pressure on people to "do things better" and made some changes in the existing process, there was improvement for a period of time. But the group felt that whenever they took their "eye off the ball" (and pressure off front-line employees), performance deteriorated. They knew they had to get a handle on what was happening because their boss would soon be calling for an explanation, especially since the ratings of other groups in the company had gone up.

When we asked the group to determine how many dissatisfied customers they had last month (based on their customer satisfaction survey), they estimated the number was between seven hundred and a thousand. When we asked if the increase in customer complaints was statistically significant, they didn't know (it wasn't) and didn't know how to make the determination. When we asked if the past changes they had made reduced the variation in the process or caused other problems to surface, they weren't sure. They also weren't sure whether or not the process was in control, or whether the group's ratings were within the control limits of the process (and therefore, not statistically different).

Soon we all began to laugh as it became obvious to us all that a natural variation in customer complaints had set off a flurry of internal activity that was, at best, wasted effort. After agreeing on a more systematic course of action, we began to build a good understanding of the magnitude of the task confronting us. But, as the group noted, a larger issue remained: how were they going to explain to their boss why they weren't reacting to the increase in complaints with the usual flurry of activity? After all, they reminded us, their boss didn't understand that the differences between this month's numbers and last month's were a natural part of the process and did not represent a significant shift in performance levels.

The first step in managing our key processes is to decide to do so. We must not underestimate the changes this will require. Who will be accountable for cycle time reduction, understanding variation, and coordinating and prioritizing improvement efforts? Who will ensure that roles are re-defined in ways that promote systematic continuous improvement instead of compliance with past practices? How will managers be educated to ensure that their performance supports the efforts?

We must remain cognizant of the fact that present levels of performance are the direct result of present practices. To underestimate the need to change the way we think and the way we're organized is to invite failure.

We're frustrated by the number of attempts at process improvement we've witnessed where organizations have been at it for a couple of years but don't track cycle time or understand the major causes of variation. Start today—give someone or some group 60 days to understand the present process and to prioritize improvement efforts. You can't systematically improve what you don't understand and understanding what you have can be done quickly—if you choose to make it a priority.

C13

---

45 DAYS: A SUGGESTED PLAN OF ACTION

Knowing that instant reorganization is unlikely in most companies, keep your organizational chart and appoint a process owner for a major process under your purview. Give that individual 45 days—no longer—and tell him or her to develop a full understanding of the process in that time. You want to know where the variation is created, what the cycle time is, how well the process serves its internal or external customers, and where the areas of major improvements should lie. If you pick the right individual, chances are the project will be accomplished within the time limit and the information that will be generated will be invaluable.

C H A L L E N G E   1 4

Making Proactive Recovery
A Strategic Issue

A well-handled problem usually breeds more loyalty than you had before the negative incident.

—Thomas J. Peters, *Thriving on Chaos*

Only Her Hairdresser Knows for Sure

We asked an executive in a large corporation to name the company to which she was *most* loyal. She told us her hairdresser. "Why is that?" we asked.

"Well, because the first time they colored my hair, it turned out green instead of blond. They then spent the entire day fixing it until it was right. They even paid my parking ticket."

We were unconvinced. "Did it ever occur to you that they were incompetent?"

"No." She seemed surprised we'd even ask.

A customer's response to an organization's extraordinary recovery effort can be irrational. In retrospect, it may even seem silly. But the fact remains that those critical minutes or hours after we make a mistake may be the best single opportunity to create cus-

C14

tomer loyalty. When something goes wrong, chances are good that our follow-up to remedy the situation will have a lasting impression on the customer. If we hesitate, resist, or stonewall, the negative impression we make with the customer may haunt us for a long time. If, on the other hand, we react impressively, we can build a degree of loyalty that under normal circumstances might be impossible. In fact, if we make a mistake, apologize, and fix the problem quickly, many customers will like us more than if we had never made the mistake at all. A customer problem brought on by our systems or employees can, therefore, be a strategic opportunity, the po-

---

WHEN CUSTOMERS CALL...

Do your customers get answers to their problems the first time they call your company? If they have to call again, they're more likely to go away unhappy even if their problem is solved. Companies that empower employees answering 800-number phone calls to respond directly to customers' questions see increased customer satisfaction.

% of Customers Completely Satisfied

	One Phone Call	*Two or More Phone Calls*
Industry sales	86%	42%
Packaged goods	77%	40%
Computers	68%	28%
Retail banking	66%	35%
Financial services	56%	22%
Auto repairs & services	50%	18%
Hotels	46%	13%

Reprinted with permission from the Technical Assistance Research Program, Inc., Arlington, VA.

tential significance of which is seldom recognized by most organizations.

When we asked a wide range of customers—in addition to the temporarily green-haired executive—which companies they were most loyal to and why, up to 70% of them described an instance where a mistake had been made and the company reacted impressively. Even when the mistake was outrageous and/or unquestionably the company's fault, many customers were willing to overlook the initial problem and focus on the company's reaction after the problem was identified.

For example, we found people loyal to airlines that reacted quickly to flight delays and reservation problems. Customers we interviewed at Nordstrom told us stories about how the retailer went beyond the call of duty to make amends when an alteration wasn't ready on time or when the altered garment turned out not to be exactly what they wanted. We all have stories of companies that have personally impressed us and most of us are not bashful about sharing our experiences—no matter how irrationally loyal we might appear. "I buy from them because I know that if there's a problem, they'll make it right," is a familiar refrain.

When we asked customers what in particular impressed them with the recovery efforts of their favorite companies, we were surprised at the consistency of the responses. In a very high percentage of cases, people told us simply, "They *care*." Most of the time when things go the way they are expected to, customers get exactly what the organization planned to deliver. However, when things go awry, we get an opportunity to show customers our "true colors." At these times, we must make the decision to either remedy the problem quickly, or debate and negotiate. The first reaction builds loyalty, the second frustration. Correcting the problem quickly and graciously communicates that we care. Debating and negotiating often suggests that we don't—or that we mistrust our customers and must protect ourselves from those who might take advantage of us. In either case, the customer gets a good view of who we really are—not just who we *say* we are or *wish* we were.

We're Only Human

A friend of ours told us about an unfortunate dining experience C14
he had with his father in a restaurant a while back. There was an
hour wait, the salad was lousy, there were no hot entrees, the
dessert was so-so, and the service was poor—a total disaster.
That is, until the manager came to the table to apologize, ex-
plaining how he had hired a new chef from out of state and his
plane had been delayed. Our friend's father's response: "Nice
guy. We'll have to give this place another chance." According to
our friend, his father still laughs at his logic, but defends it,
nonetheless.

In any event, never, never underestimate the power of caring.
Customers (like organizations) are inescapably human.

Not only does recovering from mistakes build customer loyalty
(which can increase profitability), but the amounts invested in
recovery consistently demonstrate a return that usually far ex-
ceeds the overall ROI of the company. By way of illustration,
a study of corporate complaint-handling units done by the Technical Assistance Research Program (TARP) a number of years
ago estimated that the return on investment realized by these
units ranged from 15% to 400%, depending on the industry.
And this analysis does not take into account the potential referrals
or the tendency to purchase related products resulting from recovery efforts. If investing in recovery pays—and pays so well—why
then have so many organizations been so slow to make this
commitment?

One reason is the short-term mentality endemic to most of
today's businesses. If we fail to consider the value of a given customer's revenue stream over time, then spending dollars today to
retain that customer can be viewed as an immediate loss rather
than as marketing money spent to resell that customer. A second
reason recovery isn't given the attention it should has to do with
the way many companies account for sales and the money spent in

the recovery effort. Once a sale is made and the revenue counted, we tend to become inflexible. Instead of viewing a sale as final only when the customer is delighted, we consider it final as soon as we get the "right" to the money. Any money spent to solve problems (short of a refund) must often be counted against operational budgets, not marketing budgets. And because recovery expenses were not anticipated, these "lost" dollars can make it difficult for some groups to "make their numbers." Even when managers want to do the right thing for customers, they are hesitant to do so if company policy or the cost-accounting system makes it punishing to respond impressively.

As with so much else that happens (or doesn't happen) in the organization, recovery is a systemic issue. The way the work is organized and managed, the practices that are punished, and the behavior that is rewarded all combine to send clear messages to employees that guide their actions when problems arise. No matter what the message, some employees will respond effectively with customers. However, for a company to consistently and creatively respond to mistakes, the system must recognize and reward such efforts. Maybe the secret of Nordstrom's performance in this area is reflected in the fact that there wasn't a single employee we interviewed who could recall an instance where someone got in trouble for doing whatever was necessary to serve the customer. To these employees, the company "walked its talk" when it came to doing right by its customers. We should all demand the same from our organizations.

Keeping the Reading List Short

In one group we recently visited, an executive assistant to the president bragged about protecting her boss from customers. "He's busy, he doesn't have time."

"He doesn't have time for customers even when they are calling him?" we asked.

"No," she said, "if he started that, he wouldn't have time for anything else."

Maybe if the president talked to these customers and ensured that their problems were resolved and that the cause of the problem was addressed, others in the organization might work that much harder to ensure that the president received fewer calls and letters (of the negative variety) from customers.

C14

STRATEGIC RECOVERY SELF-ASSESSMENT

To be effective, a recovery strategy must be fast and distinctive, proactive, and intelligently planned, with the findings of each recovery effort analyzed for further enhancement of the delivery process. Following are questions you can ask to determine whether your strategy is doing the job it should:

Are Our Recovery Efforts Fast and Distinctive?

- Are our efforts customer-friendly?

- Do we, or could we, guarantee customer satisfaction?

- Have we empowered employees to solve customer problems quickly and efficiently?

- Do our customers have easy access to the people they may need to talk to?

- Are our recovery efforts noticeably (to the customer) different from our competitors'?

- Do we give the customer the benefit of the doubt?

- Is the customer's perception of a problem considered a significant event at every level of the organization?

- Do employees have the ability to deviate from planned actions or operating procedures when they see the need to?

Do We Proactively Search for Potentially Dissatisfied Customers?

- Is our goal to identify dissatisfied customers before they complain? At every level?

- Has identifying customer problems been clearly defined as everyone's job?

C14

- Is identifying a problem perceived to be rewarding, or is it punishing to point out discrepancies?

- Are there multiple methodologies (surveys, call-backs, comment cards, employee data gathering) used to identify customer problems?

- Are toll-free lines available for customers to communicate with someone who has the ability to solve the customer's problem?

- Is access to the company user-friendly and well communicated to the customer?

- Is there a structure that requires the company to act quickly on customer information when it is received?

Are Our Efforts Strategically Planned?

- Are potential problems identified as part of process improvement efforts?

- Have plans been developed to quickly and efficiently deal with common problems?

- Are these plans (and the reasons for the choices that have been made) widely understood?

- Are recovery efforts perceived to be an essential part of the delivery process, rather than an afterthought?

Is Process Effectiveness Systematically Evaluated and Improved?

- Are the types and frequency of customer problems tracked systematically?

- Are the root causes of problems identified?

- Is this information used to improve delivery processes as well as organizational practices?

- Do we routinely evaluate the effectiveness of our recovery efforts from the customer's point of view?

In addition, after taking action to recover from a mistake, we should ask these questions in evaluating our performance in recovery efforts:

- Did our actions provoke the desired customer effect: i.e., did we create a loyal customer?

- Have we used the information learned through our error and in the recovery effort to improve our process?

- Did our actions send the symbolic message to everyone in the workforce that we are committed to serving—no, delighting—customers?

This is Scott Cook, President of Intuit . . .

In this age of voice mail and telecommunications, we are all used to being put on hold. Still, when senior writer John Case of *Inc.* magazine phoned Intuit Software Corporation (producers of the phenomenally successful Quicken personal finance software), he expected a reasonably quick response. Having previously called Intuit "The Last Word" in customer service in an earlier *Inc.* article, instead he was put on hold for 20 minutes! As Case describes, "Suddenly, a familiar voice came on the line. 'This is Scott Cook, President of Intuit,' went the recorded message. Cook went on to explain that he knew the wait was unacceptable. But he explained why it was happening (an unexpected jump in sales in an already busy month), and what the company was doing about it (training new support people as fast as possible, with 80 new ones recently brought on board).

As it turned out, Case was unfazed by the wait. "A little respect for the customer along with some information about the problem made all the difference between a disgruntled customer and an admiring one."

(But John, you waited 20 minutes!)

C H A L L E N G E 1 5

Create a Real-Time, Universally Accessible, Decentralized, Centralized Customer Information System

As a general rule, the most successful man in life is the man with the best information.

—Benjamin Disraeli

U.S. companies pay research firms billions of dollars every year to learn more about their customers. And for good reason. In this era, where more educated and demanding customers are being taught that they can have it *their* way, a company with a world-class customer information system has a definite advantage. On the lookout for more and better customer information, companies are investing in ever more sophisticated processes to track customer preferences, current satisfaction levels, re-purchase intention, and the willingness of existing customers to recommend the company and its products and services to others.

Consider, for example, a mid-sized company with offices in 30 states. Type in a customer's name on any of the company's PCs and up pops a screen that gives the user a number of options. Click on one icon for a status report on that customer's pending orders. Click on another for that customer's responses on past customer surveys. Choose the "Key Contact" icon and the screen fills with a list of key contacts in the customer company complete with what these contacts think are the company's most important product and service attributes. Or select the "Executive Comment" icon for a detailed description of the information received during quarterly executive visits. While having all this information on tap doesn't guarantee that the company will use it wisely, at least it affords the company's employees the opportunity to do so.

Understanding Each Customer

"Good evening, Pizza Hut. Home phone number, please...." Even though Pizza Hut is only selling twelve-dollar pizzas, they're building a data base to track your preferences and purchasing history. They're determined to get their share of your stomach and have made a significant investment in building a process to capture information to help save customers today and plan strategy tomorrow.

Frequent shopping cards at the grocery store? Sure, they're a way of thanking repeat customers for their loyalty. But is that their primary purpose? The information gathered through such programs is being used by some retailers to better identify their high-value customers. Many programs of this type already exist, and more are in the planning stages: we've seen ski resorts and gourmet coffee stores, for example, that offer frequent purchase programs similar to those offered by airlines and the hospitality industry. Identifying high-value customers is an important step toward customization and retention.

Remember when "call-backs" were unusual—when, after you purchased a product, a company representative would call you back to ensure that you were satisfied? Today, call-backs are far more prevalent—but far less likely to impress in many markets. In fact, it's gotten to the point that they're often downright annoying. "If one more company calls me during dinner . . ." is the start of a familiar refrain. The same with surveys. They're almost impossible to avoid. Get on a plane and it's not unusual to be asked to fill out a six-page questionnaire that quizzes you about everything from

C15

in-flight service to your ticket number. Shorter, often better-designed forms can be found in hotel rooms, at grocery store check-out stands, on the back of restaurant tabs, and at gas station cashiers' counters. We've even been given a response card to fill out at a professional basketball game. The capper, however, was when a friend of ours received a questionnaire from the IRS following an audit. After making his life miserable for a couple of months, they asked him to rate the quality of their service. His question: "If I give them a high rating, are they more or less likely to audit me again next year?"

In assembling this list, we're not dismissing these methods of data collection or saying that they aren't often useful and effective. We <u>are</u> suggesting, however, that as these surveys proliferate, they are becoming more intrusive and irritating to those being asked to respond. Most people simply don't have the time to give everybody the feedback they want, especially when all too many of the surveys are poorly designed and overly detailed. We expect that in the future, as return rates decline, surveys will become progressively more expensive to administer and that, even when a survey is well designed, people will not take the time to look at it, much less complete it.

This does not mean, however, that the information potentially to be gleaned from a survey is any less valuable. On the contrary, in the years to come, the success or failure of many companies will depend on the accuracy and speed at which this information can be gathered and used. The challenge, then, is to come up with a better, more efficient way to collect this data. Fortunately, in many organizations, the most critical component of such a data collection system is already in place: the front line. Also in place is the most opportune time for gathering this information: during the normal course of business.

There are a number of advantages to using the front line as a key component of your customer information system, not the least of which is cost. When data is collected by employees as part of the day-to-day conduct of business, the price tag for gathering that information is extremely low. What is required, however, is sufficient time to gather the information, categorize it, and input it into a database that can be readily accessed by others in the organization. With such a system in place, employee-collected data could be made available to others in the company within days or even hours, instead of the weeks or months it used to take, if it happened at all.

When front-line employees routinely analyze customer data, the customer, who may ordinarily be just a voice on the phone, takes on fuller dimension. Dealing with complaints and suggestions provides workers with a broader context for performing their jobs, and "customer focus" becomes more than just a company slogan. Involving employees directly in the information-collection process deepens their relationship to the customer and enhances their ability to solve customer problems that may emerge from their discussions. In addition, giving customers the opportunity to air their opinions on a regular basis, as part of the normal transaction of business, makes it easier and more comfortable for them to make their complaints known. The fact that front-line workers are always there to listen and respond to customers builds a mutual trust, while paving the way for customers to take part in the improvement process.

Internally, using employees with regular customer contact to gather customer information increases the employee role in building customer loyalty and further enhances their involvement in the business. Distinctions between functional barriers are also blurred in the wake of the greater external focus that results from front-line participation in data gathering and as more and more employees are made aware of customers' needs.

Owning Up to Information

Typically, when customer information is gathered by individuals in the organization other than customer contact employees, trouble ensues—particularly when the information reveals deficien-

cies in the customer contact employees' performance. When this happens, the at fault syndrome often comes into play, and it is common for these employees to spend as much time trying to explain why the data doesn't accurately reflect their performance as they spend learning from the data. "That must have been data about another group's performance," is a remark we've often heard.

On the other hand, if customer contact employees are allowed to collect and analyze their own data and are held accountable for identifying weak spots, they are much more likely to use the data to solve customer problems and improve the process, even if the information is not entirely flattering.

Although collecting and analyzing customer information is ultimately a complex process, particularly in large organizations, it doesn't have to start out that way. In fact, setting up a customer information system can be as simple as requiring every employee with customer contact to ask at least one customer per week for a single improvement suggestion: i.e., "If there were one thing you would change about the way we do business, what would it be?" Employing this simple, direct approach, even small companies would still be able to generate a significant number of suggestions each month. If this data was then categorized and analyzed (preferably by those who will *use* the information) and made accessible to others for whom it might be helpful, the voice of the customer would no doubt be heard loudly and clearly throughout the organization. Just imagine how much more responsive your company would be if, when you came to work on Monday, you could call up the information gathered last week (not last month) and find out what your customers want you to do differently.

There's little question that the time for collecting information in context and in real time by those who can act on that data has come. Fortunately, since the cost of implementing such a system is only a fraction of what it was just a couple of years ago, and in some cases requires only a commonly available database, money will not be the biggest obstacle. What the system <u>will</u> demand, however, is *discipline,* with each customer contact employee being responsible for gathering and categorizing data and making it available to others in a usable format. While this sounds relatively straightforward and sensible, it's amazing, given how frequently we talk about the importance of such information, how hesitant we can be in re-defining people's roles to ensure that they participate in the process.

C15

Letting Doers Think

One executive surprised us with his response to our suggestion of using the front line as information "hunter-gatherers" by noting, "These people you are asking to collect and analyze information are <u>doers</u> not <u>thinkers.</u> If they spend time thinking about these issues, they'll become less effective at what they do." It was 1993, and we couldn't believe it! But, then again, what other reason can many offer for ignoring the single most accessible, least expensive source of information available to most companies? A number of leaders told us it never occurred to them. Perhaps their not having come up with the idea themselves was not a failure of imagination, but had more to do with the long-time assumptions about the potential and the role of the front line held by many of the people in their organization.

We can't afford to delay any longer. The advantages that can be attained from involving everyone in the information gathering effort are just too great to be ignored. Collecting, analyzing, discussing, and tracking trends in the data bring focus to our talk about customer service and are also a highly effective mechanism for generating informed dialogue about the enhancements we must make in the near future to improve processes and build greater value for our customers.

80,000 Snapshots

C15 When former chief executive officer Barry Gibbons took the helm of Burger King, one of the first things he did was set up an information system to provide him with a picture of what was happening in the field. The system encompassed employee and supplier surveys and an 800-number hot line for customers to call in comments and complaints. Gibbons also saw to it that every Burger King was visited regularly by mystery eaters who reported back on their dining experiences. As a result, Gibbons' picture was actually a continually evolving composite made up of over 80,000 separate snapshots per month.

SEVEN CONSIDERATIONS FOR BUILDING AN EFFECTIVE CUSTOMER INFORMATION SYSTEM

> *Breakthroughs come from an instinctive judgment of what customers might want if they knew to think about it.*
> —Andrew Grove, CEO, Intel

In developing a more efficient, more timely way to collect customer information in your organization, there are a number of ideas, trends, and assumptions you might want to take into consideration. Here are seven:

1. Know each customer's needs. Customers having it their way will require that we have specific information about <u>each</u> customer, not just generalized information about a set of similar customers. The types of data that will have to be known for us to effectively serve these "personal niche" customers may require that we know the customer's individual purchasing history, pending sales, past delivery problems, and his or her specific priorities and needs.

2. Make customers your partners. Do you like the packaging? Can you understand the directions? Is the game *fun?* Our offices are in close proximity to those of Electronic Arts, a video and computer game manufacturer that routinely holds focus groups with kids, who get to comment on new offerings and help design the next generation of games. Not surprisingly, most of the kids in the neighborhood clamor to take part.

From jeans manufacturers to computer distributors, companies are involving customers in the design of future processes and the evaluation of present ones. More and more "customer partnerships" are the rule rather than the exception. Indeed, it has gotten to the point that if a company hasn't found a way to actively involve customers in the company's improvement efforts, they're behind the times.

3. Look for information in unexpected places. Inevitably, the most interesting things happen at the periphery of a given process or major trend. Of course, when information hits us in the face, it's imperative that we see it and act on it to stay in business. If, however, we want to scoop the competition, we must learn to capture and analyze data that is less apparent or may not seem particularly important at first reading.

4. Anticipate customer needs. When it comes to the future, customers don't always know best. In fact, they can be downright unreliable in predicting what they'll want or need next year—or even next month. Remember . . . fax machines, overnight delivery . . . and they'd never even *heard* of Post-it notes. Now it's impossible to do business without them. Sure, we have to listen and address today's concerns. But if we hope to thrive tomorrow, we've got to arrive there before the customer does.

5. The deeper we go, the more we learn. Asking customers simple, direct questions in a survey will usually yield simple and direct answers, unless the customer is willing to elaborate—which

C15

few are. On the other hand, when we have a discussion with a customer, we can probe for details and examples to enable us to better understand the customer's feelings, needs, and wants. A customer's feedback is most revealing when it is considered in light of that customer's specific circumstances.

6. Involve everyone in building your customer information system. It is altogether possible that our efforts to bring a consistent customer focus to many in our organizations have been inhibited by our limited methods of data collection. With so much at stake, the task of collecting customer information is just too large and too important to be delegated to a few, or solely to a third party. Instead, to gather, analyze, and use information effectively, the consistent involvement of everyone in the organization should be required. There is no faster, more effective way to bring reality to the words "customer focus" than to involve everyone in the process of building a customer information system and using that information to enhance the value of your organization's products and services.

7. Make information accessible to all who need it. Anyone in the organization who might have use for customer information should have access to it, right? Seems obvious, but it isn't a reality in most organizations. One would hope that the reasons for this have more to do with technology constraints than with a deliberate denial of information to certain groups. In any event, based on our observations, it is clear that when it comes to making information available to a wide range of employees, many organizations still have a long way to go.

Part **4**

Leader of People

. . . The leader starts out with the realization that he and the organization owe; they owe the customers, the clients, the constituency, whether they are parishioners, or patients, or students. They owe the followers, whether that's faculty, or employees, or volunteers. And what they owe is really to enable people to realize their potential.

—PETER DRUCKER,
Managing the Non-Profit Organization

6

Leader of People

Our people went all over the world looking at the most successful companies. The bottom line was people. . . . Whenever you begin to think something else is as important or more important, you are continuously reminded that it is otherwise.

—Richard LeFauve, President, G/M Saturn

The most exciting breakthroughs of the 21st century will occur not because of technology but because of an expanding concept of what it means to be human. . . . Apocalypse or Golden Age. The choice is ours. As we approach the beginning of the 3rd millennium, the way we address that question will define what it means to be human.

—John Naisbitt and Patricia Aburdene, *Megatrends 2000*

In virtually every company we've worked with over the years, management talks of the importance of front-line employees and how the success of the organization rests in their hands. Ironically, many of these employees (and many levels of management, for that matter) tell us they feel untrusted, undervalued, unappreciated, and unchallenged. They claim they have more to give, but no one is listening. It is difficult to believe that such an inconsistency can exist in so many organizations for so long without more people asking why.

Regrettably, the most significant waste in most organizations may be the waste of human potential that results from the way we have chosen to organize and lead. It appears that what we know about how to capture the creativity, commitment, and enthusiasm of people pales in comparison to what we don't know (or possibly just don't practice). Employee survey after employee survey demonstrates the frustration that exists in many work environments. Considerable resources are spent developing plans to address the issues identified in these surveys. Unfortunately, the actions taken to improve employee satisfaction are usually not significantly different from the actions that created the present situation—new recognition practices, more pay-for-performance systems, additional leadership training classes, and more celebrations.

Predictably, the "more of" philosophy is not working. It is wishful thinking that the road to improving our abilities to harness the potential of people lies in past practices. The fact is, we haven't been very good at capturing the commitment of our workforce. Too often, we've created narrow, uninteresting jobs, and relied on managerial control to stimulate productivity improvement. We've taught managers (by example and through leadership models based on behavior modification principles) to encourage desired behaviors by manipulating rewards and punishments, but have done little to encourage or enable them to re-make organizational structures to foster learning. We've focused more on the quantity of output per-person and less on the quality of that person's performance or his or her interest and involvement in the work. Sure, we've been talking about employee satisfaction for decades; but the importance of that satisfaction has been dwarfed by our preoccupation with short-term profits, maximizing shareholder value and, more recently, delivering value to customers.

In the future, the front-line worker will have to be able to quickly read situations and effectively adapt to diverse and rapidly changing circumstances. Thanks to beepers, personal communicators, and other advances in technology, we will be on-call to support customers twenty-four hours a day. As technology re-defines every job, the need for new and different skills will continue to evolve. Personal commitment to continuous learning will become orders-of-magnitude more important. Risk taking and effective decision making will be key competencies required of all workers as they seek new and innovative ways to tailor each customer's experience and increase their own productivity. As never before, every company will be dependent on the flexibility, commitment, persistence, and quick thinking of front-line employees.

In order to meet this future, we must first face the fact that we've been better at gaining the *compliance* of the workforce than at building their *commitment*. We have, in fact, been extremely good at getting people to comply. By adapting many of the management techniques popular in the early twentieth century, we have built a service sector economy that is, by far, the most productive in the world. The memory of these successes may, however, be the biggest obstacle to creating the kind of changes that will be required to implement and sustain future improvement. Our organizations are full of leaders who gained their positions by applying methods that will not be effective in the very different marketplace of tomorrow. We must not, therefore, let our past successes at gaining employee compliance lead us to underestimate the magnitude of the challenge of capturing the full-scale commitment from the workforce that we'll need to succeed in the future.

Gaining this commitment will often require wholesale changes in the way leaders think and manage, will meet with substantial resistance, and will be risky for many. But we can't afford *not* to act. Traditional measures of the costs of employee turnover, such as recruiting, hiring, and training, tell only part of the story. Although these costs are substantial, when you add in those associated with the lost productivity and the lost customer loyalty that typically result from having less-than-committed employees, the total price tag can be shocking. There are already numerous studies that demonstrate a significant link between customer loyalty and employee satisfaction. As the complexity inherent in most jobs multiplies and the pool of available, trained employees capable of performing independently dwindles, the correlation between customer loyalty and employee satisfaction will grow even stronger and the price of having an uncommitted workforce will continue to mount.

In a relatively high-wage country like the United States, profitability depends on a company's ability to consistently deliver outstanding goods and services. In addition to a sound strategy, this requires a "tuned-in, turned-on" workforce. Obviously, frustrated and demotivated employees can render the most effective of strategies ineffective. What is less obvious, however, is that a compliant, non-complaining workforce may be equally ineffective in the future. The pace of change coupled with the multiplication of new competitors has raised the standard. Having employees who do only what they are told will inhibit us from competing effectively in a world marked by rapid innovation and constant change. Our traditional strategies of establishing control, ensuring order, and minimizing the cost of individual labor, even when respectably realized, are too expensive when the creativity and commitment of every employee is required.

Our journey to a different kind of organization will be a rocky one. To be successful, we will have to re-design many, if not most, of our practices governing employees. We will have to overcome many of the obstacles to improvement that are the natural outgrowth of our past policies. Indeed, of all the challenges facing organizations today, re-making these practices may be among the most difficult and important to address early in the effort.

The evidence that exists of just how much better our organizations could be is compelling and the possibilities exciting. Fortunately too, barriers in this new organization are primarily within our control to eliminate. Again, we must simply *choose* to change, to build a different kind of environment in which ordinary people can make extraordinary contributions and where a shared sense of purpose provides the beacon that shows the way to substantially higher levels of performance.

TESTING OUR ASSUMPTIONS ABOUT PEOPLE

> *I believe that we have only just begun the process of inventing the new organizational forms that will inhabit the twenty-first century. To be responsible inventors and discoverers, though, we need the courage to let go of the old world, to relinquish most of what we have cherished, to abandon our interpretations about what does and doesn't work. We must learn to see the world anew.*
>
> —Margaret Wheatley, *Leadership and the New Science*

"Just do it!" Great slogan for an athletic shoe company, but not great advice for most leaders. We *are* practical people. We prefer practice to theory and, at times, have little patience with ideas that cannot be practically applied—now. In many cases, our action orientation has served us well but, in others, our aversion to theory has led us to create a number of practices that are costly and ineffective distractions that undermine improvement efforts. When it comes to creating an efficient, people-friendly organization, we simply have to "get theoretical" before we can "just do it." In order to be more effective in the future, we must first understand the reasons why, after decades of attempts to capture the potential of the workforce, we have come up far short.

In most organizations, there is alarmingly little consensus about what motivates people, how capable the workforce is, and whether the majority of employees can be trusted. For the most part, we have not wrestled with these issues long enough to create a shared set of beliefs that we can use as a foundation for building a more effective organization. And without a strong theoretical foundation, anything we build will be shaky. How many times have we embraced an improvement method that turned out to be inconsistent with our philosophies about people and organizations, then watched as this method was discarded faster than it was adopted? The expressions "flavor-of-the-month management theory" and "management-by-best-seller" are not uncommon to most of us.

The question is, what *do* we believe about people? Forty years ago, organizational behaviorist Douglas McGregor implored managers to question their personal beliefs. He warned that it was impossible to build and sustain an organization inconsistent with our fundamental beliefs. He also cautioned that some of the beliefs we held might be inconsistent with our desire to have an organization full of motivated employees. Most heard his message, but failed to examine the underlying philosophies that governed the way they led. Instead, many managers merely updated their "leadership style," changing a few of their methods.

The result of our failure to examine our beliefs has been a spotty commitment to a long list of leadership practices that are often inconsistent with the organization's, as well as our own, espoused values. Do we believe that work is of little interest to people and, therefore, people must be given external incentives to "jump start" them into action? Or do we believe that under the right conditions, work is as natural as play and that most people really want to learn at work?

Pressed for an answer, a high percentage of leaders claim that their views lean toward those of McGregor and others who believe that human beings like to work, and will readily exercise self-determination, imagination, ingenuity, and creativity on the job if it is interesting and personally benefiting to do so. Most leaders are also quick to point out that they know many individuals who are interested in and committed to their work. They can cite example after example of people who have opted to work for companies where they are paid less but where the chance to contribute is greater.

The question is, do these leaders hold these positive beliefs about the majority of the people in their organizations or only a select few? Evidence suggests the latter. Many leaders, for example, expound at length about how some individuals seem to do no more than they have to—no matter what the job. They talk of the need for more discipline and often lament that the work ethic today isn't what it used to be. Many also resist the notion that the typical employee is underchallenged and, in confidence, will admit that they simply don't trust a significant number of the people who work with them. We don't believe that these managers represent a majority of the leaders in most companies. However, a careful examination of the people practices in most organizations, with a view to the kind of assumptions that underlie these practices, can lead to serious questions, if not disturbing conclusions.

If most leaders believe that people, when interested, are capable of significant commitment, why don't most management training classes help create the skills necessary to re-design jobs to create more interest? Why, instead, do most teach that it is the manager who sets goals and monitors performance, not the employee? Why do so many classes recommend giving recognition when the employee is successful while backing off in the amount of task direction that is provided? And how are we to distinguish these classes in obvious behavior modification from those that teach methods for training dogs and rats?

If people are capable of great emotional and intellectual commitment, why do we continue to manipulate rewards and punishments as the primary way to order behavior? And why do we perpetuate job descriptions that are often narrow, uninteresting, and inflexible? If creating the "right" conditions became a leader's focus, restrictive job descriptions would be quickly dismantled—as they should have been years ago. If work is as natural as play, why have we become so enthralled with incentive compensation systems that attempt to manipulate behavior and often destroy interest in the process? We may, in other words, say that we hold only the most positive beliefs about people but, sadly, our practices often tell a different story.

Fortunately, there are large numbers of leaders who *do* hold positive assumptions about people, and many of these leaders are beginning to change the face of their organizations. In manufacturing companies, productivity and quality have been radically enhanced by reorganizing the work environment to challenge every employee, requiring learning at every level, and ensuring fairness and respect regardless of position. The NUMMI plant in Fremont, California, is one such example. Here, General Motors' partnership with Toyota brought with it new assumptions about people coupled with new leadership practices that turned a factory once dominated by less-than-committed workers into a world-class operation—and with many of the same employees. Similar examples abound. Today, people are ready to work together to build a different kind of workplace—one that provides individuals with more of an opportunity to make a difference, as well as holding out the hope of greater job security.

To be successful in remaking our organization, we will have to overcome the limitations imposed by our own past beliefs about people. It may not be that the majority of leaders hold negative assumptions about people. Rather, it may be that our preference for action over theory has led us to perpetuate practices that are more compatible with the mass-production philosophies of the early twentieth century than with the organizational needs of the twenty-first century. No matter. Whatever the reason, our practices often get in the way of building a committed workforce. We must get theoretical before we can change. We must take the time to challenge the structures that limit our ability to build a more effective organization. We must start, as Douglas McGregor advised a half-century ago, with a passionate debate about our assumptions. We must decide what we stand for and then begin to systematically eliminate those practices that are incompatible with our deᴖᴉᴜᴇ ᴛᴏ ᴄᴀᴘᴛᴜᴜᴇ ᴛʜᴇ creativity and imagination of people. Only then can we begin to build new structures to support our efforts. So, sure, let's *just do it!* But let's try and learn from our past experiences before we do more of what didn't work yesterday.

OVERCOMING A HISTORY OF LOW EXPECTATIONS

I become steadily more persuaded that perhaps the greatest disparity between objective reality and managerial perceptions of it is an underestimation of the potentialities of human beings for contributions to organizational effectiveness. These potentialities are not merely for increased expenditure of effort on limited jobs (although such potentialities do exist) but for the exercise of ingenuity, creativity in problem solving, acceptance of responsibility, leadership in the relational sense, and development of knowledge, skill, and judgment. When opportunities are provided under appropriate conditions, managers are regularly astonished to discover how much more people contribute than they had believed possible.

—Douglas McGregor, *The Professional Manager*

". . . The difference between a lady and a flower girl is not how she behaves but how she's treated. I shall always be a flower girl to Professor Higgins because he always treats me as a flower girl and always will; but I know I can be a lady to you because you always treat me as a lady and always will." Eliza Doolittle's words, in George Bernard Shaw's *Pygmalion*, echo a lesson that has been taught for generations: If we have high expectations of people and treat them as if we expect them to succeed, the chances that they will are greatly enhanced. Today, few teachers, managers, or leaders would argue this premise. Most of us, however, whether in our schools, our organizations, or our homes, have not translated it into practice. We simply don't treat people as if we expected a great deal from them—and as a result, we often get what we expect.

One of the more revealing studies about the effects of higher expectations was performed by noted Harvard University psychologist and researcher Robert Rosenthal. In this study—initially conducted at a California elementary school and reported in *Pygmalion in the Classroom*—Rosenthal randomly selected 20% of the student body and told their teachers that these children had unusual potential for intellectual growth. Predictably, the teachers had high expectations for these students and treated them differently than they did the others in their classrooms. Also predictably, the kids responded. They learned at an accelerated pace and by the end of the school year showed significantly higher gains in IQ than their peers.

These research findings may bode well for the randomly selected 20% of the children from whom more was expected. But what about the other 80% who were thought to be average or below? More to the point, how much potential has been squandered and how much damage has been done by our teachers' failure to expect more? What in our educational system leads teachers to expect so little of students who are capable of so much? Perhaps if this issue had been addressed more systematically, some of the educational problems we are experiencing today might have been avoided. Instead, over the last two decades, student requirements in many school systems have been reduced. These lower expectations have led to lower performance by many students which, in turn, reinforced the teachers' lower expectations . . . and the devastating cycle continues.

Fortunately, there are a number of organizations whose practices reveal an understanding of the importance of holding individuals to a high standard. Visit Miliken and Co., spend some time at a Federal Express office or hub, tour with one of the teams at Johnsonville Foods, or study one of the many manufacturing companies that have radically improved productivity and quality standards by challenging employees to take on greater and greater responsibility. Here, as in the classroom, the differences in performance among employees are significantly affected by how they are treated. Have high expectations of people, design systems that support their efforts, and let them know how important they are by both your words and actions, and ordinary individuals will accomplish extraordinary things.

High expectations, however, are not the norm (particularly outside the factory). For a variety of reasons, many companies have designed and perpetuated systems that ignore people's abilities and substantially underestimate the potential of most employees. In many cases, the leaders who work in these organizations are so close to the systems that they don't see or appreciate just how significantly many practices limit their ability to build an environment in which people are excited to give their best. It isn't only myopia that does us in, however. Sometimes, it's a simple lack of commitment. Our leaders tell us they believe in the importance of having high expectations, but their day-to-day actions cast doubt on those beliefs.

We wonder why it is that so many leaders feel uneasy when considering a significant (or even insignificant) delegation of authority. It seems absurd that we're willing to trust a driver we don't know to remain on the other side of a yellow line while barreling

---

THE FRONT LINE DOESN'T LIE ... (REVISITED)

A friend of ours was flying out of New York when he realized that he'd lost his plane ticket. So he asked the ticket agent for some help. The agent proceeded to outline the most absurd set of policies our friend had ever heard—including paying four times the lost ticket's face value (even though they had a record of the price he'd paid). When he spoke to the supervisor, she was quick to authorize a replacement ticket at the price he'd originally paid, and thanked him for his patience. When our friend asked why the ticket agent couldn't make this common-sense decision, the supervisor gave him a lecture about the need for control. At one point the frustrated ticket agent interrupted, "It's OK, they don't trust me with sharp objects either."

down the road in our direction at 60 miles per hour (a genuine matter of life and death) and have so little trust in the people we hire—in situations that are considerably less life-threatening. Why, for example, do we still pay supervisors to check and schedule the work of front-line workers? Do we really believe that they can't handle these tasks themselves? Are we afraid that workers will take advantage of the authority given them?

Manufacturing quality didn't improve significantly until we expected the people who did the work to measure their own performance, learn from their measurements, and use this knowledge to further improve. Still, in far too many organizations, workers are required to get a supervisor's signature to authorize a routine activity. Sure, it's time that all employees commit to improving the processes in which they work. Absolutely. But how can they—or why should they even care—given the restrictive nature of some of their jobs? Are we truly asking people to fully engage their minds as well as their hands, or do our articulations of simple tasks and restrictive practices reveal far lower expectations? More often than not, our organizations' job descriptions are a testament to just how little we expect.

In some cases, our low expectations are communicated implicitly; in others, we communicate our lack of confidence explicitly, sometimes even blatantly. We can't understand, for example, how some companies that have promulgated "respect" as a core value and pay leaders based on upward appraisals still require many of their employees to sign out to go to the bathroom. (We're not making this up! We, too, were surprised and disheartened to observe this practice in 1994.)

It is not that leaders don't expect people to work hard. On the contrary. In many jobs employees now work 8 hours per week longer than their predecessors did a decade ago. Many leaders have continually pushed people to pedal harder to do more of what they did yesterday. Few, however, have challenged employees to fully engage their minds or to fulfill their potential. The result in the workplace, as in our schools, is predictable: low

---

I'M NOT A CHILD

We sat in a meeting last year when a CEO of a mid-sized company asked his front-line employees how he could help them become more productive.

"Trust me and stop treating me like a child," one employee exclaimed. "I run a household, support myself, my son, and my father on $30,000 a year and still manage to save a few dollars. I feel like I'm pretty capable. But when I come to work, you don't listen to my ideas and you treat me like a child—and not a very smart one, at that. I'm not a child. I've got much more to contribute but you make it very difficult for most of us."

The CEO was speechless and embarrassed. He later told us that he left that room with a better understanding of how much human potential was being wasted and just how patronizing some organizational practices can be.

---

expectations lead to low performance, giving the appearance that the low expectations were accurate, and leading, in many cases, to even lower expectations and lower performance levels.

It's easy enough to say that from now on we're going to have higher expectations of people. It's far harder to deliver on that promise, however. Low expectations of some employee groups are so ingrained in most organizational cultures that it will take nothing less than a revolution in management thinking to significantly alter the situation. Changing gradually, on the other hand, has the potential for being even more damaging than staying where we are. Once we admit to the absurdity and counterproductivity of our past practices, we have to move rapidly to eliminate them; otherwise, employees will become even more cynical and frustrated. Sound familiar? In many manufacturing companies, where success has been more readily observable, we had to do it quickly. We didn't have a choice. Maybe that was the good news.

CARING IS NOT OPTIONAL

To understand the challenge of improving the productivity of service workers, we must also seek to understand why people do their work, not only what they do. This type of question requires us as managers to have a reason and purpose for our own work and for that of those we seek to lead.

—Chairman, Fortune 500 Company

In any human endeavor, there is no substitute for support and caring. When people genuinely care about each other, the synergy can be impressive. When people care, they support one another and everyone grows and profits in the process. Unfortunately, genuine caring is rare in many organizations. We are concerned, therefore, with the apparent carelessness that surrounds many reward and recognition events. We are worried that, because many employees perceive these programs to be more manipulative than caring, the programs may backfire, or produce disappointing long-term effects.

Few people like to be manipulated. Most of us don't like accepting gifts or praise (or even money) when they are given with strings attached or with the expectation of getting something in return. Sure, if the reward is large enough, we may perform as requested, but we probably won't like doing so. That doesn't necessarily mean we'll tell you. Instead, we'll often accept your reward, and just quietly resent your methods. And if at some point you decide to eliminate the reward, we may not perform at the level you desire. Veiled attempts to control people, in other words, can often have more far-ranging negative effects than those who dole out rewards realize.

We're not arguing that every reward designed to modify behavior is undesirable or will elicit a negative response. Clearly, some attempts to alter behavior are thought by most to be necessary and desirable (i.e., recognition designed to encourage ethical behavior or the fair distribution of resources). However, when the primary purpose of the reward or recognition (or threat of punishment) is to get people to do something that they don't want to do, don't feel is necessary, or don't understand the significance of, there is a risk that they will turn against the rewarder and further disparage the task.

We believe that the key to understanding or anticipating peoples' reactions to a reward or recognition event is to put yourself in their shoes. No matter what you think they *ought* to feel (i.e., motivated, grateful, scared, etc.), their perception is the only one that counts. If they feel that the person designing the event cares about them, appreciates their efforts, and supports their need to achieve personal goals, then it is more likely that any effort will be viewed positively. However, if the reward or recognition event is perceived to come with "strings attached," the result is usually far less positive—or even worse.

What would happen, for example, if your spouse (or significant other) gave you a gift, supposedly as an expression of caring but you are almost positive that the motive for giving you the gift is to get you to do something—something you don't really want to do. For most of us, the suspicion of an ulterior motive will affect our reaction to the act of giving. For some of us, this perceived manipulation may detract only slightly from the appreciation we feel. Others of us, however, may react quite negatively to this subtle attempt to modify our behavior. Our reaction may range from amusement to anger. Our trust in the other person may be significantly affected and our relationship altered.

The corporate equivalent of the "gift with strings attached" is observable in most organizations daily, in their reward and recognition events. Our attempts to capture people's best efforts and to motivate have led many to invest in these events, hoping that they will encourage greater commitment and higher levels of performance. Undoubtedly, many of these events help focus efforts and provide the all-too-infrequent opportunity to celebrate the fruits of our hard work. However, when people feel that those rewarded were unfairly selected or that the sponsoring group is insincere, these events can do more harm than good. Instead of a celebration of accomplishment and success, they become visible symbols of the problems that can plague an organization on a daily basis—favoritism, flawed measurement systems, "bossism," etc. These events worry us.

Recently, while working with a company to assess the effectiveness of their reward and recognition practices, we were told firsthand of the problems with what a number of employee groups referred to as "Trinkets and Trash" programs. Among these individuals, the mere mention of recognition events elicited comments which might generously be described as cynical. The gap between management's "walk" and "talk" was fuel for a seemingly endless list of stories that gave evidence to management's dwindling credibility. Listening to these workers, it was obvious that leadership inconsistencies lay at the root of their cynicism. Not that these employees turned down the money or the plaques or the free dinners they were awarded: they accepted them all, but not in the spirit that management had hoped. Also, after hearing these individuals' frustration, we had to wonder what the long-term effect of these events would be.

When we asked these same individuals why they thought management would go to the trouble of investing in these events if they didn't care, their reasoning varied. "They're doing it to fulfill the Baldrige criteria," was a common response, as was, "They think this stuff motivates us." Some employees attributed the best of motives to individual managers ("They really care"), but hypothesized that the way the business was organized made it very hard to care about people and still get ahead. Others believed that many managers viewed employees as a resource that had to be "managed" on the way to the really important stuff—shareholder return and stock price.

When we asked managers in this company why they held these events, they were generally consistent in their stated motives. "Appreciation for past performance" and "the events' motivational effects in guiding future performance" were at the top of most lists. By and large, we found these managers to be sincere, caring, and well intentioned. However, their failure to walk their talk on a day-to-day basis, a list of organizational structures that were perceived to be inconsistent with stated goals, the suspicion among employees that management had an ulterior motive, and a perceived lack of genuine caring by management turned many of these acts of appreciation into opportunities for building peer alliances and bashing senior management.

Noteworthy, we feel, is a comparison of this company's recognition events to those we witnessed at Disney. Ostensibly, the events at both organizations were quite similar. The speeches echoed many of the same themes, and the activities and meals were virtually indistinguishable. In many cases, however, the reactions of those in attendance were as different as night and day. In the first company, employees were cynical about the events and untrusting of the motives of the event's sponsors. In contrast, most Disney cast members viewed their events as genuine celebrations, thank-you's from the company's leaders who, the cast members felt, truly cared about them.

We're not suggesting that the celebrations at Disney were perfect or that Disney has no disgruntled cast members. But the overall mood and atmosphere at the Disney celebrations was markedly different from that at the other company. At Disney, the number of celebrators was surprising, there was a far greater number of "winners," and the involvement of individuals from all levels of the workforce was generally the rule, not the exception. Celebrations seemed to be part of the day-to-day culture of the organization and were, therefore, less likely to be perceived as an infrequent event held to "get something."

We can't, of course, pretend to know whether these employees' interpretations of management's motives were correct in every instance. We have found, however, that most people possess excellent "motive detectors." If we ever are tempted to fool those we work with, we'd be well advised to think again. That's why the next time we plan a recognition event, we should first ask:

- Do we personally care about these employees? Or are we just interested in what they can do for us?

- Do we routinely support their efforts to improve, learn, and grow, or are these goals secondary to what we want from them?

- Are the structures of the organization consistent with the values we will espouse in this event? If not, have we visibly committed to changing them?

- Have we made a firm commitment to telling the truth? Considering most organizational histories, people have a right to be skeptical. If we fudge on the truth even a little, we're in deep trouble.

As we've said before, every organization is inescapably human. Caring is not optional. Caring, not manipulation, is the currency most likely to build a good foundation for the kind of team we will need to succeed in the future.

INTRINSIC VERSUS EXTRINSIC MOTIVATION: MAKING THE CHOICE

> *Our prevailing system of management has destroyed our people. People are born with intrinsic motivation, self-esteem, curiosity to learn and joy in learning. The destruction starts with toddlers—a prize for the best Halloween costume, gold stars, grades in school—and it continues up through the University.*
>
> *On the job, teams and divisions are ranked—rewards for those at the top, punishment for those at the bottom. Management by objectives, incentive pay, bonus plans, put together and separately, cause further loss unknown and unknowable.*
>
> —W. Edwards Deming, *Out of the Crisis*

For nearly a century, researchers have been studying and analyzing motivation in the workplace. Emerging from these studies is a whole new language made up of some familiar and some not so familiar terms—"job enlargement," "job enrichment," "motivators," "hygiene factors," "deficit needs," "issues of growth," "empowerment"—to name a few. Interestingly, while the majority of this research points to a specific type of reward structure as being the most effective motivator under most circumstances, few of us have found ways to incorporate this reward into our day-to-day structure activities. Of even greater concern, however, is that the reward structure we *do* use in most of our organizations can be an obstacle to a motivated workforce and can inhibit our ability to build flexibility and foster learning.

The focus of much of this research around motivation has been to identify the relative differences between the effects of *intrinsic* and *extrinsic* motivation. When motivation is intrinsic, the rewards are inherent in the activity itself. Intrinsically motivated people then, are those who engage in an activity for its own sake. When a person learns a new skill, performs a challenging task that builds self-esteem, or engages in an event that fulfills that person's need to be socially responsible (feeding the homeless, for example), the benefits can be thought of as intrinsic.

Conversely, when a person is extrinsically motivated, he or she seeks rewards that are external to the activity. An extrinsically motivated person, therefore, does something because of what he or she might receive as a result. "If you do *this*, you will get *that*" has been a popular way of thinking about this type of reward structure. Money, promotion, time off, praise, recognition programs, and a wide assortment of other benefits are all extrinsic rewards that have been used in the attempt to generate better performance.

Taken as a whole, however, the research leans heavily in favor of intrinsic reward structures over extrinsic ones if the goal is to gain greater employee commitment and improved long-term performance. If you desire to encourage continuous improvement as a way of life, there is no substitute for developing a work environment where people are more likely to get interested in their work. There is no substitute for the opportunity to learn and to grow.

There is no substitute for the satisfaction of doing a challenging job well.

It's hard to think of a person who is very good at something who is not excited by, and passionately involved in, the task. Great ballplayers who hate playing the sport, great scientists who don't like research, or great front-line service workers who don't like serving are a rarity, if they exist at all. Of course, we're not suggesting that these people don't want to be paid—or even paid well. Nor are we suggesting that the benefits which these individuals receive from their activity fully explains their growth and success. What we are suggesting is that to be as good as they are, most of these top performers have a significant love for the activity they're involved in—and that money and other external rewards aren't the *driving force* that leads them to the highest levels of performance. People who are interested in and get pleasure from an activity tend to be more committed and better performers over time.

Over the years, however, most organizations have attempted to influence performance largely through the use of extrinsic rewards. We have focused more on building external reward structures than on building environments where intrinsic motivation could flourish. As in other areas, managers typically adopt methods they can control. Paying a few more bucks or running an incentive program is simply easier than trying to recreate a work environment to ensure that jobs are challenging and meaningful. External rewards can be manipulated and can even appear to bring about predictable results. If the reward is large enough and the task do-able, the immediacy of the result can provide what appears to be a direct link between the reward and the performance. Few would argue that external incentives can result in significant short-term improvements.

The dark side of external rewards is that their salutary effects are extremely short-lived. The need for them escalates over time. In many cases they can become virtual entitlements. Also, external rewards tend to discourage growth and learning. While the often rapid results that come with external rewards may fit into our need for short-term gains, external motivation as used by most organizations usually ignores the deeper, more essential needs of the individual employee. In fact, in many cases, external reward systems are an outgrowth of behavioral research performed on rats and pigeons and then applied to a highly complex human workforce. It's understandable, then, why such reward systems can be truly dehumanizing.

There is no doubt that money motivates people. The question is, "Does it motivate them to do a *better* job?" The answer, more often than not, is no. Money primarily motivates people to get the money. As we said earlier, pay a large enough commission on *anything*—and it will probably sell. Have a contest: the person who wins gets a huge prize. Will it get people to work harder for a while to try and win the prize? If the prize is that desirable, you bet! The right extrinsic rewards can get people to do what you want them to do—and if you want it fast, they'll do it fast. For centuries we have been experimenting with ways of using one reward or another to get people to do what we wanted. What we have overlooked, however, is how our preoccupation with employee behavior modification has inadvertently affected the quality of their work, their reasons for doing the work, and how they feel about their jobs.

People want and need money. Promotions are important. We all like to be praised. We're certainly not arguing that all extrinsic rewards should be abolished. We are suggesting, however, that if we focus primarily on extrinsic motivation, the unintended negative effects of some of our practices may make it very difficult for us to build the true commitment we desire. In fact, a preoccupation with finding the best short-term extrinsic motivators may result in an organization that is *extrinsically disadvantaged* in the future.

The Potential Unintended Effects of Extrinsic Rewards

Over the last few years, I have come in contact with any number of companies struggling with this transition from command and control hierarchy to employee empowerment and organizational learning, and every one of them is its own worst enemy. Managers embrace the language of intrinsic motivation but fail to see how firmly mired in the old extrinsic world their communications actually are.

—Chris Argyris, *Harvard Business Review*

Extrinsic Rewards:

1. Can change the way people approach their work. If the proposition is "Do this and you'll get that," people will often focus more on the "that," the reward, and less on the "this," the job. In an extrinsic environment, in other words, the task can become secondary to the attainment of the reward. Perhaps the most profound and farthest-reaching fallout that can result from the use of extrinsic rewards is a reduction in a worker's commitment to his or her work. If this is true—and study after study indicates it is—then rewards are not just innocuous incentives that may or may not entice employees. Rather, rewards can actually promote or heighten disinterest and resentment in the job to be done. Or, as author Alfie Kohn says, **"The more you want what was dangled in front of you, the more you may come to dislike whatever you have to do to get it."**

2. Can be perceived to be controlling and manipulative. Generally, extrinsic rewards put the rewarder in a position of power and control over the rewardee—or at least reinforce that power and control, with most rewards being like those "strings attached" gifts you used to get from your parents. Sure, you wanted the present, but the conditions of its giving often left a bad taste in your mouth. You knew you were being manipulated, just like workers know they are being manipulated by rewards on the job, and many don't much like it. Rewards also tend to color whatever personal relationship exists between the rewarder and the rewardee.

3. Can discourage creativity. Though initial logic suggests otherwise, rewards actually cut down on the inclination to be flexible or innovative. People working for rewards usually seek the most predictable solution that will afford them a payoff as quickly as possible, with the least chance of failure. Given the choice between striking out in new directions or using past solutions that have worked, the reward seeker will probably opt for the latter.

4. Don't lead to lasting change. If you are trying to change behavior, extrinsic rewards can work over the short term. To sustain any behavioral change over the long term, you have to keep giving rewards, and in most cases increase the ante as time goes on. As for changes in attitude or interest levels, rewards usually have little positive effect on either.

5. Encourage inappropriate solutions to complex problems. Example: If salespeople are not featuring a particular product in their sales efforts, providing a reward for them to do so may distract you from an essential problem with the product, or worse yet, may entice the sales force to find a way to sell a product to a customer who doesn't need it.

6. Impede the leader's development of leadership skills. Paying or otherwise rewarding a person to do his or her job differently is much easier than building the leadership skills necessary to engage in the kind of serious give and take required to build a shared commitment for change.

7. Are expensive. In a world of shrinking financial resources, it would seem that dangling rewards—usually in the form of bonuses or merit pay—in front of employees is contrary to the direction most organizations are seeking to take. This is underlined by the fact that today's rewards will not be adequate tomorrow, and that for rewards to continue working, they must continue to spiral upward in value. The more that rewards are used, the more they are needed.

8. Can be punishing. The effectiveness of many reward programs is evaluated by assessing the subsequent performance of those who are rewarded. But what about those who do not get the goodies? As mentioned earlier, often rewards are given to people whose performance is not substantially different from those who were not rewarded. In other cases, failures in our information systems have resulted in rewards being given to people who are *less* deserving than their peers. The demotivational effects on the many who go unrewarded frequently outweigh the motivational effects on the few who got the prize.

7

The Challenges of Creating an Intrinsically Motivating Environment

CHALLENGE 16

Sharing a Cause Worthy of Commitment

You are not here merely to make a living. You are here in order to enable the world to live more amply, with greater vision, with a finer spirit of hope and achievement. You are here to enrich the world, and you impoverish yourself if you forget the errand.

—Woodrow Wilson

C16

*We were not meant to stand alone. We need to belong—to something or
someone. Only where there is a mutual commitment will you find people prepared to deny themselves for the good of others. We, however, in
our belief in liberalism and individualism, are wary of commitments.
We look suspiciously at words like "loyalty" and "duty" and "obliga-
tion." Independence, whether we seek it or not, is being thrust upon us.
. . . Loneliness may be the real disease of the next century, as we live
alone, work alone, and play alone, insulated by our modem, our Walk-
man, or our television. The Italians may be wise to use the same word
for both alone and lonely, for the first ultimately implies the second. It is
no longer clear where we connect or to what we belong. If however, we
belong to nothing, the point of striving is hard to see. . . .*

—Charles Handy, *Harvard Business Review*

A Walt Disney theme park executive turns down a job at a
competing company that would pay her twice her current salary.
"Where else," she says, "would I be able to work for someone who
has brought more pleasure and entertainment into people's lives
than right where I am?"

At Honda's Marysville plant we met a couple who, because of
the company's policy against hiring the spouses of current employees, waited two years until they both had jobs in the company
before they got married. "We both wanted to work for the best,
simple as that!"

Over the last few decades, however, there has been a gradual
undermining of many organizations and institutions that people
have traditionally turned to for a sense of belonging. There's been
a notable de-emphasis on the extended family, and even the nu-
clear family has been diminished by separation and divorce. Many
fell away from religion when they saw their leaders not practicing
what they preached. Many more became cynical about government when the self-serving actions of elected officials were re-

vealed and when government simply no longer appeared to work. Long-time political party affiliations were also weakened as parties adopted will-o'-the-wisp platforms that were more a response to trends than a reflection of long-held beliefs. More and more of our traditional institutions have become harder to believe in.

Disappointment in our traditional institutions notwithstanding, people all over America are still looking for that worthwhile organization and cause to commit themselves to—and maybe looking harder than ever. If this weren't the case, why do one-third of the workforce volunteer more than three hours a week outside the workplace? Why do many of them work harder for that volunteer organization than they do for the one that pays them? Why would many of us die for a cause, when precious few would die for money?

These questions go to the very heart of the issue we confront in remaking the workplace into one that is intrinsically motivating. Collectively, we are a people seeking something powerful and meaningful to touch our hearts and minds. We are at our best when we are swept up by commitment and working in the service of a larger goal. We're looking for a cause that fires our imagination and excites our spirit. For the organization that can satisfy these needs—particularly today when there is a dearth of organizations that can—an enormous opportunity exists.

People want a cause that distinguishes them from others. No one gets excited about being average. If we don't stretch our goals, offer a valuable cause, and give people an opportunity to realize their potential, chances are they won't give us the best they have to give.

This doesn't mean that every biotech company has to commit to wiping out hunger and starvation on the planet, or that every retailer has to clothe the homeless. Causes can be more moderate and still make employees proud to be working for our organization. The biotech company can focus on leading the industry in the development of environmentally friendly products that replace traditional pesticides, while the retailer can content itself with striving to offer the best service in town. The measure of a worthwhile cause is not how lofty it sounds to an outsider or how it assuages the social conscience or stimulates the competitive juices of the management council. A good cause is one that excites workers, deepens their commitment, and lends meaning to their work.

> *Thus we reject the pessimism that views the future as one in which work will become increasingly meaningless to most people and in which the pursuit of leisure will become the most important end of our society. We cannot help but feel that the greatest fulfillment of man is to be found in activities that are meaningfully related to his own needs as well as those of society.*
>
> —Herzberg, Mausner, and Synderman, *The Motivation to Work*

C16

C H A L L E N G E   1 7

Beyond Empowerment: Ensuring a Challenging Role, Meaningful Responsibility, and the Ability to Succeed

> *. . . Any time we talk about accountability and about achievement, it has to be clear that we are going to delegate thoroughly. Delegate with a certain abandon so that people have space in which to realize potential, in which to be accountable, in which to achieve. . . . It is the kind of thing a follower has a right to expect from a leader. Like other aspects of the work of leadership, delegation is a serious, high risk, high potential meddling in other people's lives. It demands thorough preparation, and a loving commitment.*
>
> —Max DePree

*E*mpowerment. The "E" word. Rarely in business has one word meant so many different things to so many people. We all use it, most of us believe in it, but few of us agree on exactly what it is and how or to what extent we should make it part of our organization's improvement efforts. In theory, empowerment is about the redistribution of authority and accountability in the organization. Most often it takes the form of granting greater decision-making power to front-line employees to enable them to improve the way work is done or to customize the process for customers.

In most implementations, however, companies attempting to

empower employees still retain their traditional organizational structure, where power emanates from the top. Needless to say, this can result in confusion: the front-line has supposedly been empowered, yet the old system dictates that power be held at higher levels and that managers be held accountable for the front-line's actions. For the front-line worker, this semi-delegation of authority can be little more than an organizational tease since the true power remains with the manager and all that is actually redistributed is some of the manager's responsibility. Often too, empowered workers are frequently not given the background and training necessary to successfully carry out their new-found responsibilities.

Also hampering most empowerment efforts is that the power granted to employees is usually conferred on a provisional basis. Since in most implementations managers remain in control and ultimately responsible, they can revoke authority whenever they deem that employees are not using it wisely. This patriarchal aspect of empowerment frequently results in employees who feel that they are not genuinely trusted.

In most instances empowerment is an attempt to bring about a new result while still working from an old set of assumptions—assumptions that, in many cases, are nearly as old as the century. These assumptions, as we've said elsewhere in this book, saw labor primarily as an instrument of production and little more. Labor costs were to be minimized, job definitions kept narrow, and training costs kept low so that, in the event of a high turnover rate, the effect wouldn't be crippling and the investment in the departed workers wouldn't be too great. In a world where production was king and the role of employees and managers was simple and clear-cut, these assumptions held a definite appeal. But what could their appeal be today, when distribution and delivery of products and services to a loyal customer base by a loyal workforce are key to survival? How do these old assumptions square with management's oft-stated goal of having employees treat the company's money as if it were their own? How does empowerment, as defined today in most organizations, bring us

THE NEED FOR CONTROL

C17

"Locus of control," or the need people inherently have for being in control of what happens to them, has been studied for years. Research shows that people who believe they have a span of control over their lives are happier, healthier, and more productive.

In 1976, researcher Herbert M. Lefcourt conducted the now classic "shut off the noise" experiments. Adult subjects were split into two groups. Both groups were assigned a series of tasks such as solving puzzles and proofreading. Throughout the experiment, loud background noise was played. The subjects in one group were instructed to do their best in spite of the noise; those in the second group were told that they could push a button to turn off the distracting noise if they so desired. In the end, the button made all the difference. The group with access to the button did better and made five times more attempts at solving puzzles than the group without access to the button.

Surprisingly, no one who had access to the button actually used it during the experiment. The knowledge that they had control and could choose to use the button made the difference.

closer to this goal—or any of our other goals, for that matter? Often, it doesn't.

In most organizations, our effort to empower people simply grants too little at the same time that it demands too much. As employees, we are told that we've been given more power, but realize, soon enough, that it's only on loan. We are asked to take greater responsibility, but it seems that there is always someone looking over our shoulder. We are held responsible for results, but are not given control over our work and frequently don't have the ability to succeed. We are asked to act like *owners* but, in fact, we're thought to be and are given the responsibility of *renters*.

Not that being a renter is a foreign concept. Most of us have been renters at one time or another, having rented cars, skis, houses, or apartments, and we know that renting essentially empowers us to <u>use</u> something over a defined time period. We also know that our commitment to what we rent is limited. We may, for example, repaint our rented apartment, but we probably won't redesign the kitchen or replace the appliances. We'll make sure our leased car is regularly serviced, but probably won't add spiffy wheels or even pay a great deal of attention to preventive maintenance. On the other hand, if we owned that car or apartment, our interest in it would be greater, we'd take better care of it, and when the situation warranted, we'd likely make improvements.

Similar distinctions exist in the workplace. Generally, owners:

- Reap financial rewards from their work only when it produces value for the customer: working hard alone doesn't guarantee a paycheck.

- Readily confront problems and act quickly to rectify them.

- Continuously sell themselves and their companies to their customers.

- Design systems that keep them informed on all issues that could affect their ability to conduct the business profitably.

- Take responsibility for running the business day to day, unless they delegate that responsibility.

- Hold themselves accountable.

- Help design processes and business practices, soliciting advice and assistance when necessary.

- Put themselves at risk, often using their own capital.

- Are compelled by their work and believe they will succeed.

- Are confident in their authority.

By contrast, renters (i.e., employees who have been empowered on a provisional basis) feel that their authority is on loan, and often act accordingly. In most cases, that means that they'll do a creditable job in the exercise of that authority, maybe even a first-rate job. Still, their commitment will likely be limited, because their empowerment feels tenuous and because they are essentially thought to be, and are treated as, tenants. Frequently, for example, empowered workers are not given a context for their work, have little control over the process, are denied information that could improve their performance, and are judged by the specific task they perform rather than the value they help create. As a result, they are far less likely than owners to put themselves at risk, keep themselves informed, and do whatever is required to build value for those they serve. In other words, in many cases, "empowered" employees often won't (or can't) give their all because the responsibility they've been granted is too limited, and because they're uncertain when and if that responsibility will be taken from them.

C17

If our goal, however, is to get people to treat the company's money like their own, to treat the company's customers like their own, and to commit to their work as an owner might, then it's time to give them true title to their jobs. It's time to move beyond empowerment and create a true sense of "ownership" among our employees.

In engendering such a sense of ownership in employees, it may be helpful to think of them as independent contractors or business owners whom we've hired to produce value for the company. What is the value we expect of them? How much is it worth to us? How will we determine whether we receive the expected or greater value? Thinking of employees in these terms allows us to consider their value and importance to the company in a new light, and forces us to determine whether the tasks they perform are genuinely necessary and/or valuable.

By that same token, if employees are urged to see themselves as independent contractors with a generally defined role in the process, they will take greater responsibility for creating the value their "organization" has been asked to deliver. This may take the

DR. BOB LOVES YOU!

In the mid–1970s, Dr. Bob Gardner decided to empower each staff member of his pediatric dental practice. He gave each person in the office $1000 and challenged everyone to spend the money in ways that would help him build the practice. He knew that each person's choices would probably not mirror his, but he was not prepared when one member of the staff entered the office and proudly showed him 25,000 stickers inscribed with a red heart and the saying "Dr. Bob Loves You." Believing that these stickers would last the rest of the century, he called the person into his office to discuss the decision she had made. His point—better judgment would have been helpful, and next time she should think through the issues more thoroughly before making a decision to spend $1000. "Why 25,000 stickers?" he asked.

"Because you limited my spending authority," she responded.

Thank heaven for limits, he thought to himself.

Much to Dr. Bob's surprise, Moms and kids loved the stickers. They put them everywhere! Before he knew it, they were re-ordering even more stickers! Visit Dr. Bob today and "Dr. Bob Loves You" is everywhere. In Columbus, Ohio, if you ask about Dr. Robert Gardner, the response you are likely to get is, "You mean Dr. Bob?" Yep— weird idea, those stickers—but brilliant. What makes the stickers even more effective is that Dr. Bob really does love kids. A more giving, caring man is hard to find.

form of helping develop or improve the process, anticipating changes in customer needs and requirements, solving problems, improving productivity, and ensuring a good return on the investment that is being made in them. Although these employees may not have legal ownership of the company's assets, they will in fact own something that may be even more significant: **they will own the responsibility for making a meaningful contribution.**

TAKING STOCK OF OWNERSHIP

The organizational landscape is full of companies whose employees own stock but who don't feel (or act) like owners. That's because a sense of ownership only comes when we are convinced that our contribution is a meaningful one—when we are committed to the work we do, the customers we serve, and the teammates we work with. While stock ownership may involve us financially, it does little to involve us emotionally.

In most volunteer organizations, for example, little is actually owned that could be sold to generate wealth. Instead, the enterprise is managed to support good work and a worthy cause. Yet, in these organizations, many people work at a level that would make most paying employers jealous. Certainly, some people in these organizations are paid, but much of the work is done by people who are contributing time and effort without expecting anything in return but a sense of ownership—responsibility, accountability, and the opportunity to make a difference.

C17

A Challenging Role with Meaningful Responsibility

While being an owner may be preferable to being a renter in most cases, no one wants to own a lousy apartment in a bad neighborhood or a car that may break down at any time. By that same token, most of us don't want to own (or commit to) a dead-end job. It is, therefore, also time that we make the jobs in our organization worth owning—time to provide every employee with a challenging role and with meaningful responsibility.

As we've already said, one of the keys to winning employee commitment is to provide all workers with a cause that is worthy of that commitment. It is also critical that we provide the opportunity for learning and that we design processes that people can control to create value, instead of processes that control people. A mindset that results in employees being systematically denied training and information flies in the face of our pronounced need for the well-trained, well-informed worker. Indeed, in today's competitive, information-sensitive world, we'll have to retrain experienced workers and continuously retrain them for more complex tasks. Undertrained employees will not be able to reliably analyze information and make the real-time decisions that will be required. Uninformed, partially committed employees cannot be expected to effectively innovate delivery or ensure customer loyalty. On the other hand, if our organizations provide employees with a worthy cause, interesting work, sufficient training, and the opportunity to reach their potential, the chances are excellent that they will make the commitment we seek.

Unfortunately, most jobs have not been designed to produce value for the customer while also providing an opportunity for the development of the worker. In fact, in a large percentage of cases, just the opposite is true. We've designed jobs and written job descriptions in ways that make sense from an efficiency standpoint, but that do little to feed the needs of people to learn, grow, and be challenged. In the short run (quarter to quarter), the current system may even seem effective. However, as the organization increasingly calls on the intelligence of its people to build new capabilities, the price we're paying for these "efficiencies" is already too steep.

The question is: Is it possible to create an interesting, challenging job for every employee? Can we really organize so that every employee has a chance to grow and prosper? And, more to the point, is it even possible to accomplish this without turning the organization completely on end? The answer is yes—provided that we make the change from the old-fashioned, factory-based, production-oriented mindset to one that better accommodates flexibility and responsiveness and, above all, expects significant contributions from everyone in the company in both the planning and execution of their jobs.

Certainly, not all jobs are equally interesting, nor can every job be made to seem appealing. This is particularly true in inherently unchallenging, highly repetitive, low-paying, little-experience-required jobs, of which there are millions. However, even in most of these jobs, interest and commitment are possible for many employees if, in addition to the performance of the task, they are charged with the management of the process.

What would this entail? Here are eight responsibilities that are the foundation of process improvement efforts:

1. Gather customer information. In the normal course of business, employees should regularly ask customers what they like or don't like about the company's products and services and what they'd like to see done differently. This data should be quickly analyzed by those collecting it and then be communicated throughout the organization.

2. Help design the service delivery process. Being involved in this design, of course, must be predicated on an understanding of the entire delivery process, not just the job that the employee performs. Everyone must have a substantial understanding of the implications of their work and have the ability to influence the design of the way that work is accomplished.

3. Customize the process when necessary. Why is it that some employees don't act in the customer's best interest when common sense often dictates a different, obvious course of action? Often, it's because many workers today still aren't trusted to make even the simplest deviations in the process and must get supervisory approval to do so. For an organization to be considered responsive in the future, this must change.

4. Measure the quality of their own performance. The primary benefit to be gained from measuring your own performance is that the direct, unfiltered feedback you receive when doing so enhances learning. Whether you are or aren't allowed to measure your own performance is often an issue of trust. Many managers believe that workers are unable (haven't been trained) to measure their performance effectively and won't identify areas where they have weaknesses (too much risk). Wouldn't they be honest in their self-appraisal if fear were eliminated from the process?

5. Identify disgruntled customers. Often, the customers we lose are the ones who are marginally dissatisfied but are not particularly vocal about it. Most customers don't complain; they just move on. Customer-contact employees can often head off such losses if they are given the responsibility to seek out those quiet, unhappy customers and do something to alleviate the causes of dissatisfaction quickly.

6. Find the root cause of service problems. In most service companies, management controls the process, and only a few groups have been trained to analyze information effectively to determine the root cause of problems. Rectifying this shortcoming will require education and time. Many companies still claim that they can't "afford" to give employees time to meet for an hour or two at the end of every week to discuss what they learned that week and to set priorities for improvements in the coming week. To be successful in the future, they can't afford not to.

7. Improve the process. Innovation and continuous improvement of processes have not traditionally been responsibilities of most employees. There is a significant difference between performing a task and playing a part in managing a process. The former can get repetitive quickly; the latter is continually engaging.

8. Have the power to routinely eliminate non-value-adding tasks. In most organizations many people are involved in some unproductive activities. Typically, only managers can choose to eliminate these value-subtracting tasks. Why? If we respect people's minds, why don't we trust them to get rid of activities that waste their time—or at least build a process that enables them to point out wasteful activities without fear of retaliation?

C17

YOU CAN'T FAKE IT!

In many companies, the attempt to increase employee involvement has been more fad than passion. In the abstract, employee involvement seemed like a good idea. But when it came right down to it, re-defining jobs to make them more challenging and giving employees greater responsibility was either too daunting, too hard, or too threatening and disruptive for too many managers. The shape of tomorrow's successful organizations is becoming clear, however. Although many companies have survived failed attempts at greater employee involvement in the past, it seems unlikely that they will be so lucky in the future.

The road to creating an organization in which employees can take responsibility for making a meaningful contribution will not be an easy one to travel, however, particularly at the outset. Greater involvement in the work and in the company must become a goal for every employee at every level. All employees must become partners in productivity, improvement, and innovation. Thinking, learning, skill development, and challenge must be designed into every job.

Keep in mind, too, that people can't be *made* to feel that their jobs are valuable or that they are an important part of the business. The only way for that to happen is to give them responsible positions and let them know how their performance impacts the company, its customers, its suppliers, and other stakeholders. **The simple truth is that if employees don't play a significant role in the business, you can't fool them into thinking they do.**

More Accountability, but Not More of the Same

With the freedom to choose, comes the consequences.
—Max DePree

Of the many ways organizations are trying to improve the performance of their workers, increased accountability is one of the most important. In most cases, if people are accountable for what they do, they'll do it better. Accountability can help provide focus, communicate priorities, indicate serious commitment to an issue, create a sense of urgency and tension, and demonstrate to all those in the organization that its leaders are even-handed and fair. In addition, and perhaps most significantly, recent studies indicate that accountability may be the single most important factor in effective decision making. It's hardly a surprise that people who have to live with the consequences of their decisions tend to make better ones.

The wrong kind of accountability, however, can focus energy on the wrong kind of activities, and can lead to the formation of habits that must be broken. For example, it is common for many managers to be largely accountable for pleasing their bosses or making their bosses look good to their bosses. Often too, managers are held accountable for short-term improvements in performance measurements that are achieved by mortgaging future opportunities; or for meeting agreed-upon performance targets, which may represent an improvement over yesterday's performance, but ignore the possibility of far greater improvement. Meanwhile, at lower levels of the organization, employees are frequently held accountable for complying with standard procedures and doing their job as it was designed to be performed instead of seeking out new and more efficient ways of doing the work, innovating the process, and better serving the customer.

Left unchanged, these accountability practices wed us to the past. They make it more rewarding (or at least less punishing) to do things as they have always been done. If, however, we want to provide people with a challenging role in a changing organization, we must design accountability so that it supports that role and encourages that change. The focus needs to be less on immediate (and sometimes meaningless) results and more on continuous (even unreasonable) improvement and learning. As legendary UCLA basketball coach John Wooden advised, "Don't measure yourself by what you have accomplished, but by what you should have accomplished with your ability."

Educator and best-selling author Charles Handy describes the need to change accountability practices as moving from Type I to Type II accountability. According to Handy, Type I accountability is old-style accountability—accountability for doing things correctly, for complying to standard practice. Type II accountability is for doing things as well as they can be done. It is accountability for reaching the potential of the process, then finding a better one. It is accountability for realizing our own personal potential.

With Type II accountability, we'd always be looking ahead rather than looking back. Instead of judging our progress primarily by our improvement, we'd analyze performance in light of what was possible. Instead of valuing contributions that conform to yesterday's methods, we'd value those that re-defined products, services, and processes. With Type II accountability, we'd look at the present process as an impediment to future improvement, rather than as an end in itself. The concept is simple . . . but anything *but* simple to implement. Doing so will require a complete refocusing of individual and group goals.

Shifting the Burden of Proof

It is an injustice, a grave evil and a disturbance of right order for a large and higher organization to arrogate to itself functions which can be performed efficiently by smaller and lower bodies . . . .

—Quadragesimo Anno (papal encyclical)

C17

IF EIGHTH GRADERS CAN DO IT, WHY CAN'T (OR DON'T) WE?

Imagine an eighth grade where students spend up to half their days being lawyer, banker or congressperson, and where many of the traditional responsibilities of teachers and principals are handled by student groups. Called Microsociety™ and founded by educator George Richmond, this experiment in education began in the early 1980s in a racially troubled, poorly performing school in Lowell, Massachusetts. Here, as in the other Microsociety schools it has spawned, students, not teachers create a society to manage their learning experience. They pass and enforce laws, manage their political system, sell goods and services using internal currency, set economic policy, and act as financiers and auditors. Now in its second decade, the school tests well above the national norm in reading and math, absenteeism is below six percent, and there are virtually no dropouts. In fact, students from all over the area are clamoring to get in.

The question is, if a troubled school in a racially charged environment can dramatically accelerate learning by allowing students to design their own society and take significant control of their own education, why can't we give our own front-line employees greater latitude in the design and control of their work? Surely, if we offered them that freedom, they would use it wisely in the realization of their own potential and that of the organization.

Most organizations work from the assumption that management knows best—that managers ought to have control until a convincing argument can be made to the contrary. If lower-level employees (or teams) seek greater authority, they must ask for it, then demonstrate that they deserve it, will use it wisely, and—maybe most importantly—show that transferring the authority will lead to a preferable result. The burden of proof, in other words, lies with the employees.

What if we shifted that burden to management? In this paradigm, the assumption would be that the people (or more likely, teams) who work the process also have complete authority over it and are held accountable for its success. Meanwhile, if anyone wants to centralize authority (i.e., move authority further up the heirarchy, assuming there is one), he or she will have to convince the organization that doing so would lead to a preferable outcome. It would also be up to the team to ask for the help it needed, submit its own budgets, measure its own performance, calculate its return on investment to the company, and generally justify that it is worthy of its members' salaries and the organization's decision to entrust it with ownership of the process.

Of course, shifting the burden of proof in this manner represents a major shift in the role of management in most organizations. While incorporating "empowered" teams into a traditional environment is a significant task, shifting the burden of proof is even more of a challenge, demanding entirely different accountability practices and an entirely different environment. Still, we feel that giving people the type of knee-knocking accountability that puts them at risk—the way that owners are at risk—is an effective alternative to a system that boasts empowerment, but often delivers a great deal less.

Several years ago, we asked Ralph Stayer, then CEO of Johnsonville Foods, about team training. "Mostly unnecessary," he replied. "Just give people a real job, and the team will form and work effectively." When the responsibility is there, when the authority is "real," and when people have job competency, they will do what they have to do to deliver the value they are being held accountable for.

The Ability/Accountability Mismatch

Companies that hope to reap the rewards of a committed, empowered workforce have to learn to stop kidding themselves. External commitment, positive thinking at any price, employees protected from the consequences and even the knowledge of cause and effect—this mindset may produce superficial honesty and single-loop learning, but it will

C17

never yield the kind of learning that might actually help a company change. The reason is quite simply that, for companies to change, employees must take an active role not only in describing the faults of others but also in drawing out the truth about their own behavior and motivation. In my experience, moreover, employees dig deeper and harder into the truth when the task of scrutinizing the organization includes taking a good look at their own roles, responsibilities, and potential contributions to corrective action.

—Chris Argyris, *Harvard Business Review*

THE OTHER 'E' WORD

A friend of ours received her "Notice of Auto Insurance Rate Increase" a few months back. She was shocked to find that her premium had been raised by more than $900. Upset and furious, she immediately called the company's headquarters for an explanation.

"You were in an accident," the clerk she was connected to told her. It was not her agent, nor was it anyone she had ever spoken with before.

"Yes, but that wasn't my fault. The other driver was cited."

There was a pause on the other end of the line. "I have your file in front of me," the clerk said. Then, after a few more seconds he concluded, "You're right. We must have made a mistake. We're sorry for the inconvenience. Please disregard the notice."

When we heard this story, we were impressed with how easily the mix-up was resolved and that a front-line worker had the authority to make a $900 decision on the spot. So we called the company ourselves and spoke to one of its executives.

"Tell me about how you 'empower' workers," we asked.

"We don't use that 'E' word," he said. "We use the other 'E' word."

"Which one?"

> "Education," he said. "We ensure that every person who has contact with a customer has all of the information they need to make a business decision."
>
> He went on—"We think it's a crime to try and decentralize decision making without giving people the tools to make good decisions."

C17

Nothing is more unfair than holding someone accountable for something they can't do. Yet, in their rush to extend accountability, this is precisely what many organizations have done (and continue to do). We've asked workers, especially on the front line, to improve and be accountable for their performance. In many cases, however, we've given them little control over the process, which is frequently the cause of most of the problems that exist. In other words, the accountability is there, but the individual employee's ability to meet it is not. As a result, workers are often frustrated, customers are disgruntled, and we rarely get the improvement we're looking for.

How can this mismatch between ability and accountability be averted? How can we be certain that accountability is fair and supports our efforts to improve and change? Here are three questions to ask before assigning accountability:

1. What must be done? Before people can be held accountable, they must have a clear understanding of what it is they are being held accountable <u>for</u>. In any event, they shouldn't be held accountable for performing an activity. Rather, people should be accountable primarily for making a significant contribution.

Also, more frequently than anyone wants to admit, people are held accountable for tasks not worth performing. Every task for which an individual is to be held accountable must be examined to ensure that it adds value. If a task is not worth doing, don't hold anyone accountable for doing it. In fact, *stop* doing it!

2. Who will be accountable? Who's responsible? Is it someone or some group? Too often responsibility is unclear. Accountability should be assigned at the lowest level possible. Those closest to customers (or processes) are best equipped to deal with them, and should, therefore, be the ones who are held accountable for the consequences of their actions. When there are teams, there should be team, not individual, accountability. Team members must win or lose as a team.

We're not talking casual accountability here, but genuine "buck-stops-here" accountability. So when the question is asked, "Who's accountable here?" there's a single raised hand, not a half-dozen fingers pointing in every direction. This is not to say that accountability should engender fear, but rather that each person should be responsible for his or her actions. Besides, accountability is inevitably accompanied by a certain amount of discomfort.

3. What abilities will those being held accountable need to achieve success? The issues raised by this question are often discussed, but rarely resolved. We've seen few systematic plans to ensure that the right people in the process have sufficient control or the right skills to do the job required. This problem is sometimes compounded by a managerial mindset that often results in managers receiving the lion's share of the benefits of training and education.

The question also arises, "How much ability is enough?" There is no definitive answer. We do know, however, that the ability to succeed today will probably not be adequate a year from now, and that the best companies are focusing their training efforts 12–18 months into the future. While some of the skills that these companies invest in today may not be transferable to present processes, learning that will result from broader experiences and education, more experimentation, process improvement skills, and facility in handling information better will enable these companies to adapt to change more quickly, respond with greater flexibility, and shift course more effectively when the time is right.

What *are* the elements that constitute the "ability to succeed?" Clearly, there is more involved than the formal training we usually associate with making someone "able." Here are some questions to spark discussion about a person's or group's ability to perform specific tasks.

To what extent do these people or groups have:

Goal Clarity

- Do they understand customer and other stakeholder interests?

- Do they have a consistent vision of desired outcomes?

- Do they understand the company's strategy and their group's role in the process?

Education and Experience

- Do they understand the complexities of the task?

- Do they have the ability to anticipate potential problems?

- Do they have the ability to predict the consequences of different courses of action in a variety of circumstances?

Control of the Process

Do They Have the Authority to

- Change or redesign the process as required?

- Deviate from the process when called for?

- Influence peers and other departments to achieve needed cooperation?

Information

- Do they have access to the information needed to analyze the process (understand customer needs/trends) and make decisions regarding the most effective courses of action?

Resources

- Do they have the people, financial resources, tools, space, etc., required to efficiently accomplish the task?

Time

- Do they have a reasonable time frame?
  (Note: There are no unrealistic goals, only unreasonable time frames. However, too much time pressure can limit alternatives unnecessarily, while too little time pressure can delay change efforts.)

Shared Values

- Do they have a standard for decision making?

C H A L L E N G E   1 8

Building Organizational DNA: A Framework for Effectively Managing Risk

If we allow autonomy at the local level, letting individuals or units be directed in their decisions by guideposts for organizational self-reference, we can achieve coherence and continuity. Self-organization succeeds when the system supports the independent activity of its members by giving them, quite literally, a strong frame of reference.

—Margaret Wheatley, *Leadership and the New Science*

*I*t is currently fashionable (and entirely appropriate, we feel) to compare the organization to a huge and highly complex self-organizing physical system or organism. Looking at such a system under a microscope, we would see a stable center. Yet, at the system's periphery, where it encounters the external environment, the system appears chaotic. Keeping the organism intact and functional in the face of this chaos is the DNA molecule that is carried by virtually every cell in the system. Each of these molecules, in turn, contains a genetic fingerprint of the larger organism of which it is a part. Cells found in an animal's hair or blood, for example, share the same unique DNA pattern as those that make up its bones or skin. With DNA, in other words, every cell will always be characteristic of that system—even as old cells die and new ones take their place, they will assume the same shape, organization, and behavior.

C18

Applied to the organization, DNA can be thought of as the systemic code of information carried by every employee as well as his or her link to the organization's stable core—its vision, values, and decision-making criteria. In organizations where DNA exists, individuals—even those thousands of miles from headquarters and thousands of miles from one another—all function as members of that system. Therefore, when confronted with similar problems or requests, they will tend to make similar decisions. With DNA, in other words, the organization can support decentralized decision making, maintaining a sense of order even as it adapts to a changing environment.

Unfortunately, many of today's organizations don't have organizational DNA, either because there is no shared vision, because values aren't articulated (and lived), because decision-making criteria have not been established, or a combination of the three. In place of DNA, most organizations have extensive rules—rules that have proliferated to accommodate every possible situation. We've all seen the countless manuals and SOPs that are meant to govern every action and inform every decision made in the organization. We've also seen how referring to these manuals—in actual fact, or in our heads—often slows the process and gets in the way of delighting customers. Aware of how counterproductive rules can be, some of us have significantly reduced their number. In place of the rules, we've empowered people to act—only to find that they are reluctant to assume that responsibility because, in the absence of organizational DNA, the risk of doing so is simply too great.

Lacking DNA, how can we go about creating it in our organization? How can we genetically engineer this essential substance to enable us to decentralize our decision-making process and give people the parameters they need to act along with the power we may have already given them? Not, we're convinced, by looking to the Disneys and Nordstroms of the world, companies whose DNA has been forged through decades of experience and handed down through generations of employees. Trying to copy the methods of a Disney or Nordstrom without their history and pervasive cultures

Will quickly prove frustrating for most companies—although these organizations and others like them can serve as long-term models.

It would be far more productive to look at the experience of a division of a major power company that streamlined its installation and repair service by empowering its linemen to make decisions in the field. This organization began by adopting the following criteria to guide decision making:

1. Exceed the customer's expectations.

2. Treat every individual with respect.

3. Protect the long-term financial health of the company.

4. If you can't do it safely and ethically, don't do it.

Immediately after the field people were given these criteria, however, there were questions and confusion. "What *are* our customers' expectations?" "What does 'long-term financial health' even mean?" Also, until they were presented with these criteria, linemen had always been told that the reason they couldn't make decisions on their own was that the company was afraid of the legal ramifications of their actions. Now, suddenly, it was "all systems go." Clearly there was a notable lack of information and a great deal of misinformation standing in the way of linemen taking the initiative. A training program was devised to give these individuals the background and information they would need to make informed and intelligent decisions.

Nine months later, at a meeting that we attended and that included linemen and other employees of the company, more than a few people were still skeptical of the power company's efforts to "empower" its employees. One particularly vocal lineman from the division rose in defense of his division's efforts: "Hey," he said, "it used to be risky to deviate from standard practice. Now, all I have to do is ask four questions. If my boss doesn't agree with my decision, I know we'll be discussing these same four questions:

C18

Will the decision I made help me exceed my customer's expectations? Is what I've done respectful to all individuals? Is it in the best long-term financial interests of the company? Can I do it safely, legally, and ethically? If I made a good attempt to measure my decision against these criteria, my boss and division manager will support my taking the initiative. And if I didn't, then they'd have every right to be on my case."

In today's world, we need people willing to take risks to improve the process and better serve the customer. Without DNA coursing through the organization, there's no effective way to manage risks, so people will simply shy away from taking them. With DNA, we can all take risks, we can all fail, and we can all learn. And we can do it all knowing that we will be supported, without the fear of being branded a failure.

C H A L L E N G E   1 9

Abolishing the Corporate Caste System

I've seen knights in armor panic at the first sight of battle. I've seen the lowliest unarmed squire pull a spear from his own body to defend a dying horse. Nobility is not a birthright; it is defined by one's actions.

> —Kevin Costner as Robin Hood, *Robin Hood, Prince of Thieves*

People could feel this useful overconfidence, McClelland said, only if they thought that society was open and their lives were changeable. He wrote, "What a modern society needs for successful development is flexibility in a man's role relationships. His entire network of relations to others should not be traditionally determined by his caste or even by his occupational status." That is, he should not know his place.

> —James Fallows, *More Like Us*

*R*ecently a pharmacist told us how lucky he felt that his family had immigrated to the United States when he was young. He said that if he had remained in India, he would never have been allowed to become a pharmacist. After all, he was a shoemaker's son. In America, he went on, people are not as limited by their social status, and have a reason to stay motivated because they have more control over their future. They do not have to *"know their place."*

In many organizations today, a large number of employees are given the not so subtle message that they should "know their place." For many, there is little in the work environment that encourages them to reinvent the way work is done or to invent new roles for themselves. In fact, often the exact opposite is communi-

C19

cated. People are taught that bucking the system can be career-limiting and that obedience and being perceived as a good team player are all-important. They are expected to learn their roles quickly and not to venture too far into someone else's turf.

In the traditional command and control structures where many of us began our careers, the differential treatment of different classes of employees was at the heart of maintaining order and obedience in the hierarchy. The costly by-product of these practices, however, has been reduced flexibility, less learning, and an increased feeling of helplessness among certain groups. History and common sense tell us that we are healthier and more productive when we resist the instinct (natural or otherwise) to set ourselves apart from those with whom we work.

From G.I. Joe to Joe College

When Congress considered the GI Bill, which offered a free or subsidized college education to all returning World War II veterans, many noted educators warned that colleges would become hobo jungles and that such a lax admission policy would not ensure that the best students were selected. Several proposed restricting the program to only a carefully selected number of the most able veterans.

Wisely, our legislators passed the bill and returning veterans brought a new energy to college and university campuses. They were more mature, better motivated, and had had more life experience than most other college students. A large number also excelled academically.

The veterans who participated in this program were fortunate that their opportunities for education and future careers hadn't been thwarted by those who demanded a rigorous exclusionary selection process. The greatest beneficiary of the bill, however, was America, as many of the GI students went on to become the engineers, doctors, educators, and managers who led the nation into its greatest period of growth and expansion.

Providing inspiration and impetus for the past successes of many of our leaders has often been the distinctly American notion that anyone can be anything they want to be—that anyone can grow up to be president. Where you were born is regarded as far less of an obstacle to success in this country than in others. After all, America was built by men and women who transcended their past and who believed they could change their fate. Refusing to know their place, those who came before us dreamed a dream of unlimited possibilities and created an unparalleled level of innovation. Our recent entrepreneurial history suggests that this dream is still alive for many. However, for a growing number of people locked in certain jobs (particularly in the service sector), the American dream is just that—a dream. Where you went to school, *if* you went to school, where you entered the organization, who you worked for, and which department trained you can brand you and greatly influence your ability to grow and succeed.

The unfortunate fact is that the first impression you make may make or break your career in many companies. We've all either been there or seen it happen: the boss takes a liking to us and, therefore, gives us more responsibility, treats us as an important team member, delegates decision-making responsibility, and works hard to ensure that we are supported. The not so subtle communication is that we've been selected as a top performer and, not surprisingly, we often succeed. Even if we fail along the way, the person who "marked us for success" has a vested interest in ensuring that his or her judgment was correct and bails us out. On the other hand, we have all seen what can happen when people are branded with less favorable endorsements. They get less interesting assignments, less responsibility, less decision-making authority, and less positive support. For some employees, the result seems inevitable. They are treated as part of the underclass and success is substantially more difficult for them to achieve.

While some of the messages about our status are subtle, many are often explicit and unambiguous. Try eating in the executive dining room if you don't rate. Have we ever figured out why many

C19

promotions necessitate a slightly larger office, fancier desk, better furnishings, and maybe even "real" art? And just listen to what we call one another—"boss," "subordinate," "manager," "bargaining unit," or "hourly employee." The meaning underlying our words is worth pondering. Is it indicative of a mindset that demands visible differences in status to maintain control? We once worked with an executive who was willing to spend millions of dollars to reorganize the entire company to, as he put it, "break down barriers to communication." But he was absolutely unwilling to discuss giving up his assigned parking place. In too many organizations, having the indices of success is perceived to be more important than the quality of one's performance.

Our roles in perpetuating status differences in our organizations may be difficult to evaluate until we experience what it is like to work without them. It is hard to explain the learning that can accrue when you enter a world where status does not play as large a role. Touring Honda's assembly plant in Marysville amid a sea of white lab coats one day, we were totally immersed in a conversation with a man we assumed was a front-line team member. An hour later, our host introduced us to this individual as a Honda executive, leaving us to consider all the reasons why we had thought he worked on the front line rather than in management, and how our new knowledge altered the way we now perceived him. In fact, we had always prided ourselves on not being significantly influenced by a person's position. But we left Marysville with uncomfortable questions about our assumptions.

The full effect of the subtle (and often not so subtle) messages created as a by-product of treating people differently within an organization is sometimes not readily apparent to those who work there. If, however, we can step back far enough to get an objective view, it becomes quickly evident that the unintended caste system that has been created significantly undermines our ability to capture the potential of the workforce. Class distinctions tend to create bureaucracy, lessen self-esteem, and lead to a feeling in many individuals that they have little control over the systems in which they work. Downsizing and flattening organizational hierarchies might help cut down on the negative effects of class distinctions, but if companies don't change the structures that created the problems initially, it won't be long before a similar caste system emerges.

C19

But why? What will it buy us? The benefits of these practices are hard to comprehend, and yet there is little doubt that they can rob the organization of the very values it must have to prosper in the future. *We need to create structures which communicate that people should not know their place.* We need people eager to remake their roles in search of new ways to make a meaningful contribution. The good news is that in organizations where things have to get done, and done quickly, people have less time for and less patience with the trappings of status. In these organizations, the demonstrated ability to contribute is everything and class and status are next to nothing. The challenge then is for each of us to choose to make it increasingly more difficult to unfairly or unnecessarily differentiate among our fellow employees.

C H A L L E N G E   2 0

Developing a Persistent, Obsessive, Optimistic Environment

Life inflicts the same setbacks and tragedies on the optimist as on the pessimist, but the optimist weathers them better. As we have seen, the optimist bounces back from defeat, and, with his life somewhat poorer, he picks up and starts again. The pessimist gives up and falls into depression. Because of his resilience, the optimist achieves more at work, at school, and on the playing field. The optimist has better physical health and may even live longer. Americans want optimists to lead them. Even when things go well for the pessimist, he is haunted by forebodings of catastrophe.

—Martin Seligman, *Learned Optimism*

*M*ost of us believe that optimism in the workplace can be a blessing, pessimism can be a problem, and helplessness—that is, the sense that there's nothing we can do to improve our situation— is a feeling to be avoided. Many of us even know an optimist or two—a persistent salesperson who won't take no for an answer and is undeterred by the inevitable string of rejections that comes with the job; or the successful, seemingly obsessed leader who persists in doing what everyone tells him or her is impossible. Still, there is strong evidence that more and more people are beginning to feel pessimistic about their ability to impact the organization. Although we still believe in the importance of optimism, it is becoming an increasingly rare commodity in some organizations— despite the fact that it is critical to our efforts to adapt in continuously changing times.

The more uncertainty that exists, and the more complex the issues we face, the more experiments we must conduct, and the greater the number of mistakes that will inevitably result. To the optimist, these mistakes are speed bumps, necessary minor irritations, challenges on a road that ultimately leads to a desirable outcome. Optimists tend to be more persistent and less affected by unanticipated difficulties. Their solutions tend to be more imaginative and creative and they are usually more avid learners. On the other hand, to the pessimist, or to someone who has learned to feel helpless, mistakes don't seem like speed bumps. To these individuals, mistakes can appear as the unexpected end of the road. Demoralized, they can't even imagine finding an alternate route to success. For some, even the smallest problem is thought to be a disabling event over which they have little, if any, control. Predictably, these individuals expend less effort on the job and their successes are infrequent.

If there were only a few pessimistic employees in our organizations, their effect might not be so disabling. The fact that there are many—it is said that two-thirds of Americans today tend to be pessimists—means that the performance of virtually every corporation has been impacted. Whether the feelings of helplessness that often accompany pessimism have been learned outside the workplace or on the job as a result of past practices, employee pessimism is a gargantuan value subtractor. This is particularly the case as we increasingly rely on employees at every level to learn, experiment, and use data to innovate and improve performance. We must, therefore, refuse to give in to pessimism. We must learn to be optimistic, and help others do the same. We must also redesign those organizational structures that create a work environment in which individuals have little control and where a feeling of helplessness is perpetuated.

Unfortunately, many traditional management practices contribute to creating and perpetuating precisely such an environment. For many employees, especially those at the base of the organizational hierarchy, narrow, rigid job descriptions communicate that the individual can have little effect on the design of his or her work. Reinforcing this message are job demands for which workers receive insufficient training, information, and resources. When employees perceive that they are not trusted, or that their past efforts have not been valued, their tendency to be optimistic is inhibited and their pessimistic tendency is encouraged. Traditional practices that lead to finding fault with people instead of processes, dismantling improvement efforts before they can be successful, limiting feedback, perpetuating inflexible procedures, and creating a corporate caste system that communicates that employees should "know their place" are counterproductive. The cumulative effect of these practices fuels a sense of helplessness in many employees and reduces their ability to persevere in the face of the resistance inherent in most change efforts.

If change is what we are after, we have little choice, therefore, but to eliminate those structures that tend to increase feelings of helplessness in people. We need to build employee confidence and provide individuals with a sense of control over their environment. People should have the opportunity to participate meaningfully throughout the organization and have a significant say in the way work is done. Substantial involvement is not optional but a prerequisite to building an effective, optimistic team. Optimistic people and teams learn more, achieve more, and are more successful. Optimists usually lead happier and healthier lives and have a lot more fun.

Nevertheless, optimism isn't always preferable. Because pessimists tend to see the world more as it is, and optimists perceive it more as it suits their needs, being an occasional pessimist can be a real benefit. If, for example, you're considering a decision that "bets the company," it's better to be somewhere along the continuum between realism and pessimism. However, in approaching most tasks, the advantages of optimism can be substantial and its benefits in many organizations are largely unrealized.

We're not suggesting that it will be easy to make optimists out of people who have learned to be more pessimistic—or turn yourself into an optimist if you're not. But because optimism and pessimism are states of mind, they can be influenced and ultimately changed. All of us must resist the temptation to give in to the feeling that our actions don't matter.

TURNING FAILURES INTO LEARNING OPPORTUNITIES

To characterize a mistake as a learning opportunity—as has been recommended by many in recent years—does little good unless the person who is doing the characterizing believes it to be true. As a general rule, optimists will and pessimists won't. The more optimistic a person is in his or her ability to solve a problem, the greater the chance that person will view failure as an opportunity. However, people who believe that the problem and its causes are out of their control, that they are helpless to affect the result, and that they might even be at fault are less able to learn from their mistakes and take corrective action. How a person perceives a given situation is everything. Putting a different label on a set of facts doesn't automatically make things better. If we want to encourage people to see mistakes or failures as opportunities, we must create an environment that supports this concept and that communicates to all employees that:

- **Failure is temporary.** The result of any failed attempt can be overcome with time and hard work.

- **Failure is natural.** In most complex endeavors, there will be more failures than successes. Succeeding only once out of ten tries might be a perfectly acceptable average in some situations.

- **Failure is probably not their fault.** Yes, we should take responsibility for our actions. But a majority of the problems we encounter on the job are precipitated by the way work has been organized, not through the fault of individual participants.

C20

- **Failure is the key to learning.** Every unsuccessful attempt is a chance to increase our understanding of the system and to experiment further. Failing doesn't mean giving up; it means looking for alternatives.

Martin Seligman, author of *Learned Optimism*, has said that each of us carries a word in our heart. For some of us that word is "yes." Yes, we believe we can succeed. Yes, we can learn. Yes, we can make a difference. Others carry a "no," with all the negative baggage that accompanies it. As leaders, we must realize which word we carry and how it enhances or inhibits our ability to lead. Skills and desire are not enough to succeed. We must also be convinced that we *can* . . . and be able to convince others, as well. If we are passionately optimistic, odds are that our optimism will be contagious. In any event, our improvement efforts, no matter how well considered, will have little chance of succeeding if a significant part of the workforce feels powerless to make a difference.

A MODEST PROPOSAL: THE EMPLOYEE BILL OF RIGHTS

It is your right as an employee of this company to work in an environment that is consistent with the following values. It is your responsibility to participate in the continuous improvement of the work environment and to hold others in the organization accountable for doing the same. It is your right to voice an opinion, and any person inhibiting your feedback is subject to immediate dismissal.

It is every employee's right . . .

1. To be part of a cause that is worthy of commitment

2. To have a challenging and meaningful role

3. To be trusted

4. To be treated honestly, fairly, and respectfully

5. To have the opportunity to learn

6. To be part of a supportive and caring environment

Often we are hesitant to make these promises for fear that we can't deliver. If we choose to make the promise, we have no choice!

Leader as Hero

We find people in other organizations who have great aspirations but who are not given the opportunity to reach their potential. We hire them and then let them be themselves. We support their efforts to take us to a new level of excellence.

> —General Manager of one of the world's top five hotels responding to the question, "Where do you find these outrageous service professionals?"

8

Leader as Hero

Respect, loyalty, security, dignity—old-fashioned qualities for a new-fashioned economy. Earlier this century machines helped liberate our ancestors from the toil of the fields. In this generation, wondrous technology has freed us from the drudgery of the assembly line and enabled us to speed new products to far-off markets. As we approach the millennium, it is people who will carry us forward. In an economy built on service, the extent to which we prosper will depend on our ability to educate, entertain, empower, and ennoble ourselves—and each other.

—Fortune

In every culture, people have tried to emulate those individuals, real or imagined, who best represented the highest values of the era and who pursued a worthy cause in the face of substantial adversity. We have both revered and studied heroes—from Christ to Gandhi, from Churchill to Kennedy, and from John Wayne characters to Luke Skywalker—with the hope of becoming more like them.

Perhaps it is the hero potential in us all that drives us and fuels our fascinations. It seems that every person yearns for the opportunity to make a difference, and our heroes provide us with role models that provide guidance and a sense of hope. Coaching Little League, leading scouting programs, teaching, improving the environment, volunteering our time for charity, or in a thousand other ways, we are determined to leave our mark on the world. While most of us don't expect to have the impact of a Gandhi or the universal recognition of a Muhammad Ali, we nevertheless work diligently to have as much impact as we can. Of course, we don't expect that making the heroic effort will be easy or without risk. In fact, it is the hero's persistence in the face of adversity that captures our imagination.

If this is true, if most of us have an innate desire to be heroes, why then haven't we structured our work environment in a way that can support our aspirations? Why isn't our system one that enables us to become heroes on the job, where we spend so much time and expend so much energy? Why haven't we created a workplace that is consonant with our collective dreams, rather than one that most of us try to forget the moment we leave the office? The reasons are many and varied. For some leaders, the successes of the past have blurred their vision of what is possible. For others, the need for predictability and fear of complexity have made it difficult to rethink their basic assumptions about what works and what doesn't. Still others have simply ceased to care.

It is time now for each of us to ask, "Why?"—to question our beliefs about people, and to begin to experiment in earnest with new organizational designs that will help unleash the potential of the people who work with us. It is time to work in concert to design the organization that will enable us <u>all</u> to realize our dreams, to become heroes together. What will it take? Who will tomorrow's heroes be? For the answer, let's look first at the characteristics of the traditional hero.

Heroes

- **Deal in transformational change.** No one ever became a hero by perpetuating the status quo.

- **Adopt the highest of values** and are committed to these values even in the face of adversity.

- **Overcome a number of substantial obstacles** that threaten their ability to create the desired changes.

- **Deal effectively with uncertainty.** At most times during the hero's journey, success is in doubt.

- **Rarely work alone.** Achievement of the desired goals usually requires the hero to enlist the assistance of others.

- **Are values-driven.** The hero influences others through the strength of his or her ideas. In most cases, the hero is more driven by a sense of purpose than opportunity.

- **Are persistent** even in the face of extreme skepticism.

- **Think differently.** There are marked differences in the way the hero thinks and what is considered conventional wisdom.

- **Create a different sense of order.** Challenging the present system in order to create a system that is consistent with the hero's purpose is central to the hero's actions.

- **Are internally driven** and seem relatively unaffected by external rewards, threats, or punishments.

It's no coincidence that these characteristics are one and the same with those of the effective leader of tomorrow's organization, as discussed in this book—i.e., change agent, visionary, values-driven, persistent, participative, and creative. There is also little question in our minds that most people have the willingness and ability to develop these characteristics quickly and that given the opportunity to do so, these men and women will be the individuals who will bring about the transformational change necessary for success in the future. And, that in the days and years to come, that they, that we, can all be heroes—to those we work with, to our loyal customers, and to ourselves. For the leader as hero is no mythical figure to be viewed with awe, but a contemporary thinker and doer confident in the face of uncertainty and unafraid to take on the challenge of change in the inescapably human and complex structure that is today's organization.

Acknowledgments

For Gary Heil

I've been very fortunate to have had the help and support of many in this endeavor. I realize that thanking all, or even most, of those who helped me is impossible. However, I would like to thank a few people to whom I owe a particular debt of gratitude:

Without the support of my wife and partner, Carol, the companionship of my best friend (and son), Ryan, the smile of my baby daughter, Michaela, and the continued patience of my Dad, any accomplishment would seem less meaningful.

Tom Parker, best-selling author, Pulitzer Prize nominee, corporate communicator, popular educator, and organizational consultant. Tom brought his wit, unique experience, and inquisitive mind to the effort, and I will forever be grateful for his willingness to collaborate and his friendship.

Rick Tate's insights garnered through his diverse experiences as line manager, educator, and consultant provided a unique perspective on the issues. Rick has the unique ability to mesh the theoretical with the practical. Rick's perspectives on leadership have been a constant source of learning for me for almost two decades.

This book happened because Deborah Collins Stephens willed it to happen. She is the type of leader whom we tried to describe in the book. She is flexible, energetic, directed, and empathetic. She lives the values that most of us aspire to. She was the glue that brought together our team, challenged our thinking, demanded a continuously improving product, and showed us what is possible when a person is outrageously optimistic.

Harry Rhoads and Bernie Swain manage one of the best service companies in the world—bar none. Through their leadership, the Washington Speaker's Bureau gives meaning to the words *customer focus* and *values driven*. Their belief in me, their friendship, and their support have touched every aspect of my life. I am a fan!

I owe a special thanks to Ken Blanchard for his mentorship. Without his help and guidance, I would not have had many of the learning opportunities I experienced. I am proud to have been his student.

Celebrated discontent describes Pam Treski, Victoria Burton Taylor, and Bob Gardner. Friends and colleagues, who, for more than a decade, have challenged my thinking and helped me learn to learn. In their own special ways, they touch everyone they meet. Through their example, they teach the power of giving.

Without Joanna Donati's support in the beginning, our business would not have survived. Francesca Ruggieri was always there to organize the unorganized and to support our efforts with a smile that brightened every day.

The team at VNR provided support, resources, and guidance. They continually demonstrated a level of flexibility that is uncommon in most service organizations. We're lucky to be on their team.

Without clients, there would be no learning. I feel most fortunate to have had the opportunity to learn from some of the best and I deeply appreciate these opportunities. It is their voices that are contained on these pages. I believe all of us are struggling with the pace and nature of the changes we face, and finding a group of people we can learn from and learn with is fundamental to effective action. I can only hope that I added a fraction of the value to their endeavors that they added to mine.

For Tom Parker

Acknowledging that there are too many people to acknowledge, and that, as always, there is too little time to do so, this book is for:

> My wife, Kathy—soulmate, alter-ego, editor extraordinaire— who was always there, even when I wasn't (which was often);
> Tomorrow's (tough) customer, my seven-and-a-half-year-old son, Gabe;
> Ellen Dasher, who believed in the importance of people and communication in the workplace long before it was popular;
> David Samec whose Czech-ered past, probing intellect, and ability to transform himself make him my favorite American dreamer;
> Sandra Kurtzig, who convinced me (but didn't show me how) work could be fun; and
> Bob McIntire, whom I can always count on to be the loyal opposition.

For Rick Tate

Over the years, I've been very fortunate to have had the opportunity to work with numerous men and women from all types of organizations and institutions. Their experiences and stories have enriched my life and certainly played a major role in the development of this book. To them, I am greatly indebted. I would also like to thank the following people for their support and encouragement:

To my wife Cynthia and our children, Tiffany, Travis, Tyler, Lauren, and Haley, for the joy and balance they bring to my life.

To Carrie James for her total commitment and partnership in my efforts over the years.

To Sean Ryan, my friend and colleague who has helped me formulate ideas and thoughts.

To Deborah Stephens whose confidence in our abilities and persistence helped make this book possible.

To Sam and Maureen Shriver for their collaboration on the *Frontline Service Program*, our collegial relationship, and most of all, their friendship.

To Bill Wade of the National Park Service, Jerry Gilbert of Johnson and Johnson, Melanie Holmes and John Poland of Manpower, and Rick Baron of Rainbird, I am blessed to count you as friends, customers, and colleagues. Your loyalty has been very important and your input has always improved my work.

To Deborah Lily of our staff for her continual help and support, which have given me the time to attend to this project.

To Paul Hersey of the Center for Leadership Studies who greatly assisted me in the beginning of my career and inspired me in the early days.

To Ken Blanchard whose personal example has taught me much of what I know about organizational behavior.

And finally, to the staff and management of VNR who supported our efforts and at times our "strategically planned, unreasonable goals!"

Sources

PREFACE

"America's culture is . . .": James Fallows, *More Like Us* (Houghton Mifflin Company, Boston, 1989), p. 48.

PART 1: LEADER AS REVOLUTIONARY

"I hold it . . .": Thomas Jefferson in a letter to James Madison, 1787.

"People repeatedly overlook a new type of organization . . .": Karl Wieck, excerpted from R.T. Pascale, *Managing on the Edge* (Simon & Schuster, New York, 1990), p. 105.

"I really think you have to question the sanity . . .": Bob Allen, CEO of AT & T, "Phone Giant Answers Call of Change," *USA Today*, March 1994, cover story.

"A non-violent revolution . . .": Mohandas K. Gandhi, "Nonviolence in Peace and War," speech delivered by Gandhi, 1948.

"Do or do not . . .": Dialogue from the movie *The Empire Strikes Back*, George Lucas, Producer, Lucas Films Limited Production, 20th Century Fox Release.

PART 2: LEADER AS SYSTEM ARCHITECT

"Put simply, while traditional science . . .": David H. Freedman, "Is Management Still a Science?" *Harvard Business Review*, Nov.–Dec. 1992, p. 26.

"A system is an assembly . . .": Douglas McGregor, *The Professional Manager* (McGraw-Hill, New York, 1967), p. 39.

"It is natural for any system . . .": Margaret Wheatley, *Leadership and the New Science* (Berrett–Koehler, San Francisco, CA, 1992), p. 96.

"CBS did not pay for news stories . . .": Linda Ellerbee, *And So It Goes: Adventures in Publishing* (Berkeley Publishing, New York, 1987).

"At the end of only six days . . .": Phillip Zimbardo in Elliot Aronson, *The Social Animal* (W. H. Freeman, New York, 1980), p. 10.

"All too often, new management innovations . . .": Peter Senge, *The Fifth Discipline: The Art and Practice of the Learning Organization* (Doubleday/Currency, New York, 1990), p. 11.

"Freud said that . . .": William Caudill, *The TIBS of Bill Caudill* (CRSS, Dallas, TX, 1984), p. 25.

"The important implication . . .": Douglas McGregor, *The Professional Manager* (McGraw-Hill, New York, 1967), p. 19.

. . . An infinitesimal change . . .": David H. Freedman, "Is Management Still a Science?" *Harvard Business Review*, Nov.–Dec. 1992, p. 30.

"I have argued that . . .": Douglas McGregor, *The Professional Manager* (McGraw-Hill, New York, 1967), p. 39.

Challenge 1: Strategically Planned Unreasonableness: Building a Constituency for Change

"People who describe themselves . . .": Roger Ailes, "Break the Rules and Win," *Success*, Jan.–Feb. 1994, pp. 36–37.

"The best place . . .": Stan Davis and Bill Davidson, *2020 Vision: Transform Your Business Today to Succeed in Tomorrow's Economy* (Simon & Schuster, New York, 1991), p. 113.

"Pride and Discontent:" Microsoft information supplied to the authors through interviews conducted with Microsoft employees in Redmond, WA.

Challenge 2: "By What Method?": Learning to Learn

"I believe that human beings . . .": Ed Simon, President and CEO of Herman Miller, excerpted from Peter M. Senge, *The Fifth Discipline: The Art and Practice of the Learning Organization* (Doubleday/Currency, New York, 1990), p. 348.

"Dr. Ignoramus," *Contra Costra Times*, San Ramon, CA, March 1993.

Challenge 3: Rethinking Our Thinking: Building a Foundation for Systematic Improvement

"When we transcend . . .": R. T. Pascale, *Managing on the Edge* (Simon & Schuster, New York), p. 110.

"The surest way . . .": Peter Elbow, *Embracing Contraries: Explorations in Learning and Teaching* (Oxford University Press, New York, 1987), p. 12.

"I stand up on my desk . . .": Dialogue from the movie *Dead Poets Society*, Peter Weir, Steven Haft, Whit Thomas, Producers, Touchstone Pictures Release, Burbank, CA.

Challenge 4: Managing the Gap: Sharing a Vision, Values, and Sense of Reality

"If you ask me . . .": Mike Walsh, "Managing," *Fortune*, Dec. 14, 1992, p. 110.

"When there is no vision . . .": Charles Handy, *The Age of Paradox* (Harvard Business School Press, Cambridge, MA, 1994), p. 96.

"All my life . . .": Jane Wagner, *In Search of Intelligent Life in the Universe* (Harper and Row: San Francisco, CA, 1986) p. 35.

"The values gap . . .": Andrall E. Pearson, "Corporate Redemption and the Seven Deadly Sins," *Harvard Business Review,* May–June 1992.

"A corporation's values . . .": Max DePree, *Leadership Is an Art* (Michigan State University Press, East Lansing, MI, 1987), p. 102.

Carlson Team Pledge, reprinted with permission from Carlson Travel Group, Inc., Minneapolis, MN.

"Why do we persist . . .": Douglas McGregor, *The Professional Manager* (McGraw-Hill, New York, 1967), p. 36.

Challenge 5: Information: Changing the "Need to Know" to the "Right to Know"

"An individual without information . . .": Jan Carlzon, *Moments of Truth* (Ballinger Cambridge–Harper and Row, San Francisco, CA, 1987), p. 1.

"Of all the skills of leadership . . .": Peter Nulty, "The National Business Hall of Fame," *Fortune,* April 4, 1994, p. 118.

Challenge 6: Capturing the Advantages of Diversity: Learning to Love the Weird

". . . When I listened closely . . .": C. W. Kim and R. A. Mauborgne, "The Parables of Leadership," *Harvard Business Review,* April–May 1992, p. 4.

"Be patient toward all . . .": Rainer Maria Rilke, excerpted from J. Welwood, *Journey of the Heart: Intimate Relationships and the Path of Love.* (HarperCollins: New York), p. 10.

"The Power of Why": Information was supplied to the authors during interviews with Northern Telecom employees in the Morrisville, NC, plant.

"Paul MacCready's 'Weird' Electric Car": Reprinted with permission from Pacific Bell Corporation, Management Telesis Division, San Ramon, CA.

Challenge 7: Competitively Disadvantaged: Building Cooperation Instead of Internal Competition

"We act competitively . . .": Alfie Kohn, *No Contest* (Houghton Mifflin Company, Boston, 1986), p. 29.

"Are they the people . . .": Stan Davis and Bill Davidson, *2020 Vision: Transform Your Business Today to Succeed in Tomorrow's Economy* (Simon & Schuster, New York), p. 112.

"Old culture Americans . . .": Philip Slater, *The Pursuit of Loneliness: American Culture at the Breaking Point* (Beacon Press, Boston, 1970), p. 103.

"65 studies found that . . .": Alfie Kohn, *No Contest* (Houghton Mifflin Company, Boston, 1986), p. 48.

Challenge 8: Winning with Teamwork

"Teamwork doesn't happen automatically . . . many teams in our culture.": Peter B. Vaill, *Managing as a Performing Art* (Jossey/Bass, San Francisco, CA, 1991) p. 17.

"It helps to remember . . . of the leader.": Max DePree, *Leadership Jazz* (Currency/Doubleday, 1992), p. 190.

Challenge 9: Performance Appraisal or Development: The Need to Choose

"The performance of anybody . . .": W. Edwards Deming, *Out of the Crisis* (Massachusetts Institute of Technology, Center for Advanced Engineering Study, Cambridge, MA, 1982), pp. 109–110.

PART 3: LEADER AS CUSTOMER ADVOCATE

"Progressively waiting . . .": Information regarding Progressive Insurance Company was based on interviews with Progressive Insurance Company, Columbus, OH.

"The difference is . . .": Max DePree, *Leadership Jazz* (Currency/Doubleday, 1992), p. 80.

"Customers like companies . . . by its advertising.": Justin Martin, "Good Citizenship Is Good Business," *Fortune,* March 1994, pp. 15–16.

Challenge 10: Making Flexibility a Source of Competitive Advantage: One Size Does Not Fit All or Even a Few

"Whether you sell . . .": "Meet the New Customer," *Fortune,* Autumn/Winter 1993, p. 8.

Challenge 11: Making "Delighting" Customers Company Policy

"Our number 1 goal . . .": Nordstrom Employee Handbook, Nordstrom Department Stores, Seattle, WA.

Challenge 12: Becoming Customer-Focused: Re-Engineering the Process from the Customer's Point of View

"Join me in testing . . .": Robert H. Schaffer, *The Breakthrough Strategy* (Ballinger, Cambridge, MA, 1988), p. 54.

Challenge 13: Making Continuous Process Improvement Everyone's Job

"In knowledge and . . .": Peter Drucker, *Post-Capitalist Society* (HarperCollins, New York, 1993), p. 92.

Challenge 14: Make Proactive Recovery a Strategic Issue

"A well-handled problem . . .": Thomas J. Peters, *Thriving on Chaos* (Random House, New York), p. 91.

"When Customers Call": Reprinted with permission from the Technical Assistance Research Program, Washington, DC, for the Society of Consumer Affairs Professionals in Business, Alexandria, VA.

"This Is Scott Cook...": John Case, "Beyond the Last Word," *Inc. Magazine*, May 1993, p. 9.

Challenge 15: Create a Real-Time, Universally Accessible, Decentralized, Centralized Customer Information System

"80,000 Snapshots," *Fortune*, July 1990, p. 36.

"Break-throughs come from...": Andrew Grove, Chief Executive Officer, Intel Corporation, from speech to American Society for Quality Control, 1994.

PART 4: LEADER OF PEOPLE

"The leader starts out...": Peter Drucker, *Managing the Non-Profit Organization* (HarperCollins, New York, 1990), p. 44.

"The most exciting breakthroughs...": John Naisbitt and Patricia Aburdene, *Megatrends 2000* (William Morrow, New York, 1990), pp. 16–17.

"I believe that we...": Margaret Wheatley, *Leadership and the New Science* (Berrett-Koehler, San Francisco, CA, 1992), p. 5.

"I become steadily more persuaded...": Douglas McGregor, *The Professional Manager* (McGraw-Hill, New York, 1967), p. 43.

Robert Rosenthal and Lenore Jacobson, *Pygmalion in the Classroom* (Holt, Rinehart and Winston, New York, 1968), p. 1.

"Our prevailing system...": W. Edwards Deming, *Out of the Crisis* (Massachusetts Institute of Technology, Center for Advanced Engineering Study, Cambridge, MA, 1982), p. 149.

"The more you want...": Alfie Kohn, *Punished by Rewards* (Houghton Mifflin Company, Boston, 1993), p. 83.

"Over the last few years...": Chris Argyris, "Good Communication That Blocks Learning" (*Harvard Business Review*, July/Aug. 1994), p. 83.

Challenge 16: Sharing a Cause Worthy of Commitment

"We were not meant . . .": Charles Handy, *The Age of Paradox* (Harvard Business Review Press, Cambridge, MA, 1994), p. 259.

"Thus we reject . . .": Frederick Herzberg, Bernard Mausner, and Barbara B. Snyderman, *The Motivation to Work* (Wiley, New York, 1959), p. 138.

Challenge 17: Beyond Empowerment: Ensuring a Challenging Role, Meaningful Responsibility, and the Ability to Succeed

"Anytime we talk . . .": Interview with Max DePree, excerpted from Peter Drucker, *Managing the Non-Profit Organization* (HarperCollins, New York, 1990), p. 39 and Max DePree, *Leadership Jazz* (Currency/Doubleday 1992), p. 155.

Herbert M. Lefcourt, *Locus of Control: Current Trends in Theory and Research* (Lawrence Erlbaum Associates Hillsdale, NJ, 1982), pp. 3–5.

". . . With the Freedom . . .": Max DePree, *Leadership Jazz* (Currency/Doubleday 1992), p. 79.

"If 8th Graders Can Do It, Why Can't (or Don't) We?": Microsociety™ information was supplied to the authors from interviews conducted with Microsociety™ Founder, Dr. George Richmond.

"It is an injustice . . .": Roman Catholic Church Papal Encyclical, excerpted from *Quadragesimo.*

"Companies that hope . . .": Chris Argyris, "Good Communication That Blocks Learning," *Harvard Business Review,* July–Aug. 1994, p. 85.

Challenge 18: Building Organizational DNA: A Framework for Effectively Managing Risk

"If we allow autonomy . . .": Margaret Wheatley, *Leadership and the New Science* (Berrett-Koehler, San Francisco, CA, 1993). p. 22.

Challenge 19: Abolishing the Corporate Caste System

"I've seen knights . . .": From the movie *Robin Hood: Prince of Thieves,* Morgan Creek Productions, Warner Brothers, Los Angeles, CA.

"People could feel . . .": James Fallows, *More Like Us* (Houghton Mifflin Company, Boston, 1989), p. 66.

"From G.I. Joe to Joe College": Excerpted from James Fallows, *More Like Us* (Houghton Mifflin Company, Boston, 1989), p. 68.

Challenge 20: Developing a Persistent, Obsessive, Optimistic Environment

"Life inflicts the same setbacks . . .": Martin E. P. Seligman, *Learned Optimism* (Alfred A. Knopf, New York, 1990), p. 208.

Epilogue: Leader as Hero

"Respect, loyalty, security . . .": "The New Economy," *Fortune,* June 27, 1994, p. 60.

Index

As avid learners, we (the authors) would be delighted to hear from you regarding your comments on this book, ideas you would like to share with us, stories you would like to pass along to us, or other information. Please contact us via fax, telephone, U.S. Mail, or COMPUSERVE USA:

THE CENTER FOR INNOVATIVE LEADERSHIP
1400 Fashion Island Blvd.
Suite 601
San Mateo, CA 94404 USA
Telephone: (415) 578-9297
FAX: (415) 578-0356
COMPUSERVE ADDRESS: 74534, 3165

If you would like information on training products, the authors' speaking schedules, seminars, and/or consulting practices, please feel free to phone our toll-free number:

1-800-640-6416